International & Cross-Cultural Business Research

Dedication

To Constanze, Laurence, and Cécile, with love.
Jean-Claude

To my wonderful men: Albert Jan and Wouter.
Hester

To Vic, Alexander, and my loving parents all of whom inspire me.
Julie

Sara Miller McCune founded SAGE Publishing in 1965 to support the dissemination of usable knowledge and educate a global community. SAGE publishes more than 1000 journals and over 800 new books each year, spanning a wide range of subject areas. Our growing selection of library products includes archives, data, case studies and video. SAGE remains majority owned by our founder and after her lifetime will become owned by a charitable trust that secures the company's continued independence.

Los Angeles | London | New Delhi | Singapore | Washington DC | Melbourne

International & Cross-Cultural Business Research

Jean-Claude Usunier, Hester van Herk and Julie Anne Lee

Los Angeles | London | New Delhi
Singapore | Washington DC | Melbourne

Los Angeles | London | New Delhi
Singapore | Washington DC | Melbourne

SAGE Publications Ltd
1 Oliver's Yard
55 City Road
London EC1Y 1SP

SAGE Publications Inc.
2455 Teller Road
Thousand Oaks, California 91320

SAGE Publications India Pvt Ltd
B 1/I 1 Mohan Cooperative Industrial Area
Mathura Road
New Delhi 110 044

SAGE Publications Asia-Pacific Pte Ltd
3 Church Street
#10-04 Samsung Hub
Singapore 049483

Editor: Matthew Waters
Assistant editor: Lyndsay Aitken
Production editor: Sarah Cooke
Copyeditor: Fabienne Pedroletti Gray
Proofreader: Tom Hickman
Indexer: Martin Hargreaves
Marketing manager: Alison Borg
Cover design: Francis Kenney
Typeset by: C&M Digitals (P) Ltd, Chennai, India
Printed by CPI Group (UK) Ltd, Croydon, CR0 4YY

Library of Congress Control Number: 2016954964

British Library Cataloguing in Publication data

A catalogue record for this book is available from the British Library

ISBN 978-1-47397-588-0
ISBN 978-1-47397-589-7 (pbk)

At SAGE we take sustainability seriously. Most of our products are printed in the UK using FSC papers and boards. When we print overseas we ensure sustainable papers are used as measured by the PREPS grading system. We undertake an annual audit to monitor our sustainability.

CONTENTS

DETAILED CONTENTS

LIST OF TABLES

LIST OF FIGURES

ABOUT THE AUTHORS

Jean-Claude Usunier, Emeritus Professor, University of Lausanne, Switzerland
Jean-Claude Usunier is a professor at the University of Lausanne, Switzerland, in the Faculty of Business and Economics (HEC). His research interests are cross-cultural consumer behaviour, and cultural and linguistic aspects of international marketing and management. He serves on the editorial board of several international business and marketing journals. His research was published in *International Journal of Research in Marketing, Journal of Research in Personality, Time and Society, Journal of International Marketing, International Journal of Electronic Commerce, Journal of Business Communication, International Marketing Review, and European Journal of Marketing*. His recent books include *Marketing Across Cultures* (Pearson, 2013; with Julie Lee), and *Religions as Brands: The Marketization of Religion and Spirituality* (Ashgate, 2014; with Joerg Stolz).

Hester van Herk, Professor of Cross-Cultural Marketing Research, Vrije Universiteit, Amsterdam, The Netherlands
Hester van Herk is professor of Cross-Cultural Marketing Research at Vrije Universiteit, Amsterdam. Her recent research focuses on antecedents and consequences of personal and cultural values on consumer behaviour in developed and emerging markets and on research methodology providing insight into differences and similarities between survey responses from different nations and cultural groups. About these subjects she has published in journals such as *Journal of Marketing Research, Journal of Cross-Cultural Psychology, Journal of International Marketing, European Journal of Marketing, Organizations and Markets in Emerging Economies,* and *Multivariate Behavioral Research*.

Julie Anne Lee, Professor, Business School, University of Western Australia, Perth
Julie Anne Lee is a professor at the University of Western Australia, in the Business School. Her research focuses on cross-cultural theory, measurement and application in the tourism and consumer behaviour contexts. Most recently, she has been examining personal values across cultures. Her research was published in *Personality and Individual Differences, Journal of Personality and Social Psychology, Journal of Cross-Cultural Psychology, Journal of Personality Assessment, Journal of International Marketing, Journal of Business Research, International Marketing Review, Tourism Management, Annals of Tourism Research*, among others. Her research has attracted over \$1 million in competitive funding in recent years.

PREFACE

This book covers topics that are relevant to cross-cultural and international business research. It is aimed at researchers in business who undertake projects with comparative international designs, involving culture as a key input for explanation. It builds on the view that language matters considerably, both English as it is the worldwide language of business, and foreign languages, because they uniquely express culturally specific patterns in context-embedded situations.

An underlying assumption of this book is that the final aim of cross-cultural and international research in business is to find interesting similarities and differences, rather than universals. In the real world, a lot is *shared*, especially since there is a dominant normative model for business activities worldwide. However, a lot is *different*; people in other cultures may have diverse habits and customs, and norms may differ. We believe that cross-cultural and international research should help to increase our understanding of the influence of culture on business theories and practices. Consequently, research can help define the kinds of compromises that can be negotiated and implemented when behavioural standards, consumer attitudes, and management styles are obviously conflicting. This type of understanding may be especially important in emerging and developing nations, where open-mindedness toward different contexts and cultures can help to understand why some models in business may or may not be appropriate.

Cross-cultural and international research in business is still developing and gaining prominence. Researchers worldwide continue to employ instruments developed in the USA and other nations. In the last decade, appropriate translation techniques and the testing of measurement invariance has become an established procedure. The pursuit for measurement invariance often leads to a focus on universals, which ignores and potentially eliminates culture specific elements. This could be replaced with the pursuit of a cross-cultural dialogue with the aim of generating in-depth insights into cross-cultural differences and similarities. A dialogue based on equality is needed between researchers from different cultural backgrounds, implying full respect for the others' language and culture. Despite our best intentions, a full-fledged dialogue remains difficult when your native culture is close to the dominant values and practices of global business and management research. In this sense the process of cross-cultural and international research, which is most often limited to the contexts studied, should extend to the researchers themselves. It is only by a reflective contemplation of their own and other cultures that cross-cultural and international business researchers will be able to both search for cross-cultural equivalence and uncover and interpret true areas of non-equivalence. Openness to non-equivalence and a willingness to interpret why there may be non-equivalence will help advance the field.

Another underlying assumption of this book is that we need to understand and apply quite different research methods in order to increase the significance of findings in cross-cultural business research. This may be difficult, as our own biases have enduring, and obviously meaningful, implications if we solely focus on only one of the two distinct scientific cultures of qualitative and quantitative researcher. Generating meaning by both words and statistical evidence is necessary, even though both approaches may at times be difficult to reconcile. Furthermore, we highly recommend looking beyond primary data collection. In the last decade, several large multi-country datasets, such as the European Social Survey and the World Values Survey, have become available to researchers. Insight from such datasets may increase our understanding of other cultures and can help us design better comparative studies. In our view, methodological pluralism makes considerable sense for cross-cultural business studies.

Chapter 1 offers a general view of cross-cultural and international business research, describing the major issues in the field and offering insights on how culture can be defined and used in these research undertakings. Chapter 2 deals mostly with the researcher's own position vis-à-vis their terrain and topic, elaborating on ethnocentrism, prejudices, stereotypes, intellectual styles and the influence of language on cross-cultural research. Chapter 3 describes how cross-cultural management research should be designed, given the inherent complexity of such research undertaking. Not only is attention paid to levels of analysis researchers are dealing with, such as individuals or nations, but also to links between designs and the instruments chosen. Chapter 4 is dedicated to methodological issues that need to be addressed before data collection starts, including the search for equivalence across cultures with regard to the concepts and measurement instruments used. Chapter 5 is dedicated to establishing equivalence after data collection. We address the assessment of the comparability of data across cultures by checking response styles and measurement invariance. We also explore the potential of the growing trend toward multi-level studies in which nations and individuals within nations are analysed simultaneously. These studies have become more prevalent, since large multi-national databases, such as the European Social Survey, have become freely available. The final chapter gives advice on how to increase the relevance of cross-cultural and international business research in terms of meaning. Throughout the book, we focus on the importance of exploring diversity in our research through an examination of the similarities and differences in languages, cultures, contexts, methods and techniques. Rather than aiming at a language-free and context-free research setting, we believe open-mindedness will lead to progress in the field.

ACKNOWLEDGEMENTS

This book contains insights and ideas, shared and developed with colleagues to whom I am deeply indebted. They are: John Antonakis, Alexander Bergmann, John W. Cadogan, Ghislaine Cestre, Eric Davoine, Olivier Furrer, Michael Hay, T.K. Peng, Rebecca Piekkari, Nathalie Prime, Nicolas Roulin, Amandine Perrinjaquet, Saeed Samiee, Peter B. Smith, and Joerg Stolz.

Jean-Claude

I would like to thank the many people who have inspired and influenced me while working in the amazing field of cross-cultural and international research. First and foremost Ype Poortinga, and the many others including Ron Fischer, Geert Hofstede, Kwok Leung, Shalom Schwartz, Jan-Benedict Steenkamp, Theo Verhallen, Fons van de Vijver, and, last but not least, my co-authors on this book Julie Lee and Jean-Claude Usunier.

Hester

I would like to thank the many people who have influenced my journey into cross-cultural and international research. Among others, they include: Dana Alden, Michael Bond, Richard Brislin, Geert Hofstede, Lane Kelly, Jordan Louviere, Mark Patton, Hamid Pourjalali, Shalom Schwartz, Geoffrey Soutar, Seymour Sudman, Harry Triandis, Nancy Wong, and of course, Jean-Claude Usunier and Hester van Herk.

Julie

We all want to gratefully thank those at Sage that helped us turn our ideas into pages, Lyndsay Aitken, Sarah Cooke, and Matthew Waters.

1

INTRODUCTION AND OVERVIEW

1.0 Introduction

This first chapter begins with an overview of research in international business (Section 1.1), describing the major issues addressed, and how they have changed over time, as well as the regional or national origin of the people involved, as researchers or as informants (Section 1.2). We then introduce the importance of environmental factors in research and explore the key concept of culture in detail (Section 1.3). We address changes in the definition of culture and discuss the significant components and carriers of culture. Different conceptualisations of culture are compared and the way in which cultures are 'staged' in international business research is discussed. A major focus of this book is on the comparative research paradigm which underlies cross-cultural research rather than on substantive paradigms which are used as a central explanation and are most often borrowed from other major disciplines.

1.1 International research in business: an overview

International research in business has progressively developed over many decades. Among the early topics was the internationalisation of companies, especially their export activities, foreign direct investment and the progressive emergence of multinational corporations. A large Harvard research project in the 1960s was dedicated to the study of multinational companies and led to some breakthrough articles such as Raymond Vernon's (1966) 'International investment and international trade in the product life cycle'.[1] As the title suggests, this research relied on international economics, especially the theory of international trade and investment. For a long time, the paradigmatic focus was on why companies internationalise, why they choose specific locations and/or modes of foreign operations, production and/or sales, and what are the steps in the gradual internationalisation of businesses. However, as the body of knowledge explaining why firms internationalise grew, there was a change in emphasis to investigate 'how' they do (or should do) it. Today, research into international business has become more complex and sophisticated. The study of international business is moving from the study of specific international phenomena to the generalisability and the exploration of boundary conditions, to the creation of new theory impacting not only the field of international business but also the original substantive discipline. These three different types of research,[2] are elaborated in the following section.

1.1.1 Progression of research in international business

Most of the research in international business has focused on phenomena that are specific to international business, such as international joint ventures, foreign direct investment, entry modes, internationalisation strategies, outsourcing, and so on. This type of research was often simplistic with little insight as to what differs in the international context. If differences in the international context were considered at all, it was through the addition of a simple contextual or control variable, such as national culture. In this category, research often fails to consider what is theoretically different for international versus domestic decisions (e.g., joint ventures) or how firms in emerging economies are different from those in developed economies.[3]

The second category included a much smaller number of studies that used the international context to examine the generalisability of theories or challenge assumptions and boundary conditions. These papers often examined multiple environments and diverse institutional and cultural settings, or complexity at the individual level such as differences in values and beliefs. For instance, Carney and his colleagues[4] conducted a meta-analysis that tested the relationship between business group affiliation and performance, and hypotheses about the conditions that moderate these relationships including financial and labour market institutions. This type of research clearly extends the existing literature by making use of multiple-country contexts. However, there is also potential to move from theory extension to the development of new theoretical insights.[5]

The third category, which has the greatest potential for impact, uses the international context to develop new theories and insights where phenomena cannot be explained by existing theories from mono-cultural contexts. For example, Earley and Mosakowshi[6] argued that processes within cross-cultural teams cannot be sufficiently explained by existing theories; instead they were heavily influenced by cultural identity theory, which changed the predictions. The international context has also been used to develop new conceptualisations, such as Hedlund's 'heterarchy'[7] and Bartlett and Ghoshal's 'transnational' conceptualisations of firms.[8] In this category, opportunities exist for research to not only impact the field of international business, but also impact the original substantive discipline, such as proposing alternative explanatory mechanisms, addressing questions that can be better understood by considering the international environment, standardisation versus differentiation of strategy and practices, and exploring 'combinative' phenomena that exist only in this context.[9]

However, it should be noted that as an interdisciplinary field, international business research also has an important role in the integration of knowledge from different fields of research. In this way, international business research is more likely to be a knowledge recipient than knowledge source for other disciplines.[10]

1.1.2 Continuing and emerging research topics in international business

As previously mentioned, international business issues have progressively expanded from the theory of internationalisation of firms and foreign direct investment to, among other things, export management (especially for medium and small size firms), the relationships with host-countries, and international business negotiations. Common topics in this theme focus on multinational enterprises and their interaction with other entities, cross-border business activities, impacts of the international environment on business, international dimensions of organisational forms and cross-country comparative studies of business.[11] In this way, international business research has attracted researchers from many different fields of business studies.

Some of the continuing and emerging themes suggested in the literature[12] are listed in Table 1.1. The international and cross-cultural environments offer a rich area for exploring a wide variety of topics.

Table 1.1 Continuing and emerging themes identified in the international business literature

Topics	Examples of research questions in international business
International firm management and performance	How can we best describe firms' international evolution?
	How should firms measure success?
	How do firms balance the interests of various stakeholders?
	What is the impact of standardisation/adaptation on firm performance?

(Continued)

Table 1.1   (Continued)

Topics	Examples of research questions in international business	
	What are the returns from international expansion/diversification? How can they best be measured?	*What contextual factors moderate all of these questions (e.g., country, cultural, industry and firm differences)?*
	What are the drivers of firm competitiveness in global markets?	
	How can we assess risk in international markets?	
	What is the optimal firm size and structure in the global economy?	
	What makes entrepreneurial start-ups successful?	
	How can firms effectively staff global organisations and measure their performance?	
	What is the role of integrating mechanisms such as global teams and talent pools?	
	To what extent do tools such as the internet and intranets serve as a vehicle to provide virtual connectedness within the multinational enterprise?	
	How can we identify and validate cross-country market segments?	
	How well do global brands achieve local effectiveness?	
	What are the determinants of success in global product development?	
	How do firms design global supply chains?	
	What impact do new information, communications, and manufacturing technologies have on international business?	
Foreign market entry forms (e.g., exporting, foreign direct investment, licensing, franchising, joint ventures)	What factors impact managerial decisions on entry mode?	
	What are the antecedents and outcomes of success in different types of markets (e.g., developed and emerging)?	
	What are the antecedents and consequences of trust and commitment in international partnerships?	
	What impact does knowledge transfer have on performance?	
Globalisation	What are the antecedents, processes and consequences of globalisation?	
	What is the role of emerging markets in the globalisation process?	
	What evidence is there for the convergence of global customer preferences?	
	How does the pace of convergence differ by countries at different levels of economic development?	
	How do different forms of economic regions impact globalisation?	
	How do we measure the impact of globalisation at a country level?	
	What are the unintended consequences of globalisation?	
Public policy, ethical, and legal issues	How to best handle corporate social responsibility and citizenship issues across borders?	
	How do ethical considerations influence decision making by managers?	
	What are the performance implications of explicit vs. implicit contracts?	
	How do firms effectively safeguard their intellectual property in cross-border relationships?	
	How can firms best handle conflict resolution in international partnerships?	
	How do firms cope with the absence of formal legal institutions in emerging markets?	

Topics	Examples of research questions in international business
Security and risk issues	What is the impact of terrorism on cross-border business?
	How do managers cope with new risks in the international environment?
	What role do firms have in the security of the regions in which they are located?
Methodological issues	How can we increase the reliability of international business research?
	How can we account for partial effects of national culture from organizational culture and other variables?
	How can we establish that measures are equivalent across different cultural contexts?
	To what extent can we apply western-based research methods in emerging markets?

Adapted from Griffith et al. (2008)[13]

Some recent examples in different substantive areas are listed below, although the interdisciplinary nature of international business means that the lines are often blurred between disciplines.

- Research in the broad field of management and organisations has been compelled to understand global businesses. Recent studies have focused on many diverse aspects of international and global management including the evolution of firms in the global environment,[14] headquarters–subsidiary relationships,[15] the transfer of knowledge within the firm and from international joint ventures,[16] and a wide range of strategic management issues,[17] including cultural distance and diversity.[18] Research has also focused on the development of human capital and teams,[19] even though many aspects of human resource management are subject to national and industry regulation. There is also a strong stream of research into international entrepreneurship.[20]

- Marketing has also developed a strong international focus in strategy, business-to-business and consumer research, as well as research methodology. Some ongoing topics include the investigation of marketing strategy, marketing mix decisions and brand sales in global markets,[21] market segmentation,[22] the role of culture in international relationship marketing,[23] consumer predispositions toward foreign countries and globalisation,[24] as well as cross-country survey and research design.[25]

- Research in finance and accounting has focused on both global and country-specific topics, such as the worldwide nature of financial markets,[26] the effect of risk and volatility in global and local markets,[27] country-specific[28] and international accounting standards,[29] as well as the impact of country and institutional environments on corporate governance practices,[30] including corporate social responsibility.[31]

The *Journal of International Business Studies*, for instance, over the past five years has published studies in many different substantive areas including, strategic management (25%), economics and the political environment (15%), accounting and finance (13%), general management (11%), international business theory and methods (11%), marketing and supply chain management (9%), cross-cultural management (9%), and human resource management (7%).

1.2 Where does research in international business emanate from?

1.2.1 Geographic location

Historically international business research is overwhelmingly of western origin, most notably North America, which comes as no surprise. However, this literature is becoming more diverse in terms of authorship and the focal regions being studied. Bhardwaj (2016) found that publications included in the Social Sciences Citation Index (2004 to 2013) with listed keywords including 'international business' originated from 62 different countries; however, over 70% of these publications came from just 10 countries.[32] Figure 1.1 shows the proportion of these publications that originated from these 10 countries. It illustrates the high proportion of publications originating from English speaking countries, which is not surprising when we consider that over 98% of these publications were printed in English. However, it is interesting to note that the proportion of publications from primarily English speaking countries is declining, with the most dramatic increase coming from China.

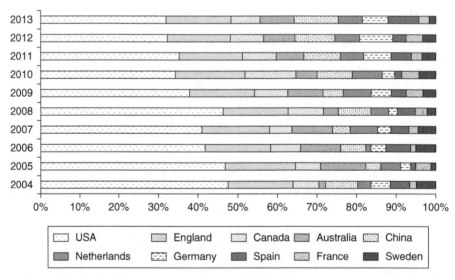

Figure 1.1 The geographical distribution of publications with 'International Business' keywords: Top 10 countries

Source: Adapted from Table 4 (Bhardwaj, 2016; p. 317)[33]

The reason for the relatively poor presence of authors from non-western countries is *not* related to some sort of structural, ethnocentric prejudice of the journal against foreign authors, rather it is more likely to be related to:

1. the language problems encountered by researchers from non-English speaking countries when they have to write and publish their research in English;
2. the predominance of business schools in the USA;
3. the relative under-investment in higher education and research in many countries in comparison to North America (e.g., most countries invest less in higher education, even when it is calculated as a percentage of GNP).

However, these factors are changing. More authors and reviewers speak multiple languages and journals openly encourage authors to have their work copyedited by local language experts. University rankings show that business schools outside of the USA are increasing in their prominence. For instance, in the World University Rankings, Asia increased its share of universities in the top 100 from 10 in 2015 to 18 in 2016. Further, external funding has targeted poorer countries, as investments in higher education are seen as a positive step toward addressing inequality. The World Bank has invested more than US$1 billion in African higher education since 2000.[34]

1.2.2 Interested constituents

The interested publics in international business research are quite disparate. Interested parties include companies, ranging from the large multinational enterprises (MNEs) to highly specialised and internationalised small to medium enterprises (SMEs), as well as entrepreneurs, public authorities in charge of export trade promotion, and faculty members or higher education institutions striving to internationalise their curricula. This interdisciplinary nature of international business research means that rather relying on a unified body of knowledge, it draws on knowledge from a wide range of areas. This is evidenced by the large number of academic associations and related journals where relevant international business research can be found, as well as the underlying disciplines cited in the international business literature (see Table 1.2). Further, many international business research publications can be found in the general business literature, as international business studies are *not* the privilege of specialised 'international scholars', who, generally speaking are not very territorial.

Table 1.2   The disciplines cited in articles published in the *Journal of International Business Studies*

Cited disciplines commonly within business schools	Cited disciplines outside business schools
• accounting	• anthropology
• business ethics	• applied psychology
• economics	• biology
• entrepreneurship	• communication
• finance	• computer science

(Continued)

Table 1.2 (Continued)

Cited disciplines commonly within business schools	Cited disciplines outside business schools
• human resource management • industrial relations and labour • international business • management • marketing • operations research and management sciences • organisational behaviour	• demography • energy and fuels • environmental sciences • environmental studies • geography • hospitality, leisure, sport and tourism • law • medicine • multidisciplinary sciences • physics • planning and development • political science • psychology • mathematical methods • sociology • statistics and probability • urban studies

Source: Adapted from the 36 disciplines / fields of cited journals in the *Journal of International Business Studies*[35]

1.3 The international environment

One of the factors that distinguish international business research from the main business disciplines is the international context in which the studies are conducted. Culture is obviously a key environmental factor that is described in some detail in this section. However, it is also important to mention other environmental factors that are often entered as independent variables; either as predictors (hypothesised to have an effect on the dependent variables) or control variables (added to hold these factors constant in the analysis). For instance, key economic and financial factors (e.g., interest rates, exchange rates, inflation, income distribution, and unemployment levels) may impact the availability of money for firms and consumers within a given country. They may also influence host governments' reactions to foreign investment and imported goods and services. Political factors, including the political system, political diversity and political stability, as well as the state of relations between the home and host countries and the general global environment can also impact business. The type of legal system can lead to differences in contractual formalism and recourse to litigation, the ways and means to solve conflicts and issues of bribery and corruption. The level of formality in addressing public and private issues in any kind of negotiated intercultural partnership, including the discussion of joint-venture contracts, the registration of subsidiaries and sensitive issues with the public authorities of the host country reflects different conceptions of institutional and legal systems. These are all interesting issues for comparative international business research, but they are also challenges to generalisability that need to be considered when seeking equivalence across countries.

Culture is an important contextual variable that has long been of interest in international business research. Various components of culture have been found to impact many areas of international business, including managerial and consumer decision making, hierarchical relationships, organisational design, motivation, communication and communication styles, and negotiation within and across organisations. Further, globalisation has multiplied intercultural encounters and created a dire need to understand foreign business environments. Cross-cultural business research is required to develop effective solutions that work across countries and respect what is culturally unique within countries. In designing cross-cultural business research, it is important that researchers understand what culture is and how it is commonly measured or examined in international business research.

1.3.1 Defining culture for international research in management

Culture has been defined as a 'collective mental programme',[36] as a shared system of representations and meaning,[37] as basic assumptions or value orientations,[38] and more recently, as a hypothetical, latent, normative values system that is external to individuals, but can be inferred from its manifestations.[39] Whereas, the earlier definitions relied on the notion of values being largely shared with a relatively high consensus between constituents of a culture as to the importance of core values, the latter definitions do not make this assumption. Viewed as a latent construct, societal culture reflects the complex meanings, beliefs, practices, symbols, norms and values that are prevalent within a society. It does not 'program' individuals, but may be considered a 'programmer', as individuals interact with their culture.[40] This view emphasises the idea that individuals may experience their culture in very different ways and the ways in which individuals experience their culture is likely to depend on the groups to which they belong (e.g., age, gender, religious, occupational, and family groups). Given this view, it is entirely reasonable that cultures will differ both within and across countries.

Culture can be viewed as a set of beliefs or standards, agreed on by a group of people, which help individuals decide what is, what can be, how one feels about it, what to do and how to go about doing it.[41] On the basis of this operational definition of culture, there is no reason why it should be equated with the whole of one particular society. It may be more closely related to norms for particular groups of people. Consequently, individuals may experience different cultures with different groups: a corporate culture with colleagues at work, an educational culture with other MBA graduates, and an ethnic culture with people of the same ethnic origin. When in a particular situation, they will switch into the culture that is operational. This perspective has the advantage of clearly highlighting the multicultural nature of many individuals in today's societies, including bicultural, multilingual people, and people who have a distinct professional culture or are influenced as employees by the corporate culture of a multinational company.

The Swedish writer Selma Lagerlöf[42] defines culture as 'what remains when that which has been learned is entirely forgotten'. In this view, culture may appear as a 'synthesis variable': serving when more precise concepts or theories have either proved unsuccessful or need to be linked together. It would also serve as an explanatory variable for residuals, when other more operative explanations have proved unsuccessful. Nevertheless, Selma Lagerlöf's definition does have the important merit of identifying two basic elements of cultural dynamics: (1) it is learned; and (2) it is forgotten, in the sense that people are largely unconscious of its existence. For example, being modest and self-effacing is a cultural norm in most Asian cultures, but people who live within these cultures are often shocked by what they consider as overly assertive and apparently boastful behaviour in other cultures. Since culture is 'forgotten', it is mostly an unconscious guide to individual behaviour in situations and institutions. Individuals within a cultural grouping often find agreed-upon solutions indicating appropriate behaviour between members of the same cultural grouping.

1.3.2 Significant components and carriers of culture

International business researchers need to be mindful of the significant components and consequences of culture. Culture is embedded in and communicated through social institutions and systems, as well as the symbolic (religious and moral beliefs such as the relationship between the physical and metaphysical world) and material (art and music, written work, machinery and tools, products and services) productions within a society. Differences in these elements of culture lead to variations in the content and distribution of beliefs, values, styles of thinking, and behaviours within society.[43]

Social institutions – relationships with groups - are extremely important sources of culture: how the individual relates to the group(s), what the dominant family and kinship patterns are, and how these relationships are framed (individualism/collectivism; patronage relationships). In anthropological research, relational patterns make sense because they are related to territoriality, kinship, etc. Relational patterns also affect international cross-cultural business research through the style of interaction between people, their decision-making process, and the way in which they mix human relationships and business matters. Contrasts between the more organic societies (collectivistic) and the more independent and atomised societies (individualistic), as well as the internalisation of these patterns, have been applied to many diverse topics in international business, including corruption in bank lending,[44] the appraisal of and reactions to work demands, such as work hours and workload,[45] and the adoption of new products.[46]

Educational institutions are also important carriers of culture. Universities are important vehicles of culture, but also can be instrumental in transmitting cultural change by exposing students to new ways of thinking and new solutions to societal problems. Education levels and education distributions are indicated by literacy levels and by the proportion of the population with the types of training emphasised in society. For instance, Japan and China tend to place relatively more emphasis on science and mathematics than western countries. This may have long-term implications for certain types of technical innovations. International business researchers need to be aware of the impact of education not only on business practices, but also on the ability to collect certain types of information from respondents, including the type of questions that can be asked and the ability of individuals to answer fairly abstract questions.

Another very influential institution is that of religion. Some societies may be fairly mono-religious with most people sharing a similar major religion, such as Christianity, Islam, Hinduism, Confucianism or Buddhism. Other societies have more religious diversity, either in terms of divisions within the majority religion or in terms of the acceptance of many different types of religion. Religious practices as carriers of culture impact the ideals to which people aspire and sometimes dictate behaviour in a more structured manner. Even within Christianity, Catholic beliefs generally downplay the personal pursuit of money, whereas Protestants beliefs emphasise hard work and the accumulation of wealth. Other religions, such as Islam, may be supportive of business, but downplay practices that are viewed as exploitative, like charging interest to borrowers. Women are also more constrained in terms of business participation, interaction with non-related males, such as salesmen, and in their participation in market research.

Naturally, language is also a carrier of culture. How people communicate (that is, both emit and receive messages) and the influence of their native language on their world views and attitudes directly affect international business. The implementation of business requires that partners write contracts in a foreign language, use interpreters, try to express ideas and concepts which may be unique in a particular language, etc. They have to communicate despite different native languages and communication styles (i.e., high context versus low context[47]). Language is important, especially for interactive cultural research. It can be seen as influencing the whole research process, including the researcher, the researched field, and the ways to address issues and to collect data. Its place in the research process is examined in detail in Chapter 2 and also discussed throughout this book. Language may be a negligible or an important element of the research paradigm, according to whether one considers language simply as a 'technical' issue, involving the mere search for translation equivalence, or as shaping the individual and collective world views of those who speak a particular language, in which case language becomes a key concern in the research process.

Each of the components and carriers of culture interacts to influence the prevailing values in a particular society, and the extent to which they are respected in the everyday behaviour of individuals. Some cultures have strong norms and a low tolerance for deviant behaviour (tight cultures), whereas others have weaker norms and higher tolerance for deviant behaviour (loose cultures).[48] Tight, as opposed to loose, nations are more likely to be religious, have more laws and regulations, more controls on the media, have fewer political rights and civil liberties, lower crime rates, and less access to and use of new communication technologies.[49] In tight cultures, people have more situational constraints on everyday behaviour (e.g., in restaurants, workplaces, and banks). Pakistan, Malaysia, Singapore, and South Korea are all considered tight cultures, whereas the Ukraine, Estonia, Hungary, Israel, the Netherlands, and Brazil are all considered relatively loose cultures.[50]

1.3.3 National culture

Social scientists have long been looking at cultural differences as they pertain to national groups. The concept of national culture has been widely used, although it may seem dangerous as it sums up a complex and multiform reality at risk of cliché and stereotype. It is legitimate to wonder (1) whether this concept is coherent and substantial enough to constitute an explanatory variable in the scientific sense, and (2) whether one should speak of national character or national culture. The answer to the first question is that the concept of national culture suffers a systematic lack of coherence. It is an 'intersection' of concepts, a merger of the culture concept, mostly derived from anthropology, and the nation-state, belonging to the political sciences. Cultures often do not correspond to nation-states but to linguistic, ethnic, religious or even organisational entities. In modern times, the most frequent mode of political organisation has been the nation-state, hence the emergence of this 'intersection' concept of national culture. The vagueness of this concept probably explains why it has been systematically underestimated, especially in international trade and international business theories. Theory-builders who generally seek to construct formally convincing theoretical explanations, tend to remove such vague variables from their models even if they have explanatory power. However, the fact that a construct is not easily measurable is no justification for ignoring it. Despite its limitations, the concept of national culture is an interesting Pandora's Box.

The second question – national character or national culture – merits consideration. Some researchers favour the idea that culture directly shapes psychological characteristics of individuals, that is, the average individual in a particular culture scores significantly higher (or lower) on certain personality traits than individuals belonging to another culture. This can be interpreted as the idea of national character or more precisely the concept of modal personality, which has been developed in greater detail by Inkeles and Levinson.[51] Their literature review is certainly the most exhaustive available. It is somewhat dated, but since national character changes over decades and centuries, their review still offers relevance. This approach largely grew out of enquiries, stemming from the Second World War, which now seem to have lost some of their relevance: why are certain people more violent, more aggressive, more domineering, collectively more prone to declare war on other nations, or to organise and implement genocide? Numerous empirical studies have been undertaken, particularly during the 1950s and 1960s, taking as a starting point the formation process of national character (where there could be a divergence between nations): rearing practices, early childhood, education systems, the socialisation process of children, etc. Generally, the results were ambiguous or not supported.

Individual personality traits are largely free from the influence of culture as expressed by Linton: 'His [the individual's] integration into society and culture goes no deeper than his learned responses, and although in the adult the greater part of what we call the personality, there is still a good deal of the individual left over.'[52] In Linton's view, individuals also have personalities quite separate from their cultural background. From a 'national character' perspective, one would expect to meet people with an average personality which reflects their culture; however, this is not the case.

Most theorists view cultural assumptions as a response to fundamental human problems. For Kluckhohn and Strodtbeck,[53] cultural assumptions provide the members of a particular cultural community with a basic framework for the evaluation of solutions to these problems, combining a cognitive dimension (*people think it works that way*), an affective dimension (*people like it that way*) and a directive dimension (*people will do it that way*).[54]

Naturally these modalities can be found in any society: people *are* and *do*, they all display temporal orientations to the past, present and future. But different assumptions result in variation as to the kind of response which is dominant in a particular society. Other approaches of the dimensions of the cultural process have been described by other authors.[55] All of them highlight common problems across cultures, depict the most important solutions and explain the dominant contrasts.

1.3.4 Large scale empirical studies using survey data

Many of the more commonly cited cultural theories, such as those by Hall,[56] Hofstede and Hofstede,[57] House et al.,[58] Inglehart,[59] Kluckhohn and Strodtbeck,[60]

Schwartz,[61] and Trompenaars and Hampton-Turner[62] propose a range of possible cultural dimensions. However, only a few of these have obtained large datasets that allow the world's main national cultures to be compared (e.g., over 100,000 respondents for Hofstede,[63] 99,000 for the World Values Survey,[64] 55,000 for Schwartz,[65] 17,000 for the GLOBE project[66]). Of these, Hofstede's cultural dimensions are still by far the most commonly applied in international business, despite the growing popularity of the GLOBE project in management and Schwartz's cultural value orientations across a number of fields. While there have been criticisms of Hofstede's dimensions that we need to be aware of, such as being overly simplified, empirically driven, and based only on IBM employees,[67] the dimensions make sense for international business studies and, as such, have been studied extensively. Further, replications show that the dimensions are fairly stable, at least in terms of the distance between cultures.[68]

Table 1.3 includes cultural dimension scores for a selected set of countries from Hofstede and Hofstede,[69] House et al.[70] and Schwartz (2008).[71] Before readers explore the table in any detail, it may be useful to consider some of the similarities and differences between these conceptualisations, which are described later in this section. We *strongly* encourage deeper reading about these cultural dimensions before they are selected as an indicator of culture for research purposes. The aim here is to touch on how the different cultural conceptualisations provide a small window into the preferred solutions to common problems that societies face.

Table 1.3 Cultural dimension scores for a selected countries: Hofstede and Hofstede, The Globe and Schwartz dimensions

Countries	Australia	China	Japan	Netherlands	Russia	Switzerland (German speakers)	Switzerland (French speakers)	United States
Hofstede and Hofstede 2001								
Power Distance	36	80	54	38	93	26	70	40
Uncertainty Avoidance	51	30	92	53	95	56	70	46
Individualism (vs. Collectivism)	90	20	46	80	39	69	64	91
Masculinity (vs. Femininity)	61	66	95	14	36	72	58	62
Long/Short-term Orientation	31	118	80	44				29
The Globe 2004								
Assertiveness								
Practices	4.29	3.77	3.69	4.46	3.86		3.61	4.5
Values	3.83	5.52	5.84	3.13	2.9		3.83	4.36

Countries	Australia	China	Japan	Netherlands	Russia	Switzerland (German speakers)	Switzerland (French speakers)	United States
Collectivism-Institutional								
Practices	4.31	4.67	5.23	4.62	4.57		4.31	4.21
Values	4.47	4.52	4.01	4.76	4.01		4.42	4.2
Collectivism-In-Group								
Practices	4.14	5.86	4.72	3.79	5.83		3.82	4.22
Values	5.82	5.12	5.44	5.39	5.9		5.54	5.79
Future Orientation								
Practices	4.09	3.68	4.29	4.72	3.06		4.36	4.13
Values	5.21	4.7	5.42	5.24	5.6		4.89	5.34
Gender Egalitarianism								
Practices	3.41	3.03	3.17	3.62	4.07		3.46	3.36
Values	5.02	3.73	4.41	5.1	4.34		4.77	5.03
Humane Orientation								
Practices	4.32	4.29	4.34	4.02	4.04		3.98	4.18
Values	5.6	5.34	5.53	5.41	5.62		5.68	5.51
Performance Orientation								
Practices	4.37	4.37	4.22	4.46	3.53		4.36	4.45
Values	5.99	5.72	5.37	5.71	5.68		6.17	6.14
Power Distance								
Practices	4.81	5.02	5.23	4.32	5.61		5	4.92
Values	2.77	3.01	2.76	2.61	2.73		2.8	2.88
Uncertainty Avoidance								
Practices	4.4	4.81	4.07	4.81	3.09		5.05	4.15
Values	3.99	5.34	4.4	3.34	5.26		3.84	3.99
Schwartz 2008								
Harmony	3.99	3.78	4.21	4.05	3.9	3.94	4.4	3.46
Embeddedness	3.59	3.74	3.49	3.19	3.81	3.34	3.04	3.67
Hierarchy	2.29	3.49	2.65	1.91	2.72	2.42	2.06	2.37
Mastery	3.97	4.41	4.06	3.97	3.96	3.97	3.74	4.09
Affective Autonomy	3.86	3.3	3.76	4.13	3.51	4.24	4.33	3.87
Intellectual Autonomy	4.35	4.18	4.78	4.85	4.3	4.66	5.32	4.19
Egalitarianism	4.79	4.23	4.36	5.03	4.38	4.92	5.06	4.68

1.3.4.1 Boundaries between people and the group

The first problem is the nature of relations between people and the boundaries between the person and group. Solutions to this problem are described by the dimensions of *individualism* and *collectivism* (e.g., Hofstede and Hofstede,[72] and the GLOBE Project[73]). Hofstede and Hofstede[74] describe these dimensions as follows:

> Individualism stands for a society in which the ties between individuals are loose: everyone is expected to look after him/herself and her/his immediate family only. Collectivism stands for a society in which people from birth onwards are integrated into strong, cohesive in-groups, which throughout people's lifetime continue to protect them in exchange for unquestioning loyalty.

Schwartz[75] (p. 129) also refers to the relationship between the individual and group in his *autonomy–embeddedness* dimension. People in autonomous cultures are encouraged to 'cultivate and express their own preferences, feelings, ideas, and abilities, and to find meaning in their own uniqueness', whereas embedded cultures expect people to obtain meaning in life 'through social relationships, through identifying with the group, participating in its shared way of life, and striving toward its shared goals'. Schwartz argues that individuals in cultures that are high in embeddedness and low in autonomy socialise their children to be obedient and hard-working and discourage imagination in order to reinforce tradition and conformity values.

Further, in individualistic societies, people are expected to take care of their own and their immediate family's needs. Relationships are said to be rational, or based on the concept of reciprocity, where an individual who gives something to another expects some sort of return within a reasonable time span. In contrast, in collectivist countries, the social structure is stronger, with people clearly distinguishing between members of the in-group and members of an out-group. In relationships, people in collectivist cultures expect their group to care for them in exchange for unwavering loyalty. These dimensions refer to concepts of the self and others, assumptions located *within* persons, as well as to a model of interaction *between* people. This is explicitly recognised by the GLOBE Project, which identified these two aspects as *institutional collectivism* (i.e., how institutions encourage and reward collective action) and *in-group collectivism* (i.e., the degree to which individuals express pride, loyalty and cohesiveness in their group). People in countries that are higher in individualism are usually more self-sufficient and less dependent on others.

Other research has identified further variants of the basic individualist and collectivist cultural dimensions by taking account of hierarchical relationship, leading to horizontal (emphasising equality) and vertical (emphasising hierarchy) dimensions of individualism and collectivism.[76] Shavitt and colleagues[77] describe the differences as follows:

1. In vertical individualist societies (e.g., USA, UK, France), people are concerned with distinguishing themselves from others to improve their standing.

2. In horizontal individualist societies (e.g., Australia, Sweden, Denmark) people are concerned with expressing uniqueness and self-reliance.

3. In vertical collectivist societies (e.g., Japan, Korea, India), people are concerned with enhancing the cohesion and status of their in-group and complying with authorities.

4. In horizontal collectivist societies (e.g., Israeli kibbutz), people are concerned with sociability and interdependence.

Shavitt and colleagues detail several areas in which this combination of values is likely to have a significant influence, including how people respond to others, and how they respond to the marketing mix, especially advertising message appeal and effectiveness.

1.3.4.2 Equality or inequality in interpersonal interactions

The second problem relates to the legitimacy of inequality, in terms of an unequal distribution of power, which is reflected in Hofstede's power distance.[78] It is shown as much by the behavioural values of superiors who display their power and exercise it, as by the behavioural values of subordinates who wait for their superiors to show their status and power, and are uncomfortable if they do not. Families in high power distance societies tend to teach children obedience and respect for parents and older relatives, whereas families in low power distance societies are more egalitarian and tend to treat children as equals. In high power distance societies, superiors and subordinates feel separated from each other. It is not easy to meet and talk with higher ranking people, and the real power tends to be very much concentrated at the top. In contrast, members of organisations in low power distance societies tend to feel equal, and close to each other in their daily work relationships. They cope with situations of higher hierarchical distance by delegating power.[79]

There is some overlap between Hofstede's power distance and Schwartz's hierarchy-egalitarianism dimensions, as Schwartz's hierarchy construct also focuses on unequal distribution of power. However, the conceptualisation of egalitarianism is broader, as it stresses a greater recognition of all humans as moral equals that leads to a concern for the welfare of all people. Cultures high on hierarchy expect individuals to adhere to rigid roles designed to ensure smooth societal functioning, and tend to value social power, authority, humility, and wealth. Cultures high on egalitarianism acknowledge the importance of interpersonal cooperation to ensure individual and collective success, and tend to value equality, social justice, responsibility, help, and honesty. Hierarchical cultures have large power distance, whereas egalitarian cultures tend toward a small power distance.

1.3.4.3 Interacting with others or for others

The third problem relates whether we interact with others or for others. In Hofstede's conceptualisation this is reflected in the assumptions behind the masculinity/femininity divide: should we help people (at the risk of their being weakened by a lack of personal effort) or should we not (at the risk, for them, of being even worse off)? This dimension roughly corresponds to the dominant gender role patterns: male/assertive and the female/nurturing roles. On average, men tend to score high on one extreme and women on the other, across societies, but there are also significant differences between societies.

In masculine societies, the emphasis is on assertiveness, money, showing off possessions and caring less about the welfare of others. Generally, there is a stronger role differentiation between males and females, but both boys and girls learn to be assertive and ambitious. In masculine societies, people are likely to be more possession oriented, and achievement is demonstrated by status brands and jewellery.[80] People in masculine societies (whether individualist like the US or collectivist like Japan) admire the strong.

In feminine societies, the emphasis is on nurturing roles, interdependence between people and caring for others (who are seen as worth caring for, because they are temporarily weak). Generally, there is less gender role differentiation and both boys and girls learn to be modest and to sympathise with the underdog. In feminine societies, the welfare system is highly developed, education is largely free and easily accessible, and there is openness about admitting to problems, such as in northern European countries. People in trouble are shown patience and hope. In feminine societies, people are more likely to share both large and small decisions, such as the choice of main car and everyday food shopping, and to purchase less expensive watches and jewellery.[81]

Schwartz's mastery construct also emphasises assertiveness and ambition, but contrasts this to harmony with the social and natural environment, rather than femininity.[82] However, these constructs show little empirical overlap, as the mastery–harmony dimension regulates how individuals relate to others and their environment.[83] Cultures that are high on mastery encourage individuals to develop and enhance their skills, using them to direct and change the environment, as well as personal and group goals, whereas cultures that are high on harmony, encourage individuals to understand and appreciate their environment in its current state.

1.3.4.4 Dealing with uncertainty

The fourth problem relates to how we deal with uncertainty. In Hofstede's conceptualisation, societies differ in their tolerance for uncertainty. High uncertainty avoidance assumes that uncertainty is bad and society must aim to reduce uncertainty. Organisations in these societies promote stable careers and produce rules and procedures to reduce ambiguity. People in these cultures tend to be better groomed as a way of organising their world and prefer purity in food, as evidenced by higher consumption of mineral water.[84] In contrast, societies low in uncertainty avoidance assume that people have to deal with uncertainty, because it is inevitable. The future is by definition unknown, but it can be speculated, and people and institutions can deal with likely outcomes. People in these cultures tend to be more innovative and entrepreneurial.[85]

Uncertainty avoidance should not be confused with risk avoidance. Hofstede and Hofstede note that risk is more specific than uncertainty and is often expressed as a probability that a specific outcome will occur, whereas uncertainty is a situation in which anything can happen. In fact, some people may engage in risky behaviour in order to reduce ambiguities, 'such as starting a fight with a potential opponent rather than sitting back and waiting'.[86]

1.3.4.5 Dealing with time

The fifth problem relates to how we deal with time, which seems universally indisputable, as we share a common clock. But, from a cross-cultural perspective, our assumptions around the concept of time and its importance have a strong influence on how we function socially. Many of the commonly cited cultural theories include time-related orientations. Some focus on perceptions of the flow of time (e.g., Hall's monochromic and polychromic task orientation[87] and time dimension as being linear versus holistic,[88]) whereas others focus on the temporal focus in society (e.g., past, present and future orientations[89]; the Chinese Cultural Connection's Confucian Work Dynamism,[90] termed Long Term Orientation by Hofstede and Hofstede[91]).

Important differences in time orientations were found in the Chinese Value Survey (CVS), which purposefully introduced an eastern bias to counter the historical western bias in value surveys.[92] The CVS proposed the dimension of Confucian Work Dynamism, which corresponds to a future orientation on one hand and a past and present orientation on the other. Later, Hofstede and Hofstede[93] referred to this as Long Term Orientation (LTO) versus Short Term Orientation (STO):

> Long Term Orientation stands for the fostering of virtues oriented towards future rewards, in particular, perseverance and thrift. Its opposite pole, Short Term Orientation, stands for the fostering of virtues related to the past and present, in particular, respect for tradition preservation of 'face' and fulfilling social obligations.

In this case, an LTO is future oriented, emphasising long-term virtues such as frugality, perseverance, saving and investment, whereas an STO emphasises short-term virtues. Short-term virtues can correspond to the past (i.e., respect for tradition and fulfilment of social obligations) or present (i.e., immediate gratification, including social consumption and spending). LTO scores are strongly correlated with national economic growth and have been used to explain the dramatic growth of the East Asian economies in the latter part of the twentieth century.[94] Many Asian countries (e.g., Hong Kong, Japan and South Korea) score quite high on LTO, whereas most western countries (e.g., Australia, Germany, USA and UK) and developing nations (e.g., Pakistan and countries in west Africa) score much lower.

Time is an important concept in business research, especially for management, for planning, strategy, for synchronising people at work, etc. Cultural attitudes towards time shape the way people structure their actions. This pervasive influence is reflected in punctuality in everyday management behaviour which may appear as the most visible consequence. Yet differences in time orientation, especially toward the future, are more important as they affect long-range issues such as the strategic framework of decision making or the trade-offs made by organisations between long-term company value and short-term profitability. Differences in the patterning of time include the dominant model of time (linear vs. cyclical), the nature and degree of temporal orientations to the past, present, and future, and the way to schedule activities according to time and people. Cross-cultural studies are increasingly carried out to understand how cultural concepts of time impact on a variety of management and business behaviours.[95]

In sum, there is a great deal of variation in different conceptualisations of culture. The important point here is that researchers need to think carefully about which cultural conceptualisation to use in their research. It should hinge on a deeper understanding of what the dimension captures, exactly was it measured and how it relates to the focal constructs of the study. Cultural dimensions

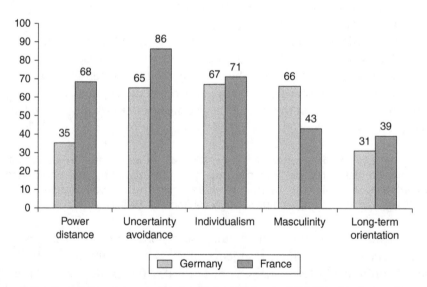

Figure 1.2 Comparison between Hofstede and Hofstede (2001) Index Scores from Germany and France

are only broad brushstrokes that capture a limited amount of information about culture. They do not convey a deep understanding of the culture, nor do they capture all of the different dimensions of culture. In many cases a deeper understanding is required.

This is illustrated with a brief comparison between the German and French language speakers in Switzerland in Table 1.4. There appears to be a large difference between these two sub-cultures in terms of Hofstede's power distance, with German speakers being low on power distance and French speakers being high. This is consistent with the scores for the home language country, with Germany being low and France high on power distance, as can be seen in Figure 1.2. This illustrates the danger in using the national culture scores as indicators of a country's culture. The assumption of homogeneity within countries is rarely a tenable one.

1.3.5 Using the construct of culture in cross-cultural business research

How the construct of culture is used in international management research is both a question of research philosophy, and a practical and operational issue. A key assumption is whether knowledge is universal or relative. A related assumption is whether business practices and knowledge are considered context-embedded or largely context-free. If the researcher's view is that business knowledge is universal and largely context-free, then the use of culture in international management research designs makes little sense.

The important question is not so much what culture is, or what cultures are, but why it is important and what impact it has. These questions lead to different research choices. The first option is to see culture as unimportant: much of the earlier international business research literature considered culture as irrelevant because business theories and practices were assumed to be universal and context-free. The second option is to consider culture as a residual explanation when (almost) all possible explanatory tracks have been used. In the third option, culture is viewed as having a significant impact on behaviour. Early research seemed to view culture as a programmer of people, where all individuals in a cultural grouping are supposed to be influenced in the same way. This leads to the study of culture as mean individuals who are supposed to display on average the modal characteristic of a given culture. However, a more reasonable position is that culture provides a guide or set of norms that are commonly understood by a segment of society, especially those who interact on a frequent basis. As suggested by McCracken,[96] in the case of consumer behaviour, 'We may see consumer goods as the vehicles of cultural meanings ... consumers themselves as more or less sophisticated choosers and users of these cultural meanings.' Consumers buy meanings and marketers communicate meanings through products and advertisements.

Many of these meanings are culture-based: they are intersubjectively shared by a social group. Intersubjective sharing of meanings implies that each person in a social group knows that others are also aware of the cognitive schema. Therefore, in the process of exchange through superior–subordinate interactions or buyer–seller relations, marketing communications or product consumption, interpretations are made spontaneously, as if they were obvious facts of the world, and a great deal of information in the process of exchange and communication need not be made explicit. Culture may be considered in this fourth option as a *meta-language* which is central in a business process viewed as exchange and communication. It works as a kind of *game rule*, a role play, indicating how people will interact in an exchange relationship, their constraints and their leeway for behaviour and decisions.

Figure 1.3 presents some basic ways to 'stage' culture in an international business research design. The first, from the upper-left corner, is the toolkit approach, which is comparative in nature, targeting individuals as basic informants of culture, and looking for values and traits of a modal personality. The second, in the bottom-left corner, has a stronger mapping orientation and defines culture in structural terms, as a way to adapt to environmental conditions. The key information comprises more factual elements and less psychometric data using respondents' self-reports. It leads more easily to a cross-national rather than cross-cultural view. The third, in the bottom-right corner, puts the emphasis on the transmission and sharing of the cultural background, a little bit in the vein of Linton[97], that is, deep seated beliefs passed through history, embedded in long-enduring institutions. The fourth, in the top-right corner, is the strongest in its emphasis on both interaction and individuals. Typically, it results in observing directly the interactions between business people or employees and their managers in different cultures as actors playing on a stage.

These approaches, though presented in this figure as different, are combined by most researchers. For example, researchers in Asia proposed a new cultural dimension (originally termed Confucian Work Dynamism[98] and later Long Term/ Short Term Orientation by Hofstede and Hofstede[99]) that helped to explain the rise of Asian countries' GDP. Research on the Confucian tradition and its impact on ways of doing business in Asia can be done in the four different ways cited above, either by studying the values of people in Asian countries based on Confucianism (toolkit); or by studying a group of countries which have a predominantly Confucianist ethic (map); by looking at what was the original teaching of Confucius and how is was transmitted to modern organisational practices in Asian countries (heritage); finally, the fourth possibility is to look at interaction between people in natural settings (business relationships, employer–employee, superior–subordinate) and try to understand how the Confucian script translates in the play of social actors (theatre).

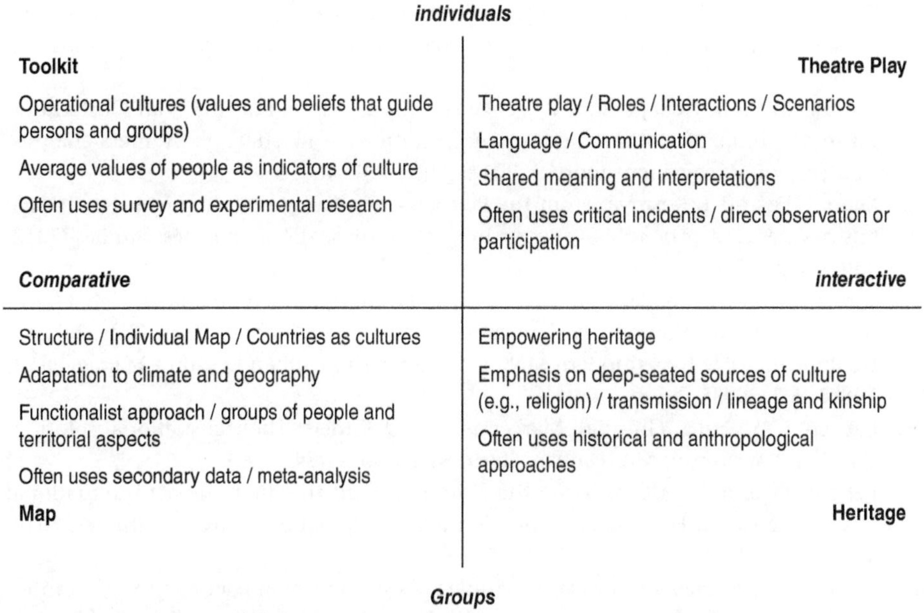

Toolkit	Theatre Play
Operational cultures (values and beliefs that guide persons and groups)	Theatre play / Roles / Interactions / Scenarios
	Language / Communication
Average values of people as indicators of culture	Shared meaning and interpretations
Often uses survey and experimental research	Often uses critical incidents / direct observation or participation
Comparative	*interactive*
Structure / Individual Map / Countries as cultures	Empowering heritage
Adaptation to climate and geography	Emphasis on deep-seated sources of culture (e.g., religion) / transmission / lineage and kinship
Functionalist approach / groups of people and territorial aspects	Often uses historical and anthropological approaches
Often uses secondary data / meta-analysis	
Map	**Heritage**

Groups

Figure 1.3 Staging culture in international management research

1.4 Conclusion

For the researcher in international business the use of culture as a prominent explanation is a conscious choice, rather than a 'scientific' obligation. Those who undertake cross-cultural business research often feel that it makes sense for them, and in fact they are members of a significant, but minority track in the field. The choice of culture-based explanations, shown in this chapter, can be staged in quite different ways, implying different research approaches and instruments. The next chapter describes the main reflective choices involved when comparing cross-nationally, because the researcher is driven, in an introspective way, to cast doubt upon their own ethnocentric views, to investigate the influence of language differences on the conception and implementation of the research design, and to put into perspective how alternative mindsets frame the way in which research issues are addressed and how the research is conducted and evaluated.

Notes

1. Vernon, R., International investment and international trade in the product cycle. The Quarterly Journal of Economics, 1966: 80 (2):190–207.
2. Roth, K. and T. Kostova, The use of the multinational corporation as a research context. Journal of Management, 2003. 29(6): 883–902.

3. Bello, C.D. and T. Kostova, From the Editors: Conducting high impact international business research: The role of theory. Journal of International Business Studies, 2012. 43(6): 537–543.

4. Carney, M., E.R. Gedajlovic, P.P. Heugens, M. Van Essen, and J.H. Van Oosterhout, Business group affiliation, performance, context, and strategy: A meta-analysis. Academy of Management Journal, 2011. 54(3): 437–460.

5. Bello, C.D. and T. Kostova, From the Editors: Conducting high impact international business research: The role of theory. Journal of International Business Studies, 2012. 43(6): 537–543.

6. Earley, P.C. and E. Mosakowski, Creating hybrid team cultures: An empirical test of transnational team functioning. The Academy of Management Journal, 2000. 43(1): 26–49.

7. Hedlund, G., The hypermodern MNC – a heterarchy? Human Resource Management, 1986. 25(1): 9–35.

8. Bartlett, C.A. and S. Ghoshal, Managing Across Borders: The transnational solution. Vol. 2. 1999: Boston, MA: Harvard Business School Press.

9. Bello, C.D. and T. Kostova, From the Editors: Conducting high impact international business research: The role of theory. Journal of International Business Studies, 2012. 43(6): 537–543.

10. Cantwell, J., A. Piepenbrink, and P. Shukla, Assessing the impact of JIBS as an interdisciplinary journal: A network approach. Journal of International Business Studies, 2014. 45(7): 787–799.

11. Eden, L., Letter from the Editor-in-Chief: Scientists behaving badly. Journal of International Business Studies, 2010. 41(4): 561–566.

12. Griffith, D.A., S.T. Cavusgil, and S. Xu, Emerging themes in international business research. Journal of International Business Studies, 2008. 39(7): 1220–1235. Hoppner, J.J. and D.A. Griffith, Looking back to move forward: A review of the evolution of research in international marketing channels. Journal of Retailing, 2015. 91(4): 610–626.

13. Griffith, D.A., S.T. Cavusgil, and S. Xu, Emerging themes in international business research. Journal of International Business Studies, 2008. 39(7): 1220–1235.

14. Zander, I., P. McDougall-Covin, and E.L. Rose, Born globals and international business: Evolution of a field of research. Journal of International Business Studies, 2015. 46(1): 27–35.

15. Hoenen, A.K. and T. Kostova, Utilizing the broader agency perspective for studying headquarters–subsidiary relations in multinational companies. Journal of International Business Studies, 2015. 46(1): 104–113.

16. Khan, Z., O. Shenkar, and Y.K. Lew, Knowledge transfer from international joint ventures to local suppliers in a developing economy. Journal of International Business Studies, 2015. 46(6): 656–675.

17. White III, G.O., O. Guldiken, T.A. Hemphill, W. He and M.S. Khoobdeh, Trends in international strategic management research from 2000 to 2013: Text mining and bibliometric analyses. Management International Review, 2016. 56(1): 35–65.

18. Dow, D., I.R. Cuypers, and G. Ertug, The effects of within-country linguistic and religious diversity on foreign acquisitions. Journal of International Business Studies, 2016. 47(3): 319–346.

19. Kim, K.Y., S. Pathak, and S. Werner, When do international human capital enhancing practices benefit the bottom line? An ability, motivation, and opportunity perspective. Journal of International Business Studies, 2015. 46(7): 784–805.
20. Terjesen, S., J. Hessels, and D. Li, Comparative international entrepreneurship: A review and research agenda. Journal of Management, 2016. 42(1): 299–344.
21. Bahadir, S.C., S.G. Bharadwaj, and R.K. Srivastava, Marketing mix and brand sales in global markets: Examining the contingent role of country-market characteristics. Journal of International Business Studies, 2015. 46(5): 596–619.
22. Kilic, C. and T. Dursun. Is Europe One? An International multiple-segmentation approach and implications for international marketers. in Proceedings of the 1999 Academy of Marketing Science (AMS) Annual Conference. 2015. Cham (ZG) Switzerland: Springer.
23. Samaha, S.A., J.T. Beck, and R.W. Palmatier, The role of culture in international relationship marketing. Journal of Marketing, 2014. 78(5): 78–98.
24. Bartsch, F., P. Riefler, and A. Diamantopoulos, A taxonomy and review of positive consumer dispositions toward foreign countries and globalization. Journal of International Marketing, 2016. 24(1): 82–110.
    Laroche, M., Advancing knowledge of the global consumer culture: Introduction to the special issue. Journal of Business Research, 2016. 69(3): 1071–1073.
25. Sintonen, S., A. Tarkiainen, J. W. Cadogan, O. Kuivalainen, N. Lee, and S. Sundqvist, Cross-country cross-survey design in international marketing research: The role of input data in multiple imputation. International Marketing Review, 2016. 33(3): 454–482.
26. Jain, A., P.K. Jain, T.H. McInish, and M. McKenzie, Worldwide reach of short selling regulations. Journal of Financial Economics, 2013. 109(1): 177–197.
27. Bekaert, G., M. Ehrmann, M. Fratzscher, and A. Mehl, The global crisis and equity market contagion. The Journal of Finance, 2014. 69(6): 2597–2649.
28. Pomberg, M., H. Pourjalali, S. Daniel, and M.B. Kimbro, Management accounting information systems: A case of a developing country: Vietnam. Asia-Pacific Journal of Accounting & Economics, 2012. 19(1): 100–114.
29. Hsu, A.W.-h., B. Jung, and H. Pourjalali, Does International Accounting Standard No. 27 improve investment efficiency? Journal of Accounting, Auditing & Finance, 2015: p. 0148558X15582087.
30. Daniel, S.J., A.P.J.K. Cieslewicz, and H. Pourjalali, The impact of national economic culture and country-level institutional environment on corporate governance practices. Management International Review, 2012. 52(3): 365–394.
31. Attig, N., N. Boubakri, S. El Ghoul, and O. Guedhami, Firm internationalization and corporate social responsibility. Journal of Business Ethics, 2016. 134(2): 171–197.
    Su, W., M.W. Peng, W. Tan, and Y.L. Cheung, The signaling effect of corporate social responsibility in emerging economies. Journal of Business Ethics, 2016. 134(3): 479–491.
32. Bhardwaj, R.K., Scientometric analysis and dimensions on international business literature. Scientometrics, 2016. 106(1): 299–317.
33. Bhardwaj, R.K., Scientometric analysis and dimensions on international business literature. Scientometrics, 2016. 106(1): 299–317.
34. MacGregor, K., Higher education is key to development – World Bank. University World News, 2015. 400: p. 2–5.

35. Cantwell, J., A. Piepenbrink, and P. Shukla, Assessing the impact of JIBS as an interdisciplinary journal: A network approach. Journal of International Business Studies, 2014. 45(7): 787–799.
36. Hofstede, G., Cultures's Consequences. 1980: Beverley Hills: Sage.
37. Goodenough, Ward H. Culture, Language and Society, Modular Publications, 1971: 7, Addison-Wesley: Reading, MA.
    Geertz, C. The Interpretation of Cultures: Selected essays. 1973, New-York: Basic Books.
38. Kluckhohn, F.R. and F.L. Strodtbeck, Variations in Value Orientations. 1961. Greenwood Press: Westport, CT.
39. Schwartz, S.H., Rethinking the concept and measurement of societal culture in light of empirical findings. Journal of Cross-Cultural Psychology, 2014. 45(1): 5–13.
40. Schwartz, S.H., Rethinking the concept and measurement of societal culture in light of empirical findings. Journal of Cross-Cultural Psychology, 2014. 45(1): 5–13.
41. Goodenough, Ward H. Culture, Language and Society, Modular Publications, 1971: 7, Addison-Wesley: Reading, MA.
42. Petit, K. (1960), Dictionnaire des Citations, Verviers: Marabout.(Our translation of the aphorism of Selma Lagerlöf by Karl Petit, p. 100)
43. Schwartz, S.H., Rethinking the concept and measurement of societal culture in light of empirical findings. Journal of Cross-Cultural Psychology, 2014. 45(1): 5–13.
44. Zheng, X., S. El Ghoul, O. Guedhami, and C.C. Kwok, Collectivism and corruption in bank lending. Journal of International Business Studies, 2013. 44(4): 363–390.
45. Yang, L.Q., P.E. Spector, J.I. Sanchez, T.D. Allen, S. Poelmans, C.L. Cooper, and A.S. Antoniou, Individualism–collectivism as a moderator of the work demands–strains relationship: A cross-level and cross-national examination. Journal of International Business Studies, 2012. 43(4): 424–443.
46. Ma, Z., Z. Yang, and M. Mourali, Consumer adoption of new products: Independent versus interdependent self-perspectives. Journal of Marketing, 2014. 78(2): 101–117.
47. Hall, E.T., The Silent Language. Vol. 3. 1959: New York: Doubleday.
    Hall, E.T., Beyond Culture. 1989: Doubleday: New York.
48. Gelfand, M.J., Culture's constraints international differences in the strength of social norms. Current Directions in Psychological Science, 2012. 21(6): 420–424.
49. Gelfand, M. J., J.L. Raver, L. Nishii, L.M. Leslie, J. Lun, B.C. Lim, and Z. Aycan, Differences between tight and loose cultures: A 33-nation study. science, 2011. 332(6033): 1100–1104.
50. Gelfand, M. J., J.L. Raver, L. Nishii, L.M. Leslie, J. Lun, B.C. Lim, and Z. Aycan, Differences between tight and loose cultures: A 33-nation study. science, 2011. 332(6033): 1100–1104.
51. Inkeles, A. and D.J. Levinson, National character: The study of modal personality and sociocultural systems. The Handbook of Social Psychology, 1969. 4: 418–506. Addison-Wesley: Reading, MA.
52. Linton, R., The Cultural Background of Personality. 1945, New York: D. Appleton-Century Company, pp. 14–15.
53. Kluckhohn, F.R. and F.L. Strodtbeck, Variations in Value Orientations. 1961. Greenwood Press: Westport, CT.

54. Kluckhohn and Strodtbeck (1961, pp. 11, 12) collected these common human problems under six main categories: (1)What is the character of innate human nature (human-nature orientation): good or evil, neutral, or a mix of good and evil? Is this state of human nature mutable or immutable? (2) What is the relation of humans to nature and supernature (nature orientation): subjugation to nature, harmony with nature or mastery over nature? (3) What is the temporal focus of human life (time orientation): past, present or future? (4) What is the modality of human activity (activity orientation): should people be (being), should people do (doing) or should they do in order to be (being in becoming)? (5) What is the modality of the relationship between humans (relational orientation): linearity, collaterality or pure individuality? (6). What is the conception of space? Is it considered predominantly private, public, or a mix of both?

55. Hofstede, G., Culture's Consequences. 1980: Beverley Hills: Sage.
   Hall, E.T., The Silent Language. Vol. 3. 1959: New York: Doubleday.
   Schwartz, S.H., Beyond Individualism/Collectivism: New cultural dimensions of values. 1994: Thousand Oaks, CA: Sage Publications, Inc.
   Triandis, H.C., Dimensions of cultural variation as parameters of organizational theories. International Studies of Management & Organization, 1982. 12(4): 139–169.
   Triandis, H.C., Culture and Social Behavior. 1994. (McGraw-Hill series in social psychology). New York, McGraw-Hill.
   Trompenaars, F. and C. Hampden-Turner, Riding the Waves of Culture: Understanding diversity in global business. 2011: London: Nicholas Brealey Publishing.

56. Hall, E.T., The Silent Language. Vol. 3. 1959: New York: Doubleday.

57. Hofstede, G.H. and G. Hofstede, Culture's Consequences: Comparing values, behaviors, institutions and organizations across nations. 2001: Thousand Oaks, CA: Sage.

58. House, R.J., P.J. Hanges, M. Javidan, P.W. Dorfman, and V. Gupta, (Eds)., Culture, Leadership, and Organizations: The GLOBE study of 62 societies. 2004: Sage publications.

59. Inglehart, R., Modernization and Postmodernization: Cultural, economic, and political change in 43 societies. Vol. 19. 1997: Cambridge: Cambridge University Press.

60. Kluckhohn, F.R. and F.L. Strodtbeck, Variations in Value Orientations. 1961. Greenwood Press: Westport, CT.

61. Schwartz, S.H., Beyond Individualism/Collectivism: New cultural dimensions of values. 1994: Thousand Oaks, CA: Sage Publications, Inc.

62. Trompenaars, F. and C. Hampden-Turner, Riding the Waves of Culture: Understanding diversity in global business. 2011: London: Nicholas Brealey Publishing.

63. Hofstede, G., Cultures's Consequences. 1980: Beverley Hills: Sage.

64. Inglehart, R., Modernization and Postmodernization: Cultural, economic, and political change in 43 societies. Vol. 19. 1997: Cambridge: Cambridge University Press.

65. Schwartz, S.H., Beyond Individualism/Collectivism: New cultural dimensions of values. 1994: Thousand Oaks, CA: Sage Publications, Inc.

66. House, R.J., P.J. Hanges, M. Javidan, P.W. Dorfman, and V. Gupta, (Eds), Culture, Leadership, and Organizations: The GLOBE study of 62 societies. 2004: Thousand Oaks, CA: Sage Publications.

67. McSweeney, B., Hofstede's model of national cultural differences and their consequences: A triumph of faith – a failure of analysis. Human Relations, 2002. 55(1): 89–118.

68. Hofstede, G.H. and G. Hofstede, Culture's Consequences: Comparing values, behaviors, institutions and organizations across nations. 2001: Thousand Oaks, CA: Sage. De Mooij, M. and G. Hofstede, Convergence and divergence in consumer behavior: Implications for international retailing. Journal of Retailing, 2002. 78(1): 61–69. Søndergaard, M., Research note: Hofstede's consequences: A study of reviews, citations and replications. Organization Studies, 1994. 15(3): 447–456.

69. Hofstede, G.H. and G. Hofstede, Culture's Consequences: Comparing values, behaviors, institutions and organizations across nations. 2001: Thousand Oaks, CA: Sage.

70. House, R.J., P.J. Hanges, M. Javidan, P.W. Dorfman, and V. Gupta, (Eds)., Culture, Leadership, and Oganizations: The GLOBE study of 62 societies. 2004: Sage Publications.

71. Schwartz, S.H., Schwartz National Cultural Value Orientation Scores, 2008, retrieved from ResearchGate https://www.researchgate.net/publication/304715744_The_7_Schwartz_cultural_value_orientation_scores_for_80_countries (August 30,2016) DOI: 10.13140/RG.2.1.3313.3040

72. Hofstede, G.H. and G. Hofstede, Culture's Consequences: Comparing values, behaviors, institutions and organizations across nations. 2001: Thousand Oaks, CA: Sage.

73. House, R.J., P.J. Hanges, M. Javidan, P.W. Dorfman, and V. Gupta, (Eds),Culture, Leadership, and Organizations: The GLOBE study of 62 societies. 2004: Sage Publications.

74. Hofstede, G.H. and G. Hofstede, Culture's Consequences: Comparing values, behaviors, institutions and organizations across nations. 2001: Sage, p.225.

75. Schwartz, S.H., Culture Matters. Understanding culture: Theory, research, and application, 2009: p. 129.

76. Singelis, T.M., H.C. Triandis, D.P. Bhawuk, and M.J. Gelfand, Horizontal and vertical dimensions of individualism and collectivism: A theoretical and measurement refinement. Cross-cultural Research, 1995. 29(3): 240–275.

77. Shavitt, S., A.K., Lalwani, J. Zhang, and C.J. Torelli, The horizontal/vertical distinction in cross-cultural consumer research. Journal of Consumer Psychology, 2006. 16(4): 325–342.

78. Hofstede, G.H. and G. Hofstede, Culture's Consequences: comparing values, behaviors, institutions, and organizations across nations. 2001, Thousand Oaks, CA: Sage. XX, 596.

79. Hofstede, G.H. and G. Hofstede, Culture's Consequences: Comparing values, behaviors, institutions and organizations across nations. 2001: Thousand Oaks, CA: Sage.

80. de Mooij, M. and G. Hofstede, Cross-cultural consumer behavior: A review of research findings. Journal of International Consumer Marketing, 2011. 23(3-4): 181–192.

81. De Mooij, M. and G. Hofstede, Convergence and divergence in consumer behavior: Implications for international retailing. Journal of Retailing, 2002. 78(1): 61–69.

82. Schwartz, S.H., Culture Matters. Understanding culture: Theory, research, and application, 2009: p. 127.

83. Schwartz, S.H., Culture Matters. Understanding culture: Theory, research, and application, 2009: p. 127.

84. De Mooij, M. and G. Hofstede, Convergence and divergence in consumer behavior: Implications for international retailing. Journal of Retailing, 2002. 78(1): 61–69.

85. Steenkamp, J.B.E.M., F. ter Hofstede, and M. Wedel, A cross-national investigation into the individual and national cultural antecedents of consumer innovativeness. Journal of Marketing, 1999. 63(2): 55–69.

86. Hofstede, G.H. and G. Hofstede, Culture's Consequences: Comparing values, behaviors, institutions and organizations across nations. 2001: Thousand Oaks, CA: Sage, p. 148.
87. Hall, E.T., The Silent Language. Vol. 3. 1959: New York: Doubleday.
   Hall, E.T., The Hidden Dimension. 1966. New York: Doubleday & Co.
   Hall, E., The Dance of Life. 1983, New York: Anchor Press/ Doubleday Books.
88. Trompenaars, F., Riding the waves of culture: Understanding cultural diversity in business, 1993. London: Brealey.
   Briscoe, D.R., and R.S. Shuler, 2004. International Human Resource Management.
89. Kluckhohn, F.R. and F.L. Strodtbeck, Variations in Value Orientations. 1961. Greenwood Press: Westport, CT.
90. Chinese Culture Connection, Chinese value and the search for review and proposal for an integrative theory. Journal of Marketing, 1987. 54: 66–79.
91. Hofstede, G.H. and G. Hofstede, Culture's Consequences: Comparing values, behaviors, institutions and organizations across nations. 2001: Thousand Oaks, CA: Sage.
92. Chinese Culture Connection, Chinese values and the search for culture-free dimensions of culture. Journal of Cross-Cultural Psychology, 1987. 18(2): 143–164.
93. Hofstede, G.H. and G. Hofstede, Culture's Consequences: Comparing values, behaviors, institutions and organizations across nations. 2001: Thousand Oaks, CA: Sage, p.359.
94. Hofstede, G.H. and G. Hofstede, Culture's Consequences: Comparing values, behaviors, institutions and organizations across nations. 2001: Thousand Oaks, CA: Sage.
95. Usunier, J.-C. and P. Valette-Florence, The Time Styles Scale: A review of developments and replications over 15 years. Time & Society, 2007. 16(2-3): 333–366.
96. McCracken, G., Culture and consumer behaviour: An anthropological perspective. Journal of the Market Research Society, 1991. 32(1): 3–11, p. 5.
97. Linton, Ralph (1945), The Cultural Background of Personality, Appleton-Century: New York.
98. Chinese Culture Connection, Chinese value and the search for review and proposal for an integrative theory. Journal of Marketing, 1987. 54: 66–79.
99. Hofstede, G.H. and G. Hofstede, Culture's Consequences: Comparing values, behaviors, institutions and organizations across nations. 2001: Thousand Oaks, CA: Sage.

2

LANGUAGE AND THE ROLE OF THE DOMINANT CULTURE

2.0 Introduction

This chapter makes the argument that international research is by its very nature comparative for the simple reason that the researcher has a different cultural background than both the field and the informants being studied. Therefore, basic differences in cross-national research designs must be made clear as early as possible during the research process. Some of the questions that should be asked are presented in Section 2.1, which highlights the underlying assumptions of comparative international research designs: What is being compared? Across which units? Who is making the comparisons? What is the cultural origin of the theories being used? What is the reference point in the comparison process? In Section 2.2, we focus on the researcher as a central agent in the process. It emphasises the researcher's background as a central element in the comparative setting. It also discusses the diversity of intellectual styles across cultures and how these styles impact views on what appropriate research is, how it should be conducted and how it should be evaluated. Section 2.3 deals with the issue of language which is a central, and most often ignored, element in the comparison process[1]: translation, although possible, is an undertaking which obscures most of the culturally obscure materials; *traduttore traditore* as the Italian saying goes (translator, betrayer). The last part explains how language can be used as a tool for the discovery of potential meaning.

It is important to make the point that even monolingual researchers can meaningfully deal with language issues in cross-cultural business research, provided that they are aware of language issues. Rather than adopting an instrumental paradigm of language, they can rely on language insiders, ask questions, use dictionaries to check for meaning differences as well as applying qualitative or quantitative methods, as described in Chapter 4. Fluency in multiple languages is not needed to be language aware.[2]

2.1 Research perspectives and world views

Do business researchers favour the search for differences or similarities? Personal interests and beliefs may be a source of bias, 'colonial' designs favouring the emergence of similarities. A common mindset, shared knowledge, recognised scientific approaches, anonymous reviewing, and academic journals tend to favour the similarity view, or at least favour the discovery of differences in *degree* rather than in *nature*. An identical research design may not be appropriate for the discovery of both similarities and differences across national/cultural contexts. Qualitative research designs favour the discovery of differences because they emphasise local meaning and interpretation. On the other hand, quantitative *etic* research designs favour similarities because they assume shared concepts, and use directive research instruments that channel the informants' insights into the researcher's pre-established frames. We have to take into account not only actual versus perceived similarities/differences but also differences in *nature* (incommensurable) versus differences in *degree* (commensurable). Incidentally, qualitative research may work as a magnifying glass and lead to the overestimating of differences in nature, because similarities are often far too substantial to be ignored.

Should researchers start with the search for differences or for similarities? Searching first for similarities is likely to tone down differences, most of which will remain unnoticed. Most differences are unimportant in the sense that late discovery does not impair the success of a locally implemented business policy because *ex-post* adjustment is feasible. Searching first for differences is likely to unveil key differences, sometimes with a magnifying glass effect. The next step is to take the true measure of such differences and to progressively discover that much is in fact shared.

Most researchers will argue that they look for both similarities and differences. However, in the real world, they tend to have a preconception of what they will (or even 'want' to) find at the end of the process. Those who emphasise similarities will favour the traditional search for 'cross-cultural equivalence', while those looking for differences will favour open enquiry and act deliberately as 'meaning explorers'. Consequently, those who search for differences and unknowingly use research strategies that favour the discovery of similarities will be deeply disappointed and discuss their findings in great detail to highlight their cherished differences. In any case, the researcher must be aware of what is predominantly being looked for because it will influence the research design, favouring the discovery of similarities or the emergence of differences. The divide in pictures of the world is partly located in the observer's eye.

A classic distinction, emic versus etic cross-cultural research, was originated by Sapir[3] and further developed by Pike.[4] The emic approach holds that attitudinal or behavioural phenomena are expressed in a unique way in each culture. Taken to its extreme, this approach states that no comparisons are possible. The etic approach, on the other hand, is primarily concerned with identifying universals. The difference arises from linguistics where phon*etic* is universal and depicts universal sounds which are common to several languages, and phon*emic* stresses unique sound patterns in languages. In general, research approaches and instruments adapted to each national culture (the emic approach) provide data with greater internal validity than tests applicable to several cultures (the etic approach, or 'culture-free tests'). But it is at the expense of cross-national comparability and external validity: results are not transposable to other cultural contexts. This is why many researchers try to establish cross-national or cross-cultural equivalence in a way which is inspired by the etic rather than the emic perspective.

Researchers should start with the search for differences if they want to later assess meaningful similarities. This can be done through *thick description*, which Geertz explains in his 1973 paper: 'the essential task of theory building here is not to codify abstract regularities but to make thick description possible, not to generalise across cases but to generalise within them.'[5] Generalising (i.e., largely 'forgetting' about differences in favour of emergent similarities) from *within* cases rather than *across* cases is related to thick description. Thick description is explicitly borrowed by Geertz from the English language philosopher Gilbert Ryle (1968).[6] The notion of thickness deals with fine-grained accounts, contextualisation, the combination of multiple perspectives, and reflexivity. Language is an instrument to put cultural experience in comparative perspective.[7] To take a geometrical metaphor: thick description, rather than describing phenomena in a two-dimensional surface, tries to offer a description in a three-dimensional space or, even better, in a multi-dimensional hyperspace. For Geertz, the notion of 'found in translation', rather than 'lost in translation' is part of thick description.

Table 2.1 highlights different cross-cultural research perspectives that considers the universal/specific aspect of both the subject (the researcher, his/her theories), and the object being studied (the field, the firm, managers or consumers as informants, the country/culture being studied). The *global perspective* is typified by looking at phenomena with the 'same eyes', meaning that theories, underlying models, concepts and views of managers and employees, their motives, and how they behave, are assumed as universal. In the *foreign/imported perspective*, the researcher travels to foreign business contexts with the same eyes and no glasses; with this perspective, there is obviously a risk of myopia. In the *ethnic perspective*, one adds glasses to the same eyes, so that part of what was previously invisible comes into light. The *cultural meaning perspective* requires 'looking with other eyes', that is changing the very instrument of vision; the metaphor suggests the difficulty of the process.

Differences can be in nature. For instance, one might argue that the concept of 'decision making' is a completely different concept (incommensurable) in certain cultures, since the word does not really exist, for example, in Japanese. Differences can also be in degree. The dimension of uncertainty avoidance in Hofstede's study, for example, assumes that national cultures can be scored on a common scaling instrument expressing the degree of tolerance to ambiguity. The researcher's practical question for such concepts is whether they are scalable, ordinally (rankings of countries/cultures) or cardinally (scores by countries/cultures). However, uncertainty avoidance has been shown to be the least robust in replications[8] with national scores varying across studies; and is also the most difficult to define conceptually. Therefore, the search for differences in degree does not preclude an exploration of differences in nature.

Table 2.1 should not be interpreted with the view that a particular cell corresponds to a better perspective than the others. However, each cell displays a strong contrast in researcher perspective. First, the *global perspective*, in its purest form, is rarely found, except when organisations and markets are viewed as truly global and unified. It may make sense for particular classes of business people, such those travelling worldwide, and their families ('the global nomads'). What does the global perspective mean for comparative business research practices? A single questionnaire is used, and only in English, assuming that all respondents understand English either as a native or as a second language; there is no questioning of the equivalence and comparability of the major concepts used in the research across cultural and linguistic contexts. This

Table 2.1 Comparative research strategies

Underlying theories ⇒ Informants/field ⇓	Universal (*etic*)	Specific (*emic*)
Universal	**(1)** Global perspective No differences in nature	**(2)** Ethnic perspective Differences in nature
Specific	**(3)** Foreign/imported perspective Assumed universality biased by creolisation	**(4)** Cultural meaning perspective Differences both in degree and nature

may be relevant if respondents are business people who are proficient in English and for countries where English is widely used in everyday living. In this perspective, lead researcher(s) dominate the research process with local collaborators who simply administer the instrument in their own national/cultural area, rather than participate in the research design.

Kotler's *Marketing Management*, in its fifteenth edition in 2016, is a worldwide success which started in the beginning from a *global perspective* and has steadily shifted to a *foreign/imported perspective* by being adapted in many languages and to various national contexts. In the imported perspective, the examples are tailored to the local markets and marketing environments, but the basic theories do not change. It may sometimes, but is not always sufficient to, allow discovery of significant differences in behaviour that require adaptation. For instance, from a global perspective, behavioural intentions models were assumed to be universally applicable: attitudes and expectations of important others influence intentions to perform a behaviour. Some insights were gained from taking an imported perspective when the 'universal' relationships between these variables were examined at a cultural level. For instance, consumers in individualist cultures appeared to be more strongly influenced by attitudes than they were by expectations of important others, while the reverse was true in collectivist cultures.[9] In this perspective, multiple research instruments can be used, possibly including more qualitative techniques, such as in-depth interviews. Comparability is assumed both *ex-ante* and *ex-post* (see also Chapters 4 and 5). The team of researchers design the research project together; however, the team often has a leading researcher who has a democratic approach to cross-national collaborations.

However, not all theories can be assumed universal. In this case, further insight can be gained from the emic viewpoints, namely the *ethnic perspective* or the *cultural meaning perspective*, which can uncover new constructs and new relationships between these constructs that leads to a better understanding of the behaviour in question. In the ethnic perspective, dominant theories are questioned, but the researcher still looks for similarities and strives for progressive convergence in the nature of the conceptual dimensions across cultures, while assessing differences in degree. This perspective attracts both quantitative and qualitative researchers. For instance, Hirschman[10] challenged researchers' assumptions about American consumers – acting as active information seekers who make personal decisions, which lead to pragmatic goals – in her examination of the primitive aspects of consumption in specific ethnic groups (Blacks, Italians, Wasps [white anglo-saxon protestants], Jews). The ethnic perspective, often uses common instruments that are adapted to each cultural concept and carefully translated to relevant languages (see Chapter 4), while checking for possible inequivalence in concepts, data collection methods, etc.

Finally, the *cultural meaning perspective* corresponds to the view that underlying theories and concepts have to be actively challenged. It is predominantly emic in style and tries to 'stage' research in unique ways, based on unique concepts and practices. Leadership, for instance, can be treated as unique to a particular culture or a phenomenon which shares some common traits cross-culturally.[11] The key objective here is to derive emic meaning; singular and specific to each particular context. Local meaning is privileged, which implies that different concepts and different research instruments are used in particular contexts, at the likely expense of cross-national/cultural comparability. However, a team of emic researchers can coordinate by meeting before the research process takes place and combine their findings *ex-post* to the extent that it is possible to do so.

The emic/etic divide is, however, a simplified perspective. Most etic-oriented researchers are still looking for differences, but these differences are in degree, while emic researchers look for differences in nature. Typical questions for etic-oriented researchers are: Is it scalable? Can the constructs be operationalised? Are the differences across countries/cultures measurable on common conceptual dimensions?

Often purportedly cross-cultural research designs use nationality as a surrogate variable of culture. Many such designs are in fact not cross-cultural (see Vaiman and Holden[12] on non-cultural factors as challengers for cultural explanations), although they claim to be; they are simple cross-national designs, providing little if no theoretical indication of how culture causes such differences. Cross-cultural comparative designs are more content oriented, describing values as components of culture, whereas cross-cultural interactive designs, emphasising interaction between managers or organisations from different cultures (e.g., expatriation, culture shock or intercultural business negotiations issues) tend to explain more about the process. There is an obvious complementarity between both types of designs.

2.2 The role of the dominant culture in international business research

To conduct comparative studies, researchers must question the role of a 'dominant culture' especially when the researcher either implicitly or explicitly assumes that one's culture is superior to other cultures in ways of solving business research issues. In fact, there has long been a dominant culture in business research, that of the United States, which many (including non-US researchers) spontaneously consider superior, because it has legitimately dominated the field over the last 70 years; however, there have been significant challenges from Europe and Asia in recent years. Vaiman and Holden[13] phrase it as follows 'One country stands out above the rest, namely the US, as the benchmark business culture for not only good practice, but also methodologies for the scientific study of business and management worldwide'. Saying that it is dominant does not imply any negative value judgement. The American domination of management research lies much more in the latent and unavowed feeling of researchers from other countries of being inferior, rather than in the rarely expressed feeling by Americans of being superior. 'Is it because they develop second-class research? In this case, this is fuelled by their US colleagues who either do not read other languages than English or may consider that the dominant and only relevant form of scientific achievement is to publish in their own domestic journals and according to routine established criteria.'[14] Being from a monolingual, English speaking culture can be a somewhat limiting factor in international business research.

Management concepts and practices, although partly originating from Europe, have been developed largely in the United States, and later enthusiastically borrowed and adopted in many countries, because these concepts appeared as powerful tools for developing and controlling businesses. In so doing, the importing cultures have often transformed management concepts and integrated them into their own culture. For instance, the success of the word 'marketing' gave a new image to trade and sales activities in many countries where it had often previously been socially and intellectually devalued. Despite the success and the seemingly general acceptance of English-based business-related vocabulary, many examples indicate that there have been some basic misconceptions,[15] especially in developing countries. For instance, in many countries, business people have a clear lack of understanding as to what the word 'marketing' really means. Either managers do not understand what marketing is all about or, if they do, they tend to believe that it has little relevance to their business. In fact, marketing is still seen in most parts of the world as mere selling, or as advertising and sales promotion. Although 'marketing' has been imported as a word, and even as a sort of slogan, its former cultural roots and its precise meaning have been partly misunderstood.

Most of the books in business studies were borrowed from the United States and then translated directly without much adaptation. Moreover, survey techniques, the underlying concepts and the wording of questions, as well as questionnaire, interview and sampling techniques, were all widely imported. In reality, it was common practice to import the words rather than their whole sense and the social practices involved. The imported nature of management and business concepts and practices is clearly evidenced by the vocabulary, information and reference sources, and the origin of literature on the subject, all of which demarcate it as an area of knowledge. Data, information sources, and professional consultancy businesses (for auditing, advertising or market consult-ants, etc.) are mostly of American origin, even though many are not. Last but not least, academic journals and associations are largely based in the United States. Academic journals also exist in many other places (e.g., the United Kingdom, Europe, Canada and Japan), but most of the research literature depicted in the reference section of the published papers is based on American materials. The quantity of US content in the bibliographies of British, German and French reference lists often amounts to as much as 90%.

That there is a dominant culture in business is merely a fact. However, it implies that the researcher has to address the issues of who compares what/whom, for whom, using which theories, and what kind of proofs are relevant? The research design is a compromise between the respective cultures of the researcher, the research field that informs him/her and the research publics who read the report, use the results, evaluate the findings and/or finance the research (Figure 2.1).

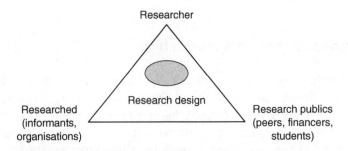

Figure 2.1   Influences on the research design

As Table 2.2 indicates, comparative designs result from the researcher's more or less conscious choices, from opportunities and constraints related to the researched field (e.g., the cultural distance between researchers and their infor-mants) and from the underlying theories which must fit the intellectual style of the clients in the research, that is, anonymous reviewers in a peer review process, or evaluators of a research project.

Researchers who undertake cross-national or cross-cultural comparisons are personally involved in the research and in the researched. Previous knowledge of the cultural area being studied is often a factor in the choice of a culturally familiar field of research. Researchers often want to explain their own cultural context and act as 'cultural mediators' in the area of academia. Such is the case of comparative management researchers who study the Arabic/Muslim style of management and leadership.[16] Sympathy between researchers from different

Table 2.2 Cultural influences on research design

	Theories (World views/languages/ frames of reference/codes/ instruments)	Data (Facts/figures/ information/ evidence/ statistics)	Proofs (Hypothesis testing/ applicability)
Researcher	Home-country 'theories' versus dominant theories	Culturally accepted images of reality	Self-confirmation
Researched	Field – host country world views	Respondents' own views	Sympathy/ relationships
Research Publics	Colleagues' own knowledge, paradigms, and research methods	Research reports: theses, articles, books, reports	Reviews/peer evaluations /readers

cultures also helps them form a cross-border 'joint-venture' research project. Such relationships as those between ex-PhD students and their former advisor/ supervisor who have developed a common understanding, are key assets in comparative management research.

2.3 The researcher as comparison base

The issue of ethnocentrism in international business research is an important one. Since a cultural conditioning is largely unconscious, it is important to be aware that the researcher's own background creates the real 'starting point' for the research process, implicitly or explicitly. Researchers in international business have to therefore address issues of ethnocentrism, stereotyping and prejudices and question their own motivation to research cross-nationally.

2.3.1 Researcher ethnocentrism and self-reference criteria

The concept of ethnocentrism was first introduced by Sumner[17] over a century ago, to distinguish between *in-groups* (those groups with which an individual identifies) and *out-groups* (those regarded as antithetical to the *in-group*). Sumner defined ethnocentrism as a tendency for people to perceive their own group as the centre and to scale and rate out-groups with reference to their own group. In its most extreme form, ethnocentrism relates to beliefs about the superiority of ones' own culture, which may lead to disinterest in and even contempt for the culture of other groups.[18] In a more mild form, ethnocentrism has been used to describe self-referencing, which is the natural tendency to spontaneously refer to the symbols, values and ways of thinking of one's own ethnic or national group; the in-group. The automatic and unconscious tendency to refer to one's own thought framework is mainly tied to national culture, which people do not generally choose but which allows them to interpret situations, evaluate people, communicate, negotiate, or decide.

Self-referencing is somewhat inevitable. Obeying the norms of one's culture is almost unconscious and the cost of adopting the cultural demeanour of the environment in which one has been raised *seems* minimal because the costs incurred in their rearing, socialisation and education are implicitly considered by accultured adults as *sunk costs*. On the other hand, the understanding and adoption of the traits of another culture are generally perceived as costly, as evidenced by the difficulties encountered by immigrants.

Ethnocentric self-referencing is not a cognitive limitation; it is also cognitive empowerment in the source culture. Multinational companies deliberately keep cultural control by maintaining an emphasis on the home language in the overseas location. Underlying this is the tough issue of who adapts to whom when economic and intellectual dominance play a key role.

Ethnocentric self-referencing tendencies can be reduced or eliminated with some effort. Lee[19] suggests the following steps in order to try to correct the decisional bias related to self-referencing, when dealing with international operations:

1. Define the problem or the objectives, as would be done according to the customs, behavioural standards and ways of thinking of the decision maker's country.

2. Similarly, define the problem or the objectives as would be done according to the customs, behavioural standards and ways of thinking of the foreign country.

3. Isolate the influence of the self-reference criterion on the problem, and identify the extent to which it complicates the decision-making problem.

4. Redefine the problem (and often the objectives) without the bias related to the self-reference criterion and then find the solutions and make decisions that fit with the cultural context of the foreign market.

The first two points are illustrated in the following situation. People are standing in line at an amusement park, such as Disneyland, where there are some very popular attractions. In the original context in the US, respect for queues is strong. They are usually well organised and there are even tangible indications for this (e.g., yellow lines on the ground indicating where people should stop to queue, tape or bars that are visible to help form queues). In the foreign context of France, where there is a developed sense of 'free-for-all' and less of a habit of organised queues (combined with a reluctance towards anything that seems too socially structured), discipline with respect to queues cannot be assumed. If Americans in France rely on their self-referencing criteria, they are likely to become rapidly frustrated. However, if they redefine the problem and objectives outside of their self-reference, they may be better placed to find an amicable solution to overcome the problem. However, this depiction of self-referencing includes some degree of naivety, as it assumes that a culture's mysteries can be easily understood.

2.3.2 Stereotypes and self shock

International, comparative business research can induce culture shocks in the researcher. A early example of such a shock is given by Clifford Geertz,[20] when he quotes a long passage from a nineteenth-century Danish trader, L. V. Helms, who accurately reports the ritual of the cremation of a dead man and his three (living) widows in India. Helms very carefully describes the background to the incident, which takes place in India around 1850. He is horrified by the ritual, amazed by the absence of reaction of the crowd attending the event and stunned by the lack of fear of the three women who throw themselves alive into the flames. Geertz emphasises the relations of culture to moral imagination: what is seen as barbarous by one culture is experienced as completely normal by another. Implicitly researchers always compare and confront their own views to the foreign reality they are observing. This is why traditional international business research is unknowingly comparative.

Stereotypes are important constructs in the researcher–research field relationship. Stereotypes represent a useful simplification, but their function of reducing and conserving differences can make them dangerous. Stereotypes have both a cognitive function and an emotional function of self-defence against a difference that creates anxiety. It seems easier to stick to one's own values and to force foreigners to change their views than to decentre oneself, that is, to leave one's system of reference and put oneself in the place of the other.

Stereotypes are often used to capture the salient traits of a 'foreign' national character; however, they are seldom very accurate, as Soutar and colleagues[21] found when they asked experienced Australian and Japanese international business people to estimate the most important values of their own culture, as well as those of other culture. For instance, Japanese business people reported that their relationships with others was the most important value listed, whereas Australian business people felt this was much less important to the Japanese than other values, such as being well respected, having a sense of belonging, and security.[22]

Self shock extends the concept of culture shock, which is considered to be a reaction to difference, to a reaction to differences with and within the self.[23] When people from different cultures meet, such as expatriate managers meeting local executives or international sellers meeting local buyers, the interaction can create uncertainty. At first it may seem that the basic problem is simply reducing uncertainty by 'getting to know the other', but as Adler[24] describes, there is in fact a 'progressive unfolding of the self' in an intercultural encounter, which can be attributed to 'a set of intensive and evocative situations in which the individual perceives and experiences other people in a distinctly new manner and, as a consequence, experiences new facets and dimensions of existence'. Experiencing how others actually are may be somewhat destabilising: identity confusion is a typical feature of culture shock. The cross-cultural researcher is therefore constantly confronted with issues in 'self-research', that is, enquiring into one's own prejudices, mindset and reference frame, which may be a disturbing task.

2.3.3 Variation in intellectual style across cultures

Many authors have noted distinct approaches to business research. Whether they speak about different 'intellectual traditions' or different 'research approaches', they highlight differences in the way issues are addressed, the role of theory is assigned, and the role data plays in the whole process. Researchers, tend to stick spontaneously to the values and representations of their national or disciplinary cultural grouping. Those who wish to enlarge their world view by freeing themselves, at least partially, from the mental programmes brought to them by culture, risk being misunderstood. By trying to escape their cultural programming, such people may be resented as exhibiting a lack of humility in setting themselves apart from the community. Furthermore, relatively homogeneous human groups, including academics belonging to scientific associations, organising conferences and running journals, may feel threatened when members of the group overstep the threshold of non-conformism.

Indeed our relation to the real world is heavily filtered by a series of convergent factors:

- our perceptual apparatus is partly formed by our culture;

- we implicitly privilege certain categories of facts *lato sensu* (emotions, thoughts, actions and/or situations) and interpret them based on our particular cultural background;

- the truthfulness of these facts is based on a cultural consensus about their being a part of reality;

- even when facts have been established as true, there still remain different readings and interpretations of them, depending on culture-based values and social representations.

Culture, among other factors, appears to influence the investigation methods and the criteria of good management research and good researchers. People may favour either *actual/empirical* reality, that is, the ways in which we experience reality here and now (or the way it is revealed by empirical science), or *potential reality*, that is, reality based on interpretation, speculation and imagination. Galtung[25] uses the distinction between actual reality and potential reality to contrast what he calls the 'intellectual styles' of four important cultural groups: the 'Gallic' (prototype: the French), the 'Teutonic' (prototype: the Germans), the Saxonic (prototype: the English and the Americans) and the 'Nipponic' (prototype: the Japanese and most generally Far East Asians).

Saxons prefer to look for facts and evidence which results in factual accuracy in abundance. As Galtung states when he describes the intellectual style of Anglo-Americans:

> ... data unite, theories divide. There are clear, relatively explicit canons for establishing what constitutes a valid fact and what does not; the corresponding canons in connection with theories are more vague.... One might now complete the picture of the Saxonic intellectual style by emphasising its weak point: not very strong on theory formation, and not on paradigm awareness.[26]

To the 'Teutonics' and the 'Gallics', the US (Saxonic) research orientation sometimes appears excessively data driven. Galtung contrasts the Saxonic style with the Teutonic and Gallic styles, which place theoretical arguments at the centre of their intellectual process.[27] Data and facts are there to illustrate what is said rather than to demonstrate it. However, Teutonic and Gallic intellectual styles do differ in the role that is assigned to words and discourse. The Teutonic ideal is that of the ineluctability of true reasoning *Gedankennotwendigkeit*, that is, the perfection of concepts and the indisputability of their mental articulation. The German language is probably the richest in the world for abstract words. It favours pure conceptual thinking. The construction of *Gedankennotwendigkeit* is itself an illustration of this: *denken* means 'to think', *Gedanken* are 'thoughts'; *Not* means 'necessity', *wenden* is 'to turn', *-keit* is a suffix which abstracts the whole as 'the state of being'. As a result of this mindgame, *Gedankennotwendigkeit* is something like *'the state of being turned into necessary (unavoidable, pure) thoughts'*. The Gallic style is less preoccupied with deduction and intellectual construction. It is directed more towards the use of the persuasive strength of words and speeches in an aesthetically perfect way (*élégance*). Words have an inherent power to convince. They may create *potential reality*.

Finally the Nipponic intellectual style, imbued with Hindu, Buddhist and Taoist philosophies, favours a more modest, global and provisional approach. Thinking and knowledge are conceived of as being in a temporary state, open to alteration. 'The Japanese rarely pronounce absolute, categorical statements in daily discourse; they prefer vagueness even about trivial matters ... because clear statements have a ring of immodesty, of being judgements of reality'.[28]

2.4 The issue of language in international business research

Cross-cultural business research tends to borrow more from psychology than from language studies and linguistics,[29] questionnaires and instruments, clients or research evaluators. The resulting Tower of Babel is often simplified by the use of English as International Language (EIL), or by means of translation as a cross-language comparison process supposed to lead to similar meaning, leaving aside idiosyncrasies and irreducible differences. However, the hope of doing language-free cross-cultural research is futile. Comparing across cultures, without awareness of language always results in biased and impoverished findings. At least three elements in language have an influence on the research process:

- words in as much as they signal specific meaning;
- words, as they are assembled in sentences and text through grammar and syntax, and work as codes that must in some way be 'translated' into other codes, when the researcher and the 'researched' do not share the same linguistic background;
- language, in general, provides the speaker with a particular world view.

2.4.1 The Whorfian hypothesis

Language tends to simultaneously reflect and shape our world views. It contains pre-shaped images of the real world which partly condition our experiences and perceptions. The first proponent of the idea that language has a decisive influence on culture was the linguist Edward Sapir. Language creates categories in our minds, which in turn directly influence the things we judge to be similar and those which *deserve* to be differentiated. It is our *Weltanschauung* that will be determined: our way of observing, of describing, of interacting and finally the way in which we construct our reality. Sapir writes:

> The fact of the matter is that the real world is to a large extent unconsciously built up on the language habits of the group. No two languages are ever sufficiently similar as to be considered as representing the same social reality. The worlds in which different societies live are distinct worlds, not merely the same world with different labels attached.[30]

The linguist and anthropologist Benjamin Lee Whorf developed and extended Sapir's hypothesis, which contends that the structure of language has a significant influence on perception and categorisation. However, the argument that language alone is responsible for these differences is largely rejected by most linguists. For example, the gender given to words is not necessarily indicative of a particular cultural meaning (e.g., the gender of the earth, the sun and the moon, or of vices and virtues); for most it often seems to reflect an arbitrary choice. There is a growing body of research that indicates that culture, rather than language alone, is responsible for differences in categorisation. For instance, regardless of the language in which they were asked, bilingual Chinese categorised objects according to their *relationship* more often than European Americans, who more often categorised the same objects according to their category membership.[31]

The vocabulary of time reveals much about the linkage between language and cultural representations. For those who have doubts about the existence of differences in cultural representations of time that are revealed, conveyed and reproduced by language, the example of the English (US) word 'deadline' is illustrative. A quick translation into French would give 'échéance [temporelle]' or 'délai de rigueur', but would not render the intensity of this word. Taken literally, it seems to suggest something like 'beyond this [temporal] line, you will [there is a danger of] die [dying]'. It therefore gives a genuine notion of urgency to what was originally a very abstract notion (a point which has been agreed upon on a line of time). The word deadline is used in French by many businesspeople as such (un deadline), even though it is not in the official dictionary, because it conveys a typically Anglo-American sense of urgency that French people do not find in their own language.

Language also reflects (and pre-shapes) how people envision the future. In some African languages (Kamba and Kikuyu), there are three future tenses which express (1) action in two to six months; (2) action that will take place immediately; (3) action 'in the foreseeable future, after this or that event'. Commenting on the uses of these African tenses, M'biti demonstrates how coherence and sophistication in the accurate use of the near future, are important to African people.

> You have these tenses before you: just try to imagine the tense into which you would translate passages of the New Testament concerning the Parousia of Our Lord Jesus Christ, or how you would teach eschatology... If you use tense no. 1, you are speaking about something that will take place in the next two to six months, or in any case within two years at most. If you use no. 2, you are referring to something that will take place in the immediate future, and if it does not take place you are exposed as a liar in people's eyes. Should you use no. 3 you are telling people that the event concerned will definitely take place, but when something else has happened first. In all these tenses, the event must be very near to the present moment: if, however, it lies in the far distant future – beyond the two-year limit – you are neither understood nor taken seriously.[32]

Levine, researching on Brazilian versus US perceptions of time, highlights the way concepts of punctuality are reflected in the language. He takes the example of the translation from English to Portuguese in a questionnaire containing the verb 'to wait':

> Several of our questions were concerned with how long the respondent would *wait* for someone to arrive versus when they *hoped* the person would arrive versus when they actually *expected* the person would come. Unfortunately for us, it turns out that the term *to wait, to hope* and *to expect* are all typically translated as the single verb *esperar* in Portuguese. In many ways our translation difficulties taught us more about Brazilian-Anglo differences in time conception than did the subjects' answers to the questions.[33]

There is a sort of continuum across languages in the accuracy of describing the waiting phenomenon (a fundamental issue in time experience!). French, which lies somewhere between English and Portuguese in terms of temporal accuracy, uses two words: *attendre* (to wait) and *espérer* (to hope). To expect has no direct equivalent in French and must be translated by a lengthy circumlocution (*compter sur l'arrivée de*).

2.4.2 Languages in relation to actions, thoughts, and emotions

Another example of the language–culture link is the Anglo-American way of dealing with action, especially in business. There is a rich vocabulary to be used, which is often difficult to translate into many other languages, if real equivalence of meaning is sought. The words might include, for instance: *problem solving, issue, matter of fact, down to earth, (empirical) evidence, to complete, to achieve, feedback, to perform, achievement, individual, data, to check, to plan, deadline, cognitive, emotional, successful.* Even such an elementary word as *fact* is demanding: in English it must be an *established* piece of reality; its French equivalent, *fait*, is less demanding in terms of unanimously agreed-upon reality (*les faits peuvent être discutés,* corresponding to a spirit of the facts being 'challenged' rather than just discussed); in German, a fact may be translated by *Tatsache, Wirklichkeit, Wahrheit,* or *Tat* – it can mean equally a *reality,* a *truth,* or an *action.*

When translating, the difficulties extend far beyond the pure lexical and grammatical issues: they are *cultural translation* difficulties, corresponding to what is often called the spirit of a language (in French, *Le génie de la langue*). Far from being merely an inter-linked chain of words, a language contains a series of stands taken on the nature of our relationship to reality. Let us compare, for instance, how the three most important western European languages express ideas, facts, and moods. One can tentatively suggest that German is stronger than English in the expression of abstractions. In German, word endings such as *-heit, -keit, -ung, -schaft, -tum, -nis,* etc. allow the 'abstractification' of concrete notions. English is not only less able to express pure concepts, it is also less prone to do so. English is more action- and more outward-oriented, with a view that data-orientation and facts-based approaches allow a separation between feelings (inner) and actions (directed toward the outside). French expresses inner states more accurately, with an emphasis on emotions rather than pure thoughts, describing the relationships between the self and others with an underlying view that any action is related to emotions and affectivity. Stereotypically, we could say that English is predominantly a language of action, French a language of emotions, and German a language of thoughts. The same languages can be slightly different in other nations, leading to miscommunication. For instance, the German language is slightly different in spelling in Germany, Austria and Switzerland. The same holds for Dutch in the Netherlands and in Flanders in Belgium; some similar words may have a different meaning though: in spoken language in Flanders people may use 'tas' for a cup (in addition to the word 'kop'). A 'tas' in the Netherlands refers to a bag, a 'kop' is a cup; the word 'tas' is not used in two different meanings. Translations into Dutch therefore need to be checked in both the Netherlands and Flanders.

Language also reflects status, hierarchy and a vision of what constitutes appropriate social relationships. The way to address other people is another example of how language reflects social hierarchy. There is only one word used in English for addressing other people, 'you' most often with the first name; this is considered as reflecting strong assumptions about equality and a preference for informality. By contrast, the French often use the formal *vous* for people they do not know very well and people of higher status, while the informal *tu* is reserved for family and friends. Thus, the French are reputed to be more formal. The Germans use *du* (second person singular) in informal and personal settings and *Sie* (third person plural) in formal address. The Germans, like the Spaniards have three forms of address: while the second person plural (*ihr*) has been lost in practice in German, it remains in Spanish. In fact, a closer look at these forms shows that the English 'you' was not originally a second person singular, which was 'thou' in old English (as in Shakespeare's plays), but the more polite second person plural. That means that the only address kept in English is based on an assumption of respect and formality and not on the everyday and less formal form of 'thou.' In fact, the assumed informality of Anglo interaction, advocated by many native English speakers, is difficult to grasp for a Latin. In people being called by their first name and together with 'you', the Latin sees a different kind of formalism rather than true informality. Language reflects quite complex assumptions about equality between people. The French address *vous* reflects the strong emphasis on hierarchical and status differences in French society, but it can be nuanced, adding for instance *Monsieur* (formal *vous*) or simply the first name (informal *vous*). It is not simply because they have long used the polite form that the French have a fairly hierarchical society; the language context contributes to constantly reframing culture-bound assumptions about hierarchy in French society.

2.4.3 Consequences of the Whorfian hypothesis for translation

The first consequence of the Whorf–Sapir hypothesis is that people from different cultures not only communicate in different ways, but also perceive, categorise, and construct their realities differently. This therefore supposes a 'state of alert' in communication, a readiness to accept that words, even when translated well, offer only an illusion of sharing in the same vision of reality. As many foreign words as possible should be kept in their original form, in order to recognise culturally unique concepts in the native language. Questioning translators, informants or foreign research associates about meaning in the local cultural context will allow areas of shared meaning to be identified. For instance, an

English term such as 'Act of God' can be (poorly) translated through Google Translate as 'acte de Dieu', when in fact the (apparent) French equivalent is *Force majeure*. *Force majeure,* a common clause in contracts essentially frees both parties from liability or obligation when an extraordinary event or circumstance beyond the control of the parties prevents one or both parties from fulfilling their obligations under the contract. However, *Force Majeure* is not a strict equivalent of *Act of God*, because its coverage is larger than *Act of God*, *Force majeure* is therefore used in French in English and US contracts.

An unfortunate consequence of the Whorf–Sapir hypothesis is that linguistic ethnocentrism is largely inevitable. Famous anthropologists belonged to the cultures of their publishers and readers, not to the cultures they observed. The same holds true for area specialists. A cultural outsider makes more objective observations than a cultural and linguistic insider in reporting those observations; however, as provocative as it may seem, it is more important to be understood than to understand. What is said by genuine cultural insiders is often difficult to understand unless their words have in some way been recalibrated in the linguistic/cultural background of the readers, which means a lot more than simple translation.

Fortunately, international business researchers are not required to have full command of several foreign languages to be linguistically astute. What is important is the ability to catch what is unique in the structure of foreign languages and word, which does not require fluency in reading and speaking. Consulting a basic grammar book and paying attention to specific words are a good start. Very often words are also borrowed, to create hybrid languages, such as Chinglish and Japlish that combines words from both languages to create a new meaning. It is sometimes important to keep original words as they are, understand meaningful elements in the grammar (such as gender, tenses, sentence construction etc.), and try to behave as 'explorers' of the meanings and world views expressed by different languages.

2.4.4 Translation equivalence: questionnaires, checklists and briefings

Three metaphors related to translation have been used by Janssens, Lambert, and Steyaert[34] to describe language strategies in international companies, which also apply to cross-cultural business research. The first avenue, dominant in cross-cultural business research, is the 'mechanical' use of back-translation to ensure equivalence with a strong emphasis on the source, rather than the target, text. Most cross-cultural business research is concerned with establishing full invariance of research instruments. This is inspired by a willingness to make data fully comparable across cultures. This is a purely etic perspective. It is based on universalist assumptions, a strictly instrumental view of language, and a mechanical approach based on back-translation.[35] This approach is often at the expense of unique cultural meaning. Some contributions convincingly demonstrate that the mere borrowing of research instruments with mechanical back-translation ends up masking significant cross-national differences.[36] As emphasised by Polsa,[37] conceptual non-equivalence across languages, cultures, and nations may be a source of unexpected findings leading to the discovery of new dimensions in established constructs.

The second approach, the cultural perspective on translation, builds on different underlying assumptions regarding language and culture, emphasising both language diversity and linguistic relativity. Rather than 'walking through dictionaries'[38] like the mechanical perspective, the cultural perspective on translation considers deviation from the source text not as a 'mistake' but rather as a 'window' opening onto the target language and culture. Translation is considered a cultural, rather than technical, message transmission process, resulting in active inscription into the new context. It is accepted that different texts may be created through each translation.[39]

The third perspective on translation is political and considers that languages may compete against each other to express meaning. It emphasises the power games between different languages to express values, to legitimise attitudes, behaviours, and shared practices. In cross-cultural business research, the political perspective is meaningful, as it concerns the forms of cross-national research collaboration, the equality versus inequality in cross-national research teams, and the opportunity given to local researchers and informants to express their views on research instruments.

Translation equivalence may be divided into the following subcategories: lexical equivalence, idiomatic equivalence, grammatical-syntactical equivalence and experiential equivalence.[40] Lexical equivalence is provided by dictionaries. For instance, the English adjective 'warm' translates into the French '*chaud*'. The issue of idiomatic equivalence arises when translating a sentence such as 'it's warm': French has two expressions, either *il fait chaud* (literally, 'it makes warm' meaning 'it's warm (today)') or *c'est chaud* (meaning 'it (this object) is warm'). An idiom is a linguistic usage that is natural to native speakers. Idioms are most often non equivalent. For instance, the English present progressive (i.e., I am *doing*) has no equivalent in French, except *je suis en train de...* which is highly colloquial.

Grammatical-syntactical equivalence deals with how words are ordered, sentences are constructed and meaning is expressed in a language. English generally proceeds in an active way, starting by the subject followed by the verb and then the complement, avoiding abstractions, as well as convoluted sentences. Many languages, including German and French start by explaining the circumstances in relative clauses, before they proceed into the action. This results in complex sentences, which start with relative clauses based on when, where, even though, although, and so on. The Japanese language has a quite different word order compared to western languages since verbs go at the end of the sentence.

Experiential equivalence is about what words and sentences mean for people in their everyday experience. Referring back to *chaud*, it translates into two English words 'warm' and 'hot': the French do not experience 'warmth' with two concepts as the English, the Germans and many others do. Similarly, the special experience of coldness expressed in the word 'chilly' cannot be adequately rendered in French. Translated terms must refer to real items and real experiences, which are familiar in the source as well as the target cultures. Expressions such as 'dual career couple', or 'decision making', or even 'strategic plan' may come across experiential equivalence dilemmas.

Another example of experiential non-equivalence is apparent in the Japanese numbering system which reflects a special experience of counting, where the numbers cannot be fully abstracted from the object being counted. Chinese is similar to Japanese in this respect. Most often, the Japanese add a particle indicating which objects are counted. *Nin* for instance is used to count human beings: *yo-nin* is four (persons). *Hiki* is used for counting animals, except birds for which *wa* is used (meaning 'feather'), *satsu* for books, *hon* for round and long objects, *mai* for flat things such as a sheet of paper, textiles, coins, etc., and *hai* for cups and bowls, and liquid containers in general.

2.5 Language as a tool for the discovery of potential meaning

The dominant position of the English language in business and international trade must be the starting point of a discussion about language as a tool for the discovery of cultural meaning. It is also a fantastic avenue for deconstruction. The special qualities of English – fairly simple from a grammatical point of view, precise, action and facts oriented – make it an ideal language for business, in fact the ideal language, because there is no other competitor for worldwide language leadership. It is not by chance that English has become the true universal language of business. It is built mostly on the merger of a Latin language, French, and a Germanic language, spoken by the English before the Norman Conquest. However, the constant recourse to English as *lingua franca* tends to blur differences across cultural contexts.

In considering English as the *lingua franca* for business research (EIL stands for English as an International Language), it is essential to differentiate between native and non-native Anglophones.[41] Non-native English-speaking researchers often have to learn English and one or two other languages. For instance, the Swedes, Finns, Danes and Norwegians often speak three or four foreign languages: English, another Nordic language, and French, German or Spanish. The situation is very different for native Anglophones. Taking Australia as an example, it is a vast, linguistically homogeneous country where almost everyone speaks English. Australia is also geographically remote. The major city of Melbourne is around 3200 km from the nearest major non-English-speaking population centre (in Papua New Guinea). In Australia, it is not necessary to learn foreign languages, whereas in Europe most large cities are located less than 330 km from a foreign-speaking region and learning one or more foreign languages is a real asset. Even in English speaking countries with large second language communities, such as the US, which is now the fourth largest Spanish-speaking country in the world, most Americans do not feel they have to learn Spanish. Rather, Hispanics have more need to learn English.

Moreover, learning foreign languages is asymmetrical in terms of effort; a westerner learning Chinese or Japanese has to master the characters, which implies a much larger effort than for the Japanese or Chinese to learn the Roman alphabet with its 26 phonetic characters. The *gaijin* (non-Japanese) has to learn two syllabaries of about one hundred characters each (*hiragana* and *katakana*, phonetic symbols) and about 1850 *kanjis* (ideographic symbols). Lastly, Americans easily find English speakers during their travels, they can count on their foreign partners to speak English, and they are tolerant towards the mistakes of their non-native counterparts.

Understandably, therefore, the impact of language differences has been systematically underestimated in international business research because of a single bias in Anglo-American culture. Most international business literature does not include a single fully foreign reference, that is, a foreign author in a foreign language. Foreign authors, when translated, will not be read in their original linguistic context and when not translated into English will not be considered. However, this regrettable situation also results from practical reasons for maintaining language homogeneity in sources, namely that the reader would not be able either to find or read references in foreign languages.

What is unfortunate however, is that native English speakers are at a disadvantage in the long term, although it may appear to be the exact contrary over the short term. The main disadvantage for them is that they cannot grasp the features of a foreign language in terms of world view and communication style. Many native English speakers cannot imagine what it implies for their foreign respondents or research associates to express their thoughts in English with limited proficiency unless the native English researchers have themselves tried to learn and speak a foreign language. Thus native English speakers have to develop an awareness of language barriers. The message to be conveyed cannot be simply and plainly to learn foreign languages. There is a difference between understanding and speaking a foreign language and grasping the consequences of languages being different. Management researchers do not need to be multi-lingual, but rather they need to have an in-depth awareness of what language differences imply.

On the other hand, many foreign researchers or informants who are non-native English speakers, although they seem to have a good command of English, still hold the kind of world view shaped by their native language. They may be somewhat misleading people in comparisons groups; looking quite the same, while being fairly different. In addition to their different mindset, they may be more proficient in oral than written communication, which may cause problems in discussing the written details of research or when writing for publication.

2.5.1 Language: a window on world views

There is a definite need to use language beyond the simple need to reach equivalence between business concepts expressed in different languages.[42] How languages other than English try to express responses to common problems can be contrasted by the mean of *untranslation*,[43] that is, avoiding translation when the meaning would be fundamentally altered by the translation process (and keeping the original word or expression in the source language) or translation when the meaning is only slightly altered (and keep note of the meaning lost or distorted). The Italian proverb *traduttore traditore* (translator traitor) contains a moral and a pragmatic message: it is better to adopt a form of sophisticated honesty and try to uncover the meaning lost in the translation process. The objective of *untranslation* is not to search for immediately applicable, practical solutions in terms of just finding the – supposedly – right translation. The benefits to be gained from *untranslation* are indirect and take time to be reaped. They consist basically in an increased understanding, a profound rather than superficial knowledge of why other people behave and interact differently in situations which are largely similar.

If we start from a metaphor of *mise en scène*, language may be seen as staging the scenario or scripts of our lives: individuals and groups, as carriers of culture, are players and they have to learn their text by heart before the dress rehearsal. Culture indicates the stage setting as well as, through language, a shared text, composed of scenes and acts, and it explains to the players the ways in which scenes begin as well as end. Culture stages people, because they have learned their roles, and people are staged by cultures because individual roles fit together in the whole theatre piece. That is why intercultural communication is not an easy task. If language was strictly about differences in words, there would be no or little differences, and in some rare cases this may be the true. We simply do not act in the same plays.

Language is especially useful to investigate conceptual and functional equivalence and hence instrument equivalence. It allows the generation of insights into possible differences which can be progressively verified. Meaning differentials can be investigated across languages for apparently similar words and utterances in the following areas:

1. Multiple meanings of a word.

2. Central, most important meaning (modal meaning).

3. Frequency of use of certain words.

4. Latent value judgements put on words, positive and/or negative, and in which context; pejorative meanings indicate a normative orientation.

5. Meaning subtleties: context of use of words and experiential aspect (for this, insert individual words in sentences which are culturally typical).

6. Idiomatic expressions.

7. Sometimes even phonology can be useful because it may be suggestive.

8. The study of grammar can be enlightening because it expresses a relationship to rules and exceptions, simplicity, and formalism, tenses and time orientations, prepositions and space orientation, active and passive modes.

9. Etymology: looking at the origins and roots of words can also provide insights.

Finally, metalinguistic aspects, such as the use of rhetoric, silence, conversational style, overlapping, body gestures accompanying language activities, are more difficult to investigate, but they are no less important. However, language proficiency is by no means a necessary condition for being able to deconstruct world views through linguistic investigation.

A practical solution for investigating world views, as they are reflected by language is to interview native speakers, local collaborators and informants, observe, discuss with them, check meaning differentials and, if possible, try to speak their language even modestly. Words often have multiple meanings and it is easy to discover in dictionaries meanings which are in fact rarely used. This testifies to the fact that world views have a large degree of intersection, especially among European languages. However, the dominant usage of a word and the special way of assembling words into specific sentences does singularise what in pure dictionary terms seemed at first much alike.

Glen Fisher,[44] a distinguished scholar in the field of intercultural relations, recounted a conversation with a Latin American friend about the words used in English and Spanish for business relations. His friend first remarked that in English the word 'business' is positive. It connotes the fact of being 'busy' and emphasises doing things. Expressions such as 'getting down to business' denote people who have a responsible concern for their work. Fisher further explains that:

> In Spanish the word is 'negocio' … The key is the 'ocio' part of the word, which connotes leisure, serenity, time to enjoy and contemplate as the preferred human condition and circumstance. But when harsh reality forces one from one's 'ocio,' when it is negated, then one has to attend to 'negocio.' The subjective meaning is obviously much less positive than in English … It is the subjective meaning of words

and expressions that needs to be captured. Time spent exploring why a given utterance does not translate well may be more productive for the one who is actually trying to communicate than concentration on technical excellence.[45]

A translator can be technically skilled enough to find the very nearest equivalent in the target language. This requires a high level of linguistic competence and a profound knowledge of both source and target language. However, the whole process may blur meaning differences because lexically equivalent words do not have exactly the same experiential meaning in the target as in the source language. If hidden, the meaning differential cannot be understood by the researcher, who loses valuable insights. Language both shapes and reflects our world views. Words and expressions reflect unique experiences and patterns of thought and action that are shared by members of a particular culture when they have a common language. The meaning of these words and expressions informs us about differences, whereas translation tries to find a similar meaning across languages, or in some way to rebuild it. When translation fails to establish meaning equivalence, we are in front of something unique, worth being understood. That is why it is worth exploring why a given utterance does not translate well and it may be dangerous to hide it by 'technical excellence'. Let us now turn to some examples.

2.5.2 Flexibility vs. structure and rules in organisational life

A French word, *se débrouiller*, is quite often used to explain that people 'manage' as in 'you will have to manage it on your own'; in French, *se débrouiller* refers to a form of personal flexibility. This emphasis on flexibility refers to quite typical situations in a high power distance and fairly bureaucratic society where people, more often than not, have to achieve while facing multiple obstacles and being given poor resources. *Se débrouiller,* and the alternative terms often used (*débrouillardise, système D, s'en sortir, faire avec*) are in general fairly positive. There is, at least, no negative value judgement. The German equivalent is a colloquial word, *sich durchwursteln*, something like to 'sausage (*wurst*) oneself through', which is negatively loaded, while the official translation (*sich zu helfen wissen*, 'to know how to help oneself') is very rarely used. Some English–German dictionaries do not even mention the word *durchwursteln*, because, although both the English and German speaking cultures know this kind of opportunistic behaviour it is neither familiar enough nor positively valued by either culture.

In the German society the rules are made to be respected, whereas in French society they are made to be explored. The French often explore the rule in order to test whether it is meant seriously. A questionnaire devised by Geert Hofstede to investigate 'business goals', was translated and administered in France by

Jean-Claude. He proposed translating 'staying within the law' to *ne pas enfreindre la loi* (that is, 'not trespass the law'). This kind of double negative expresses the dynamic of the respect of rules for the French much better than the simple positive expression used in the original English questionnaire.

2.5.3 Communication styles in intercultural business interactions

Much cross-cultural and intercultural literature mentions and sometimes investigates communication misunderstandings across cultures. A framework for explaining these misunderstandings is that of Edward Hall,[46] contrasting high context/implicit messages (prototypes: Japanese or Middle Eastern cultures) and low context/explicit messages cultures (prototypes: US or Northern European cultures). However, this framework is language free: *it works as if language never mattered*. A quick look at a book of Japanese grammar reveals that in Japanese there are no articles either definite or indefinite. *Hon*, for instance, means either 'the book', 'a book', 'the books' or 'books'. When the Japanese want to express their thoughts, they cannot communicate without taking cues from the context: *what is said explicitly is simply not enough*. The correspondence between high context communication and the general structure of a language is a feature of the Japanese language. For instance, in Japanese:

1. A predicate always comes at the end of a sentence (meaning that if I say 'I study Japanese at the College of Arts of the University of Nagoya', 'study' will come at the very end of the Japanese sentence).
2. A verb has no ending to indicate person or number.
3. There is no article used with nouns in most cases.
4. One and the same form of a noun may mean both the singular and the plural form.
5. The grammatical case of a noun or pronoun is indicated by means of various particles occurring after the noun or pronoun.
6. Subject and object are often omitted if they are understood from the context.

If we add that there are several plain and polite styles in Japanese and that, in daily conversation, either of them may be used depending on the situation, the role of the context in Japanese appears to be considerable. The language basically 'under-signifies' what the speakers are willing to say, providing insufficient linguistic cues for the listener to understand the message only on a purely digital basis. The listener must therefore 'reconstruct' the relevant meaning by searching for additional explanatory cues such as: Who speaks? What did he say previously? How does s/he say it? Where is it said?

Watashi no hon (my book) will be interpreted as the book authored by the speaker (if s/he has already published books) or the book that somebody has in his hands if it takes place in a library, etc. When the Japanese want to express their thoughts they refer constantly to the context to interpret the inexplicit aspect of messages. As a consequence, they are accustomed to guessing what others say in a fairly sophisticated mental process where they constantly have to search for meaning rather than find it nicely packaged in a full phrase. This high context sophistication exists to a certain extent in most languages when they are spoken in their colloquial form whereby people 'save' words and use contextual cues. This may explain also why Japanese are good 'listeners' compared to most westerners.

2.5.4 Specific words revealing unique concepts

A good example of such unique words is the Japanese word *ningensei*, the importance of which is emphasised by Goldman.[47] *Ningensei* literally translates into an all encompassing and overriding concern and prioritising of 'humanity' or *human beingness*. According to Japanese specialists of international marketing negotiations:

> The North American and UK negotiators failed to communicate *ningensei* at the first table meeting. Rushing into bottom lines and demanding quick decisions on the pending contract they also overlooked the crucial need for *ningensei* in developing good will ... Hard business facts alone are not enough ... *Ningensei* is critical in getting Japanese to comply or in persuading Japanese negotiating partners. (Nippon Inc. Consultation quoted in Goldman[48])

Ningensei exemplifies four interrelated principles of Confucian philosophy: *jen*, *shu*, *i* and *li*. Based on active listening, *Jen* is a form of humanism that translates into empathetic interaction and caring for the feelings of negotiating associates, and seeking out the other's views, sentiments and true intentions. *Shu* emphasises the importance of reciprocity in establishing human relationships and the cultivation of 'like-heartedness'. According to Matsumoto's (1988)[49] it is 'belly communication', a means of coding messages within negotiating social and corporate channels that is highly contingent upon affective, intuitive and nonverbal channels. The *i*, also termed *amae*, is the dimension which is concerned with the welfare of the collectivity, directing human relationships to the betterment of the common good. 'The *i* component of *ningensei* surfaces in Japanese negotiators' commitment to the organisation, group agendas and a reciprocity (*shu*) and humanism (*jen*) that is long-term, consistent, and looks beyond personal motivation.'[50] Finally, *li* refers to the codes, corresponding to precise and formal manners, that facilitate the outer manifestation and social expression of *jen*, *shu*, and *i*. The Japanese *meishi* ritual of exchanging business cards is typical of *li* coded etiquette.[51]

2.6 Conclusion

Language barriers, and differences in intellectual styles and academic systems are major deterrents for cross-cultural business research. True international research, which is still quite rare, should always be the product of collaboration between native researchers coming from diverse cultural and linguistic contexts. The purely instrumental view of language in business studies, that is, seeing language as a neutral vehicle for conveying representations, ideas, and concepts[52] has helped develop an artificially homogeneous body of knowledge. Such assumptions have underlain the practices of both global business and global academia in business for several decades, leading to a self-fulfilling prophecy. Non-English speakers have been obliged to adjust their words and their mindsets and to adopt a world view, which is highly impregnated by Anglophone concepts. Actively ignoring the world views present in other languages was, and still is, a way to avoid challenging dominant business theories and knowledge by foreign concepts. Very few foreign concepts have been imported by the US, except some key Japanese words because of the impressive achievements of Japanese companies in the world market.[53]

However, the deep impact of ideographic East-Asian writing systems (i.e., Chinese and Japanese) on knowledge creation has rarely been addressed. This suggests that the philosophical issue of whether language is a neutral instrument of communication or whether we are also instrumented by language deeply intermingles with ideological interests.[54] Comparing across cultures, without being aware of language differences may result in biased and impoverished findings. Any cross-cultural study in business should include a preliminary phase of conceptual equivalence assessment based on linguistic cues. Core etic meanings and key emic meanings should be explored before the cross-border transfer of research instruments. The conceptual equivalence of some key concepts should systematically be investigated across major linguistic contexts and the findings shared among researchers (see Chapters 4 and 5). Part of the cross-cultural research agenda should focus on the progressive emergence of a set of etic and emic meanings for key concepts across major linguistic areas as suggested by Holden.[55]

Notes

1. Pudelko, M., H. Tenzer, and A.-W. Harzing, Cross-cultural management and language studies within international business research: Past and present paradigms and suggestions for future research. Routledge Companion to Cross-cultural Management. 2014. London: Routledge, pp. 85–94.

2. Janssens, M. and C. Steyaert, Re-considering language within a cosmopolitan under-standing: Toward a multilingual franca approach in international business studies. Journal of International Business Studies, 2014. 45(5): 623–639.
   Steyaert, C. and M. Janssens, Translation in Cross-Cultural Management: A matter of voice, Routledge Companion to Cross-cultural Management, 2015, pp. 131–41.
3. Sapir, E., The status of linguistics as a science. Language, 1929: 5: 207–214.
4. Pike, K.L., Language in Relation to a Unified Theory of the Structure of Human Behavior (2nd rev. 1967), Mouton: The Hague.
5. Geertz, C., The Interpretation of Cultures: Selected essays. Vol. 5019. 1973: Basic Books, New York, p. 24.
6. Ryle, G. The thinking of thoughts: What is 'le Penseur' doing? University Lectures, no.18, 1968, University of Saskatchewan.
7. Usunier, J.-C. and S. Sbizzera, Comparative thick description: Articulating similarities and differences in local consumer experience. International Marketing Review, 2013. 30(1): 42–55.
8. Hofstede, G.H. and G. Hofstede, Culture's Consequences: Comparing values, behaviors, institutions and organizations across nations. 2001: Sage.
9. Bagozzi, R.P., N. Wong, S. Abe, and M. Bergami, Cultural and situational contingen-cies and the theory of reasoned action: Application to fast food restaurant consumption. Journal of Consumer Psychology, 2000. 9(2): 97–106.
   Lee, J.A., Adapting Triandis's model of subjective culture and social behavior relations to consumer behavior. Journal of Consumer Psychology, 2000. 9(2): 117–126.
   Lee, C. and R.T. Green, Cross-cultural examination of the Fishbein behavioral inten-tions model. Journal of International Business Studies, 1991. 22(2): 289–305.
10. Hirschman, E.C., Primitive aspects of consumption in modern American society. Journal of Consumer Research, 1985. 12(2): 142–154.
11. Dorfman, P., M. Javidan, P. Hanges, A. Dastmalchian, and R. House, GLOBE: A twenty year journey into the intriguing world of culture and leadership. Journal of World Business, 2012. 47(4): 504–518.
12. Vaiman, V. and N. Holden, Cross-cultural management: Arguing the case for non-cultural explanations in N. Holden, S. Michailova and S. Tietze (Eds) The Routledge Companion to Cross-Cultural Management, 2015: p. 58.
13. Vaiman, V. and N. Holden, Cross-cultural management: Arguing the case for non-cultural explanations. in N. Holden, S. Michailova and S. Tietze (Eds) The Routledge Companion to Cross-Cultural Management, 2015: p. 64.
14. Koza, M.P. and J.-C. Thoenig, Organizational theory at the crossroads: Some reflec-tions on European and United States approaches to organizational research. Organization Science, 1995. 6(1): 1–8, p. 6
15. Holden, G., Who contextualizes the contextualizers? Disciplinary history and the discourse about IR discourse. Review of International Studies, 2002. 28(02): 253–270.
16. Randeree, K. and A. Ghaffar Chaudhry, Leadership-style, satisfaction and commit-ment: An exploration in the United Arab Emirates' construction sector. Engineering, Construction and Architectural Management, 2012. 19(1): 61–85.

Sidani, Y. and A. Al Ariss, Institutional and corporate drivers of global talent management: Evidence from the Arab Gulf region. Journal of World Business, 2014. 49(2): 215–224.

17. Sumner, W.G., Folkways, Ginn. Boston, MA, 1906.
18. LeVine, R.A. and D.T. Campbell, Ethnocentrism: Theories of Conflict, Ethnic Attitudes, and Group Behavior. Oxford: John Wiley & Sons, 1972.
19. Lee, J.A., Cultural analysis in overseas operations. The International Executive, 1966. 8(3): 5–6.
20. Geertz, C., Local Knowledge. New York: Basic Books. 1983.
21. Soutar, G.N., R. Grainger, and P. Hedges, Australian and Japanese value stereotypes: A two country study. Journal of International Business Studies, 1999. 30(1): 203–216.
22. Soutar, G.N., R. Grainger, and P. Hedges, Australian and Japanese value stereotypes: A two country study. Journal of International Business Studies, 1999. 30(1): 203–216.
23. Zaharna, R.S., Self-shock: The double-binding challenge of identity. International Journal of Intercultural Relations, 1989. 13(4): 501–525.
24. Adler, P.S., The transitional experience: An alternative view of culture shock. Journal of Humanistic Psychology, 1975, p.18.
25. Galtung, J., Structure, Culture, and Intellectual Style: An essay comparing Saxonic, Teutonic, Gallic and Nipponic approaches. Social Science Information/sur les sciences sociales, 1981, 20(6): 817–56.
26. Galtung, J., Structure, Culture, and Intellectual Style: An essay comparing Saxonic, Teutonic, Gallic and Nipponic approaches. Social Science Information/sur les sciences sociales, 1981, pp. 827–828.
27. Galtung, J., Structure, Culture, and Intellectual Style: An essay comparing Saxonic, Teutonic, Gallic and Nipponic approaches. Social Science Information/sur les sciences sociales, 1981.
28. Galtung, J., Structure, Culture, and Intellectual Style: An essay comparing Saxonic, Teutonic, Gallic and Nipponic approaches. Social Science Information/sur les sciences sociales, 1981, p. 833.
29. Chabowski, B.R., S. Samiee, and G.T.M. Hult, Cross-national research and international business: An interdisciplinary path. International Business Review, 2016, 26(1): 89–101.
30. Sapir, E., The status of linguistics as a science. Language, 1929: 5: 207–214, p. 214.
31. Unsworth, S.J., C.R. Sears, and P.M. Pexman, Cultural influences on categorization processes. Journal of Cross-Cultural Psychology, 2005. 36(6): 662–688.
32. M'biti, J., African concept of Time. Africa Theological Journal, 1968. 1: p. 13
33. Levine, R.V. The pace of life across cultures, in J.E. McGrath (Ed.), The Social Psychology of Time, Sage Publications: Newbury Park, CA, 1988, pp. 48–49.
34. Janssens, M., J. Lambert, and C. Steyaert, Developing language strategies for international companies: The contribution of translation studies. Journal of World Business, 2004. 39(4): 414–430.
35. Janssens, M., J. Lambert, and C. Steyaert, Developing language strategies for international companies: The contribution of translation studies. Journal of World Business, 2004. 39(4): 414–430.

36. Douglas, S.P. and E.J. Nijssen, On the use of 'borrowed' scales in cross-national research: A cautionary note. International Marketing Review, 2003. 20(6): 621–642.

37. Polsa, P., Comparability in cross-cultural qualitative marketing research: Equivalence in personal interviews. Academy of Marketing Science Review, 2007. 8(1): 1–18.

38. Janssens, M., J. Lambert, and C. Steyaert, Developing language strategies for international companies: The contribution of translation studies. Journal of World Business, 2004. 39(4): 414–430, p. 418.

39. Janssens, M., J. Lambert, and C. Steyaert, Developing language strategies for international companies: The contribution of translation studies. Journal of World Business, 2004. 39(4): 414–430.

40. Sechrest, L., T.L. Fay, and S.H. Zaidi, Problems of translation in cross-cultural research. Journal of Cross-Cultural Psychology, 1972. 3(1): 41–56.

41. Louhiala-Salminen, L., M. Charles, and A. Kankaanranta, English as a lingua franca in Nordic corporate mergers: Two case companies. English for Specific Purposes, 2005. 24(4): 401–421.
Brannen, M.Y., R. Piekkari, and S. Tietze, The multifaceted role of language in international business: Unpacking the forms, functions and features of a critical challenge to MNC theory and performance. Journal of International Business Studies, 2014. 45(5): 495–507.

42. Chidlow, A., E. Plakoyiannaki, and C. Welch, Translation in cross-language international business research: Beyond equivalence. Journal of International Business Studies, 2014. 45(5): 562–582.

43. Usunier, J.-C., Language as a resource to assess cross-cultural equivalence in quantitative management research. Journal of World Business, 2011. 46(3): 314–319.

44. Fisher, G., Mindsets. 1988, Yarmouth, ME: Intercultural Press.

45. Fisher, G., Mindsets. 1988, Yarmouth, ME: Intercultural Press, pp. 148–9, 172.

46. Hall, E.T., The Silent Language. Vol. 3. 1959. New York: Doubleday.
Hall, E.T., The Hidden Dimension. 1966. New York: Doubleday.

47. Goldman, A., Doing Business with the Japanese: A guide to successful communication, management, and diplomacy. 1994. New York: SUNY Press.

48. Goldman, A., Doing Business with the Japanese: A guide to successful communication, management, and diplomacy. 1994: SUNY Press, p. 31.

49. Matsumoto, M. The Unspoken Way: Haragei – silence in Japanese business and society, 1988, Kodansha International: New York.

50. Goldman, A., The centrality of 'Ningensei' to Japanese negotiating and interpersonal relationships: implications for U.S.–Japanese communication, International Journal of Intercultural Relations, 1994, 18(1): 29–54.

51. Goldman, A., Doing Business with the Japanese: A guide to successful communication, management, and diplomacy. 1994: SUNY Press, pp. 32–33.

52. Leung, K., Methods and measurements in cross-cultural management in Peter.B. Smith, Mark F. Peterson and David C. Thomas (Eds), The Handbook of Cross-cultural Management Research, 2008: pp. 59–73.

53. Ahmadjian, C.L. and U. Schaede, The impact of Japan on Western management: Theory and practice in N. Holden, S. Michailova, and S. Tietze, (Eds), The Routledge Companion to Cross-Cultural Management, 2015 London: Routledge: p. 49.

54. Janssens, M., J. Lambert, and C. Steyaert, Developing language strategies for international companies: The contribution of translation studies. Journal of World Business, 2004. 39(4): 414–430.
55. Holden, N., Reflections of a cross cultural scholar context and language in management thought. International Journal of Cross-Cultural Management, 2008. 8(2): 239–251.

3

DESIGN AND IMPLEMENTATION

3.0 Introduction

Research designs in international and cross-cultural business research are understandably complex. The diversity of topics, levels, cultures, and context variables that need to be taken into account makes them complex to conceive and to keep under control both at the conceptual and at the data collection stages. Overly complex designs may result in failures during the implementation process when a researcher cannot collect the required data or cannot appropriately control the data collection process, leading to either 'flat' data (almost no variance) or fuzzy data (variance is mostly measurement error). This can be true of qualitative as well as quantitative approaches: if the design requires in-depth interviewees to elaborate beyond their real experiences and their own mindset, they may smother their responses in a blanket of irrelevant statements that are difficult to untangle and find insight.

This chapter addresses the natural complexity inherent in international and cross-cultural business research by discussing the, *somewhat*, conscious choices around the selection of paradigm (Section 3.1), research question (Section 3.2), complexity (Section 3.3) and data collection techniques (Section 3.4). In fact, the choice of an appropriate avenue for explanation presupposes that alternative paradigms are carefully considered, investigated and their implications assessed before the researcher chooses the one that is most appropriate. However, more often than not researchers choose the paradigm they are most comfortable with and that choice of paradigm somewhat limits the questions they choose and the way they conduct their research.

3.1 The choice among substantive paradigms and associated methods

A research paradigm focuses on a set of fundamental assumptions and beliefs about how the world is, for which certain research methodologies seem more appropriate. It is important to choose among paradigms, not because one is superior to the other, but because they have different implications in terms of the type of questions they can answer, the way in which they are answered, and research publics likely to be interested. This choice results in observing the same reality from quite different perspectives, which are not necessarily compatible. Paradigmatic choices are also strong determinants of the 'labelling' of researchers. They largely define the abstract territory which the researcher shares with others who have a common world view. Last but not least, the personal appeal of a particular paradigm to the researcher makes sense in his or her choice.

The main paradigms in international and cross-cultural business research generally relate to either a more etic or more emic view of the world. As previously touched on in Chapter 2, etic researchers seek relatively universal frameworks that allow countries or cultures to be compared and their similarities and differences examined, whereas emic researchers seek culture-specific frameworks to uncover what is unique about a culture, group or individual. These two paradigms should not be viewed as dichotomous extremes. They are different and equally valid perspectives that are used to answer very different questions. For instance, if a manager wants to know what strategies and practices should be standardised across countries, as etic orientation is appropriate. In contrast, if a manager is interested in finding the optimal strategies or practices for a given country, an emic orientation is appropriate.

Most of the international business literature was based on an etic paradigm in the early years, when many researchers were extending studies from the western context to other regions. The emphasis was on finding universals and tested boundary conditions. The basic position was somewhat ethnocentric, where western management was seen as 'best practice'.[1] After the rise of the Japanese economy in the 1980s, there was a stark realisation that business success could also be achieved with very different management practices.

Around this time, Hofstede[2] introduced a set of cultural dimension scores that provided a relatively easy basis to test for differences not only between countries but between cultures. Hofstede translated the vague, complex construct of culture into a more manageable and concrete system. Cultural dimensions, and the distance between these dimensions, were introduced as an independent variable that could be used to explain a wide range of dependent constructs. Inevitably, this dimensional model of culture met with increasing criticism, as being too simplistic, deterministic and observed at only one point in time (see the contributions in Cheryl Nakata[3]). Despite these criticisms, a great many studies from the etic perspective still rely on these or other dimensions of national culture. At its most aggregate, cultural dimensions are used as an indication of cultural distance;[4] however, recent studies have examined differences in less aggregated forms. For instance, Siegel and colleagues found that the distance between country scores of Schwartz' egalitarianism value had a negative impact on foreign direct investment flows from multinational firms.[5] The disaggregation of cultural distance to more theoretically justified relations has increased interest in this area. Further, disaggregation to sub-cultures, such as regional, language, ethic and economic groups, is also likely to bring further insight from the etic approach.

In parallel, other researchers adopted a more emic view of culture, which has been gaining momentum.[6] In this paradigm, researchers view culture as being embedded within context and time. This view favours qualitative techniques, based on observation and face-to-face interviews, to get a more in-depth description of the context and processes within a single sub-culture, or the dynamic interaction processes between people of different cultures. In international business, this type of research has focused on the interplay between national and organisational culture being complementary instead of separated.

Case-based research,[7] ethnography[8] and grounded theory[9] are all examples of emic approaches to the study of international business. In this research, the phenomenon in context is far more important than generalisability. This means that some studies appropriately focus on just one organisation,[10] whereas others choose a sample of multiple cases (e.g., individuals, teams, organisations, regions, countries) within which they investigate a phenomenon. For instance, Lamb and colleagues[11] shed light on the process of internationalisation by focusing on small companies with a variety of international experiences and histories within wine export networks.

Pudelko and colleagues[12] contrasted the etic 'reductionist' and emic 'differentiated' culture-specific paradigms as outlined in Table 3.1. They also highlighted a growing interest in the study of language as an alternative differentiated concept of culture. Like culture, language use and impact can be studied across many nations, at all levels of analysis, such as in mergers and acquisitions,[13] between different organisational units,[14] within multi-language teams,[15] and across individuals.[16]

Table 3.1 Paradigms in international business: Comparing the etic and emic culture-specific paradigms

	Etic 'reductionist' culture-specific	Emic 'differentiated' culture-specific
Cultural concept	National culture scores	Cultural complexity
Study objectives	Comparison of cultural values	Description of interactions
Time orientation	Static	Dynamic
Reasoning	Deductive	Inductive
Theoretical perspective	Theory testing	Theory generation
Knowledge perspective	Confirmation/similarities/differences	Exploration
Context perspective	Abstraction of specific contexts	Embedded in a specific context

Source: Based on Pudelko and colleagues[17] *p. 5*

3.2 Formulating cross-cultural research questions and approaches

3.2.1 Some basic rules

Five rules have to be followed when formulating international research questions:

1. they must be clear;
2. the addition of an international/cross-cultural dimension to a management research question must make sense, otherwise it simply increases the complexity with little or no additional contribution;
3. the research question(s) must be meaningful not only to the researcher but also to the target audience;
4. the research questions should be 'researchable', that is, grounded in some kind of theory and related to data or facts that can be collected;
5. they must result in insightful results for both managers and academic audiences.

It is also very important to phrase the research question(s) clearly because international research designs are complex and unclear research questions will lead to confusion at the stages of theorisation or data collection.

Check 1: Is the research question clear enough? A clear research question is often reflected in the title of a paper, which includes a question mark and/or qualifying phrase. For instance, the title '*How product category shapes preferences toward global and local brands: A schema theory perspective*'[18] is clear and concise. In the article, the authors build on current knowledge about brand and consumer related determinants of global/local preference to uncover product category effects. In two studies, across multiple product categories and developed and emerging markets, they found support for the hypothesis that local/global preference is largely formed at the product category level. Similarly, in the article *'Explaining intermittent exporting: Exit and conditional re-entry in export markets'*,[19] the authors develop a conceptual model to explain how firm characteristics and market conditions interact to affect the decision to exit and re-enter exporting and test this model in an extensive dataset of French manufacturing firms. To be clear, the research question must be adequately formulated in the introduction of the research, linked to the theory development, as well as to the method and the reporting of results.

Check 2: Does it make any sense to add the international dimension? The researcher must think about whether it makes sense to add the international dimension to a research question or domain which does not necessarily need it. Cost accounting methods, for instance, are fairly universal: the concept of direct costing and the methods for computing complete costs cross the borders of nations and cultures, but the management control systems that derive from cost accounting can be more susceptible to cross-national variance. There should be a reason to examine the international and possibly cross-cultural dimension, based on expectations of cross-national variance. Recruitment techniques, for instance, would be a better exemplar of cross-national variance than cost accounting systems. The birthplace of applicants, their marital status, age, citizenship, or language competencies are standard, non-discriminatory, enquiries in most cultures where there is still some *being* orientation. Such questions asked to applicants or photographs required from them or hand-written letters (for graphological analysis) are popular in countries around the world, but they would be considered as discriminatory when recruiting people according to a US affirmative action compliance programme. The 'affirmative action, equal opportunity' motto lies on extremely strong *doing* and *outgroup* orientations, whereby it is seen as almost wrong to describe persons as they *are*.

Check 3: Is there a public, an audience? There is a clear problem if, after reading the research report or article, the reader asks 'so what?' Cross-cultural and international research often has higher costs, in terms of time and money, that should be justified. If there is a clear public in mind, the end insight should be clearer. Good research questions often have a specific public in mind, but not necessarily all potential publics. In the example of recruitment techniques, the researcher has to a certain extent choose the employer's side or the employee's side. This will help to clarify and focus the knowledge conveyed by the research, any suggestions for action, managerial implications, and future directions.

Another problematic category is the 'self-destroying questions' which have to be avoided because they lose their audience at a definite point in time, for instance, research questions with a deadline such as how will strategies of companies in the UK be impacted by the withdrawal of the United Kingdom from the European Union. Given the time required for the research to be completed, it may happen that the final answer is not given by the research itself but by the actual strategic moves of companies in the UK.

Check 4: Is it 'researchable'? Some meaningful and interesting research questions cannot be researched easily. Business ethics, for instance, seem to lend themselves 'easily' to a cross-cultural perspective because it makes sense. However, business ethics are not easy to research because the difference in world views of the underlying morals can vary considerably across cultures and religions,[20] morals can be personal versus impersonal, group-oriented versus individualistic, lenient vis-à-vis the sinner as in Catholicism versus relatively tough as in the Protestant ethic, internal morals versus externally regulated, etc. Further, there are methodological questions as to whether people can and do respond in a manner that uncovers their true position on moral issues: Do they know it? Does it change relative to many different situations and conditions? Are they influenced by social desirability? And so on. Further, much of the data on ethical infringements is not publicly available, or only partly accessible, such as for international bribery.

When the research design implies collaborations or cooperation that cannot be reached or obtained, the topic should be considered as less researchable. It usually takes a great deal of time to gain collaboration from firms in the international environment, and then if the 'champion' of the project leaves, the project may be lost. Similarly, designs which require hard-to-organise experimental designs are also difficult to research. For instance, field experiments are difficult to organise and coordinate; however, some multinational companies may run a pilot programme in certain subsidiaries, or roll out changes in practice in different locations over time. Laboratory style experiments can also be difficult to run, when business people and business teams (e.g., business negotiators, senior managers, medical specialists) are important to external validity. However, when samples are difficult for researchers to obtain, sometimes using students in study samples can be justified. For instance, Ryan and Tipu[21] examined the Arab work ethic with business students in the United Arab Emirates. They justified their sample as being 'future business leaders', with the caveat that business students from a single university cannot be viewed as representative of all Arab states. However, for many research questions that we would like to answer in international business, the added complexity of studying subjects in different locations, who speak different languages, can make the study very difficult to conduct.

Check 5: Is everything new? Is anything new? If everything is new in the whole design, from research question, theories, data collection, and countries covered, the researcher should worry about research feasibility. Conversely, if everything is old, outdated or over-researched, the questions have already been answered and there is no need for further research. For beginners, replication *with extension* at the international level of theories validated at the national level is a very straightforward way of generating valuable international/cross-cultural management research, if the questioning on the equivalence across contexts is properly managed (see Chapter 4). One way to manageably approach a topic is to link constructs of interest in boxes to help structure the logical order (see Figure 3.1) and clearly articulate what is known (e.g., grey boxes and arrow) and what is new (e.g., white arrow).

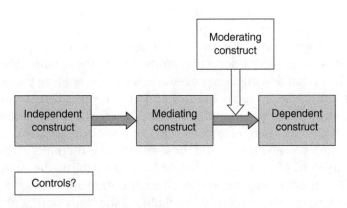

Figure 3.1 Basic conceptual model

3.2.2 Replications and extensions

An important function of international business research is to examine whether phenomena of interest carry over to other samples and settings, and to identify potential boundary conditions. Replications, although not always considered as major contributions, have the immense merit of verifying the accuracy of a given knowledge base: Hofstede's study for instance has been the object of numerous replications in different types of samples (e.g., cross-sectional[22] and longitudinal changes over time[23]). The research question is whether the replication provides the same findings; positive results promote confidence in the reliability of the original results.

Cross-national or cross-cultural replications have the special status of a replication *with extension* because they try to assess whether the outcomes of the original study can be extended beyond the original context. The research question is then: does it still hold true from here (source context) to there (target context)? Naive cross-cultural replications, which ignored the extension aspect, have been useful because they have been a major driver for the search for cross-cultural equivalence, discussed in more detail in the next chapters. However, in general there is a very limited focus on replications within international business research. Some reasons include the use of proprietary data which is difficult to reproduce, and a general lack of interest from major journals that focus more on novel ideas and methods. However, to be fair, these journals expect researchers to demonstrate that the research is trustworthy.

Despite the quest for generalisability, international business theory and practices are rarely universal. One of the roles of research in international business is to examine the transferability of phenomena into the international and cross-cultural settings. For instance, can a particular type of management practice, or an organisation structure, or an employee motivation system be transported from its original context where it proved efficient, to another context which imports it? Do the phenomena differ in nature or by degree (as discussed in Chapter 2)? Researchers might argue, or find, that phenomena of study might be limited to a particular context (e.g., those with efficient market system or a relatively high level of education). In extending the boundaries of existing knowledge, Cuervo-Cazurra and colleagues[24] identify some questions that researchers might fruitfully ask: Under which conditions do the arguments hold? Are there complementary or substituting factors or characteristics at various levels? How could these relations be alternatively explained? Are there any control groups that would help to establish the limitations in relations? Are there important control variables that need to be taken into account? If these questions are addressed during the study design phase, there are less likely to be problems with interpretation of results after the data has been collected.

3.2.3 Controls and confounds

One way to keep the complexity of international business research manageable is to concentrate on a few focal influences and include controls to hold the other relevant factors constant. However, the inclusion of the wrong, or exclusion of relevant, controls can seriously affect the results of a study. For instance, studies that examine the impact of culture on firm performance will likely find very different results if they include controls for economic development. Further, the results will likely differ, depending on their operationalisation of the control variables (e.g., GDP in current US$ or purchasing power parity or dividing by the estimated census population). This means that the inclusion of control variables should be theoretically justifiable and relevant (as a potential bias rather than a substantive variable). Similarly, the exclusion of related variables should be considered carefully. Studies that include one aspect of culture (e.g., individualism/collectivism) as a key variable, but fail to include other aspects (e.g., uncertainty avoidance, power distance, etc.) as control variables, might see a spuriously inflated effect of the one dimension of culture that is included.[25] Control variables should be included as alternate explanations of the dependent variable.

3.3 Dealing with complexity

The problems involved in monitoring the degree of complexity of international/ cross-cultural research designs cannot be solved by mere simplification. Simplification is tempting, and to a large extent, done by real-world researchers, in order to make the research project *feasible*. However, rather than to simplify, the initial task of the researcher is to *disentangle* all the constructs, fields, variables, informants, etc. involved and try to make reasonable trade-offs as to what should be kept, given the key objectives of the study.

Researchers generally have an initial *thesis or research question;* something they want to bring into light. The disentanglement process must aim to reach a point where the chances to successfully confirm or disconfirm their thesis will be high. There are basically two strategies behind the disentanglement task. These correspond roughly to criteria which are popular in operations research: maximin and minimax. The *maximin* approach starts from a very large (max) number of variables, concepts, units, etc. and reduces it to the minimal set which can optimally achieve the set research objectives. The other criteria, minimax, begins with a feasible minimum set of variables, concepts, units, etc. and progressively increases the set (and degree of complexity) to improve the relevance and feasibility up to a maximum point where marginal increases in complexity would be detrimental to the project.

Figure 3.2 illustrates three dimensions that differ in their level of abstraction. Thinking about which level of abstraction is most appropriate for a given research question can help researchers simplify the process, as much as possible. The more

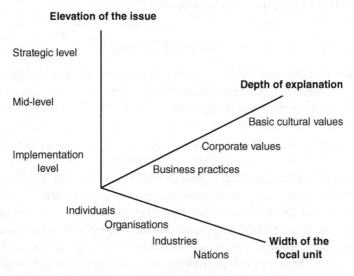

Figure 3.2 Three levels of abstraction in the research design

layers involved along any of these dimensions, the more complex the research project will be. At the most simplistic level, a research project would examine differences between individuals in the implementation of business practices across countries or cultures. Adding another level adds complexity, such as the examination of differences between individuals within organisations in the implementation of business practices across countries of cultures. Further, as the level of abstraction increases, so too does the difficulty in adequately addressing the research question.

3.3.1 What type of decision is being investigated: from strategy to implementation

The level of abstraction in the type of decision or issue being investigated refers to the level of aggregation or disaggregation in the whole management process (elevation of the issue). For instance, investigations of strategic decision making, leadership and organisational design are typical 'high key' issues and long term in their impact, whereas reporting, accounting, motivating salespeople or adapting products to foreign markets are 'lower key' issues. The impact of lower level implementation issues are more immediate and therefore easier to assess in a given timeframe than higher level strategic issues. Further, the different levels of abstraction on this dimension should relate to one another. Top level strategy decisions also need to be implemented at lower levels to be effective. The possibilities of discrepancies in the process for higher level issues are far greater. For instance, imitation and cultural borrowing at the top management level may be contradicted at implementation levels by actual behaviour inspired by local cultural patterns. Any discrepancies in the implementation of strategic or mid-level decisions will compromise the research.

3.3.2 How deep to go: from sea level to deep abyss

The question of how deep to go depends on whether the explanatory variables from the international environment are more or less deep-seated and, therefore, relatively far away from the behaviour or practices they are supposed to explain. At the highest level of abstraction, one may wonder how basic cultural assumptions or values – possibly from their roots such as adaptation to climate and geographical conditions – can be related to business practices, company rules and management procedures. Assuming that the variable to be explained is efficiency/performance or satisfaction or motivation, researchers typically need to decide how deep they will go into a particular level of explanation, or successive layers of explanations, such as relating culture to values, or corporate values and then to business practices. There is a flow or continuum from very deep-seated explanations to the final aspects of management concerned, with profound explanations at one extreme and daily managerial reality at the other.

If the researcher decides to examine cultural values and fundamental basic assumptions, he or she incurs the risk of being far from any implementable recommendation, at least as perceived by an audience of business people or even colleagues. If the eventual aim is to provide managers with operative knowledge about concrete behavioural and organisational differences and the way to deal with them in interactive settings, a choice to be 'nearer to the surface' (not to be equated with superficial) can make more sense.

When defining the depth of the cross-cultural investigation the researcher needs to decide how specific his or her analysis will be: 1) to look only at *whether* there is an impact (i.e., does the specific phenomenon being examined differ across cultures), 2) to examine the *way in* which it differs (the direction and/or level of difference) and 3) to examine *why* it differs (the causal relationship). These choices progressively add more complexity. It is important to keep in mind that question 1 'does it differ?' may be a significant research issue and that questions 2 and 3 may be better examined as follow on research, perhaps using different techniques.

To keep the research project manageable, researchers often use an existing explanatory framework (i.e., national cultures scores, such as Hofstede's dimensions) to account for deep cultural explanation in a manageable and implementable way. The use of an existing explanatory framework helps to avoid the trap of going so deep that it becomes difficult to find convincing rationales for linking the profound explanation to the behavioural outcomes.

Problems related to the operationalisation of abstract constructs, with a potentially large set of explanatory variables, explain why researchers tend to be somewhat parsimonious about the scope of their studies. For instance, historical explanations (e.g., the hypothetical view that human resource practices in Japan would be linked to the feudal system in ancient Japan) have little success in explaining business practices between cultures. However, historical, sociological, political or legal explanations may surface at times in the interpretive part of the research. The relative lack of appeal of historical explanations (except in specialised journals such as *Journal of Business History*) is probably explained by the fact that they are not really testable. However, some reasonable abstract constructs, such as religion or religiosity, have been successfully used to provide a deeper rationale for observed differences. For example, differences in religiosity have been shown to affect bank earnings management[26] and audit firms' pricing decisions.[27] Similarly, religion has been show to impact managerial decisions concerning the environment,[28] as well as the development of specific types of industries, such as Islamic banking.[29]

Not surprisingly, the easier it is to measure the construct, the more likely it is to be used. This can be seen in explanations that relate to economic systems, as there are a wide range of easily accessible economic indicators, such as gross domestic product (GDP), gross national product (GNP), unemployment rates, inflation rates, interest rates, exchange rates, and so on, as well as a myriad of adjustments to various indicators (e.g., purchasing power parity, current international dollar, per capita, etc.), accessible online from the World Bank and many other sources. Naturally, researchers need to examine each one and decide which indicators are more appropriate. They also should be cautious about believing that these are hard facts, rather than indicators. For instance, GDP is an indicator of consumption (durable and nondurable) + government expenditures (e.g., roads, schools, defence) + investments (residential and non-residential) + exports – imports. These figures are not easily obtained and tend to differ in accuracy across countries. Yet, they are all well used indicators of economic development.

A further problem for cross-cultural and international business researchers is the potential overlap or confound between constructs at the highest level of abstraction on this dimension. For instance, there is a significant positive correlation between GDP per capita and many cultural dimensions. Exactly, which comes first is a chicken and egg situation; however, how to deal with this is complex.[30] For instance, where egalitarianism was theorised to impact foreign direct investment, researchers controlled for GDP per capita (in the form of the log product of origin-host GDP) and many other factors. In contrast, in other fields of study they do not control for related economic variables, as their stated interest is in the cultural effect. Thus, results from other fields sometimes seem 'stronger'.

3.3.3 The focal unit of analysis: from individuals to nations and the world...

Width choices concern the possible units of analysis, ranging from individuals, organisations and industries to mega-groups, such as nations or regions. Width is important because it has a lot to do with the complexity of conceptualisation and data collection, that is, with the implementability of the research project. At the lowest level of abstraction, one may interview individuals about their own behaviour. At other levels of abstraction, individuals may still be interviewed, but they need to report for another entity (e.g., their company) or their responses are aggregated to form a proxy for country-level norms. This somewhat complicates the interpretation.

Typical contrasts in width at a high level of abstraction will be between large-scale surveys such as Hofstede's, with large samples both of individuals and countries, and small-scale, two-country designs (e.g., comparing the USA and China), or the study of a single organisation in several countries (e.g., McDonald's employees in the USA, Australia, China and Malaysia). However, there is some discussion on the issue of whether two-nation studies constitute a cross-cultural design. Researchers favouring the etic approach consider that a larger number of countries will provide a better and deeper understanding of the effects of culture on behaviour. When there are enough countries (usually 20 or more) to allow correlations between observed means of different national or cultural groups with the dependent variables of interest, it is referred to as an 'ecological correlation' (i.e., correlation among mean national scores ignoring within group differences).[31]

Further, at higher levels of abstractions researchers need to consider whether the entity is coherent. It might come as no surprise to cross-cultural researchers that there is a great deal more variance at the level of individuals than at the level of countries.[32] Nationality is only one very broad macro grouping to which individuals belong. It is relatively easy to identify – although getting harder with mass migration – and as such, operationally convenient. However, the direction of causality between the concepts of nationality and culture is not self-evident. Historically, shared culture has been a fundamental building block in the progressive construction of modern nation-states. As soon as these states began to emerge, they struggled against local customs, cultures and patois and tried to homogenise institutions. As argued earlier, an attempt to equate culture directly with the nation-state, or country, would be misguided for a number of convergent reasons:

1. Some countries are deeply multicultural, for example India which is made up of highly diversified ethnic, religious and linguistic groups.

2. Some nation-states are explicitly multicultural – Switzerland, for instance, with a strong emphasis on the defence of local particularisms in the political system.

3. Colonisation and decolonisation have resulted in borders which are sometimes straight lines on a map, with little respect for cultural realities; for African countries, 'ethnic culture' matters whereas 'national culture' is in many cases meaningless.

Few countries are truly homogeneous, especially when different types of homogeneity are considered, such as:

1. Linguistic homogeneity;

2. Religious homogeneity;

3. Ethnic homogeneity;

4. Climatic homogeneity;

5. Geographical homogeneity;

6. Institutional and political homogeneity; and

7. Social/income homogeneity.

Researchers who favour higher levels of abstraction should consider whether nation is the most appropriate unit of analysis for their research.

There is increasing interest in the examination of sub-cultures, such as ethnic, language, regional and religious groupings within and across countries in international business research.[33] The availability of large datasets, such as the European Social Survey and the World Values Survey, has enabled researchers to begin to examine issues of sub-cultures on a larger scale. For instance, Kaasa and colleagues[34] explored sub-cultures within 20 countries, where data were available in the European Social Survey. Arguing that culture, as a latent variable, can be measured in different ways, they used available items as indicators of Hofstede's main culture dimension (e.g., power distance was measured with indicators that related to the attitude toward politicians, institutional trust and work related power distance). They found significant correlations between their scores and the corresponding Hofstede dimension scores for some, but not all, of the dimensions (e.g., power distance $r = .69$, $p < .001$; uncertainty avoidance $r = .84$, $p < .001$; masculinity $r = .47$, $p < .05$; individualism and collectivism were not significant). However, they also found significant differences in cultural emphases between regions within countries.

Multilevel studies (see also Chapter 5) are advancing our understanding of the interplay between cultures, sub-cultures and individuals in international business research. Some of the hierarchical models used in international business research have traditionally focused on firms nested within industries nested within countries using large subscription-based datasets. However the availability of large scale, free, public domain data (e.g., the European Social Survey http://www.europeansocialsurvey.org; the International Social Survey Program http://www.issp.org; the World Values Survey http://www.worldvaluessurvey. org), has promoted other types of hierarchical models (e.g., individuals nested within sub-cultures/firms nested within countries. There are many illustrations of these approaches in the literature and books, such as 'Multilevel analysis of individuals and cultures' by Van de Vijver, Van Hemert and Poortinga.[35] One recent example by Luo and Bu[36] examines the value of information and communication technology in emerging enterprises. They argue that information and communication technology (ICT) improves the productivity of emerging economy enterprises because it facilitates effective knowledge sharing and integration. They obtained data from the World Bank's Enterprise Surveys to test their hypotheses using hierarchical linear modelling analysis of 6,236 firms from 27 emerging economies. They show that ICT generates satisfactory returns for these enterprises and adds more value to productivity when the emerging economy is less economically developed, and reaches foreign markets, or has superior quality control and assurance. They also examined six control variables, including country-level, industry-level and firm-specific variables that could potentially impact firm efficacy (e.g., GDP growth, firm size and age, foreign ownership etc.) in order to rule out alternative hypotheses. The estimation of cross-level interaction effects, such as an examination of whether individual-level demographics, attitudes and behaviour, potentially differ as a function of cultural or contextual factors (availability of infrastructure and societal wealth) has great potential for extending our understanding of existing phenomena in international business.

This type of research is likely to have interesting implications for international business research. However, as with other dimensions, including multiple levels of abstraction greatly increases the research complexity.

Choices of parsimony must often be made. For industry or organisation, one can control the complexity by taking the subsidiaries of the same multinational company on a worldwide basis[37]. If samples of individuals are considered, rival explanations by socio-demographic variables can be controlled, especially for gender, education or age, and their remaining influence must be assessed by techniques described in the next chapter. The relevance of the units examined must be carefully assessed.

When combined, the three levels of abstraction express the necessary trade-off between what would be desirable and what is feasible. The quest for the Holy Grail is an illusion common to many cross-cultural researchers who would like to find both profound and universal dimensions that would explain behaviour across a wide array of countries. If starting from a rather positivistic perspective, a reasonable strategy is to posit the design at only one level on each of the three dimensions and attempt to control variables intervening at other levels. Hofstede, for instance, chose nations as units and controlled at the individual level by similar composition of national samples from IBM. Another way of dealing with complex research designs is to use an in-depth, grounded approach which privileges internal validity at the expense of possible claims for external validity.

3.4 Data collection techniques

Once the research question and the focal variables of interest have been decided, the research continues with developing the research instrument. The same research instruments are available to international and cross-cultural business research as are available for domestic research but they face a problem of cross-cultural equivalence which has been discussed in great detail in the literature (see Chapters 4 and 5). Further, instruments become more difficult to implement, especially where local informants lack familiarity with survey research. Figure 3.2 posits various data collection techniques as they pertain to key aspects of the research design. The vertical axis opposes the phenomenon to the ideas: if the researcher is deeply engaged in describing and respecting the realities of the phenomenon under investigation, he or she will tend to choose research instruments that favour a thick description of the phenomenon. Conversely, a strong emphasis on pre-set theories (ideas), including not only the concepts and their articulation but also their operationalisation, will lead the researcher to choose an instrument which reflects a more abstract, intellectual picture of the phenomenon, suitable for measuring key pre-set dimensions rather than for coming directly to grips with reality.

The right side of the horizontal axis highlights a preoccupation of the researcher with informants, when and if, he or she consider them as the key element of the research process. In this view, the data collection process must allow informants, as much as is possible, to reveal their world views, deliver their true mind and give their own interpretations; however, this is most likely at the expense of codifiability, since the collected information cannot be easily transformed into quantified variables. At the opposite side on the horizontal axis, the research design is instrument centred to collect the informants' views in a codified form. In this case, operationalised variables are a direct output of the data collection process; however, this is at the expense of relevance (the categories proposed in the questionnaire may be far from the informants' own views), and exhaustivity (significant pieces of information may be lost because of an imposed research instrument).

The upper-right quadrant of the Figure 3.3 corresponds to context-embedded research designs where the emphasis is on the phenomenon and the informants. Their application to cross-cultural business research implies a great deal of observation, including participant observation, diaries and journals which are then analysed for generating new insights. This is rarely used in international/cross-cultural research because it is highly demanding in terms of familiarity with and knowledge of the research context.

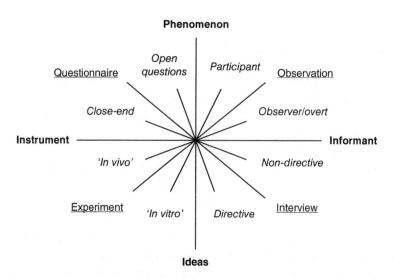

Figure 3.3 Research instruments as they pertain to key aspects of the research design

The lower-left quadrant of Figure 3.3 features decontextualised studies. The choice of context-free research instruments does not imply that the researcher is unaware of cultural issues, nor that apparently context-embedded approaches are automatically taking their context into full account. Participant observation can be undertaken with little understanding of the field's culture, while experiments can be organised so that they take into account some influences related to culture, by explaining the instrument, organising the experiment differently, or observing the subject's behaviour during the experimental process. Among the quasi-experimental research instruments, the *in vivo* category tries to reproduce real life situations while the *in vitro* category is nearer to a 'scientific' experiment. Typical in vivo instruments are vignette research or 'in-basket instruments'.

Experimental vignettes usually present participants with realistic scenarios, such as a short description of a person, object, or situation, representing a combination of characteristics prior to a series of focal questions. Vignettes are designed to enhance experimental realism and allow researchers to manipulate and control independent variables. There are various forms of vignettes, but two of the more common forms are aimed at assessing explicit (i.e., paper-people studies) and implicit (i.e., policy capturing and conjoint analysis) processes and outcomes.[38] Explicit vignette research was used by Sauer[39] in an examination of the causal effects of leadership status and style on team members' perceptions of leadership effectiveness and team performance. He used video vignettes to increase the realism. Participants watched the video and completed a questionnaire about their perception of leadership effectiveness and self-confidence in their own environments. An implicit vignette was used by De Meulenaer and colleagues[40] who used conjoint analysis to investigate the relative importance of different cues in creating perceptions of brand globalness. Aguinis and Bradley offer recommendations and advice for researchers interested in experimental vignettes in international business research.[41]

The upper-left quadrant of Figure 3.3 is very common in cross-cultural management research. Those adopting the 'toolkit' approach described in Chapter 1 tend to generate survey data through questionnaire administration. Finally, the lower-right quadrant is common among cross-cultural researchers who undertake in-depth interviews which are often within the framework of complete case studies.[42] Observation data, documents, meeting reports and contracts, can be typically triangulated with in-depth interviews in order to generate reliable insights into the phenomenon under investigation.

The real world of cross-cultural data collection and research instruments is fortunately more complex than this discussion would lead us to believe. First, the same research issue can be approached in all of the above ways, but generally in different research projects, by different researchers, as it is much more difficult to combine data collection techniques which are in opposing quadrants. They imply quite different underlying research philosophies.

As a very general and highly provisional conclusion of this section, we suggest the following advantages and drawbacks for each of the four broad categories (outlined in Figure 3.3). Observation is most likely to allow cross-cultural discovery, but also the most difficult because it needs both familiarity with the research context and an ability to distance oneself from the observed phenomenon. Experiments (or quasi-experimental instruments) are most likely to be adopted when universality is assumed. Respondents are considered as subjects of the experiment and the test is (supposed) to be culture free, which may result in diminishing cross-national differences. Questionnaires are typically used when cross-cultural equivalence is expected. They are widely used with common conceptual dimensions that appear valid across cultures. Here, differences are expected in degree but not in the nature of the construct. Their main disadvantage is that they may hide some of the conceptual differences across cultures, or if conceptual differences (inequivalences) are found there is little that can be done about it. Finally, interviews are less popular in cross-cultural research than they are in domestic settings because language is often a significant barrier. If undertaken through interpreters, there is likely to be more 'noise', artificiality and an absence of tempo in the conversation, which can be quite detrimental to the quality of the materials collected. However, cross-border research cooperation, implying a multinational research team, can overcome these limitations. We discuss this in greater detail in Chapter 4.

3.5 Conclusion

The great danger in international and cross-cultural business research is the quest for the Holy Grail, that is, the search for simplified frameworks that would nonetheless allow a deep understanding of a wide range of cultures. This quest is, fraught with danger, because it results in very complex designs which are hard to implement. The few large empirically supported frameworks, such as Hofstede, Schwartz and the World Values Survey, have been developed over a great many years and are more the exception than the rule. In order to generate cross-culturally valid knowledge, it is advisable to start from a more limited research question and find robust ways to address the issue, find collaborators in other cultures, and have with them a truly equal cooperation.

Notes

1. Pudelko, M. and A.-W. Harzing, The golden triangle for MNCs: Standardization towards headquarters practices, standardization towards global best practices and localization. Organizational Dynamics, 2008. 37(4): 394–404.

2. Hofstede, G., Cultures's Consequences. Beverley Hills: Sage, 1980.
3. Nakata, C., Going beyond Hofstede: Why we need to and how, in Beyond Hofstede. 2009, Palgrave MacMillan, New York. p. 3–15.
4. Shenkar, O., Cultural distance revisited: Towards a more rigorous conceptualization and measurement of cultural differences. Journal of International Business Studies, 2001. 32(3): 519–535.
5. Siegel, J.I., A.N. Licht, and S.H. Schwartz, Egalitarianism, cultural distance, and foreign direct investment: A new approach. Organization Science, 2013, 24(4): 1174–1194.
6. Ybema, S. and P. Nyíri, The Hofstede factor: the consequences of culture's consequences. 2015, in N. Holden, S. Michailova and S. Tietze (Eds), The Routledge Companion to Cross-Cultural Management. Routledge, New York, Chapter 5, pp.37-48.
7. Welch, C., R. Piekkari, E. Plakoyiannaki, and E. Paavilainen-Mäntymäki, Theorising from case studies: Towards a pluralist future for international business research. Journal of International Business Studies, 2011. 42(5): 740–762.
8. Westney, D.E. and J. Van Maanen, The casual ethnography of the executive suite. Journal of International Business Studies, 2011. 42(5): 602–607.
9. Gligor, D.M., C.L. Esmark, and I. Gölgeci, Building international business theory: A grounded theory approach. Journal of International Business Studies, 2015. 47(1): 93–111.
10. Jonsson, A. and N.J. Foss, International expansion through flexible replication: Learning from the internationalization experience of IKEA. Journal of International Business Studies, 2011. 42(9): 1079–1102.
11. Lamb, P., J. Sandberg, and P.W. Liesch, Small firm internationalisation unveiled through phenomenography. Journal of International Business Studies, 2011. 42(5): 672–693.
12. Pudelko, M., H. Tenzer, and A.-W. Harzing, Cross-cultural management and language studies within international business research: Past and present paradigms and suggestions for future research. 2014 Routledge Companion to Cross-Cultural Management. London: Routledge.
13. Slangen, A.H., A communication-based theory of the choice between greenfield and acquisition entry. Journal of Management Studies, 2011. 48(8): 1699–1726.
14. Harzing, A.-W. and M. Pudelko, Language competencies, policies and practices in multinational corporations: A comprehensive review and comparison of Anglophone, Asian, Continental European and Nordic MNCs. Journal of World Business, 2013. 48(1): 87–97.
15. Klitmøller, A. and J. Lauring, When global virtual teams share knowledge: Media richness, cultural difference and language commonality. Journal of World Business, 2013. 48(3): 398–406.
16. Volk, S., T. Köhler, and M. Pudelko, Brain drain: The cognitive neuroscience of foreign language processing in multinational corporations. Journal of International Business Studies, 2014. 45(7): 862–885.
17. Pudelko, M., H. Tenzer, and A.-W. Harzing, Cross-cultural management and language studies within international business research: Past and present paradigms and suggestions for future research. 2014 Routledge Companion to Cross-Cultural Management. London: Routledge, p.5.

18. Davvetas, V. and A. Diamantopoulos, How product category shapes preferences toward global and local brands: A schema theory perspective. Journal of International Marketing, 2016.

19. Bernini, M., J. Du, and J.H. Love, Explaining intermittent exporting: Exit and conditional re-entry in export markets. Available at SSRN 2620208, 2015.

20. Demuijnck, G., Universal values and virtues in management versus cross-cultural moral relativism: An educational strategy to clear the ground for business ethics. Journal of Business Ethics, 2015. 128(4): 817–835.
    Morales-Sánchez, R. and C. Cabello-Medina, The role of four universal moral competencies in ethical decision-making. Journal of Business Ethics, 2013. 116(4): 717–734.
    Usunier, J.-C., O. Furrer, and A. Furrer-Perrinjaquet, The perceived trade-off between corporate social and economic responsibility: A cross-national study. International Journal of Cross-Cultural Management, 2011. 11(3): 279–302.

21. Ryan, J.C. and S.A. Tipu, An empirical alternative to Sidani and Thornberry's (2009) 'Current Arab work ethic': Examining the multidimensional work ethic profile in an Arab context. Journal of Business Ethics, 2016. 135(1): 177–198.

22. Minkov, M. and G. Hofstede, A replication of Hofstede's uncertainty avoidance dimension across nationally representative samples from Europe. International Journal of Cross-Cultural Management, 2014. 14(2): 161–171.

23. Beugelsdijk, S., R. Maseland, and A. Van Hoorn, Are scores of Hofstede's dimensions of national culture stable over time? A cohort analysis., 2015, Global Strategy Journal, 5(3): 223–240.

24. Cuervo-Cazurra, A., U. Andersson, M.Y. Brannen, B.B. Nielsen, and A.R. Reuber, From the Editors: Can I trust your findings? Ruling out alternative explanations in international business research. Journal of International Business Studies, 2016: 1–17.

25. Cuervo-Cazurra, A., et al., From the Editors: Can I trust your findings? Ruling out alternative explanations in international business research. Journal of International Business Studies, 2016: 1–17.

26. Kanagaretnam, K., G.J. Lobo, and C. Wang, Religiosity and earnings management: International evidence from the banking industry. Journal of Business Ethics, 2015. 132(2): 277–296.

27. Leventis, S., E. Dedoulis, and O. Abdelsalam, The impact of religiosity on audit pricing. Journal of Business Ethics, 2015: 1–26.

28. Cui, J., H. Jo, and M.G. Velasquez, The influence of Christian religiosity on managerial decisions concerning the environment. Journal of Business Ethics, 2015. 132(1): 203–231.

29. Iqbal, M., P. Molyneux, and S. Conermann, Thirty years of Islamic banking: History, performance and prospects. 2016: Bankhistorisches Archiv, 32(2): 155–158.

30. van Herk, H. and Y.H. Poortinga, Current and historical antecedents of individual value differences across 195 regions in Europe. Journal of Cross-Cultural Psychology, 2012, 43(8), p. 1229-1248.

31. Hofstede, G., Cultures's Consequences. Beverley Hills: Sage, 1980.
    Hofstede, G.H. and G. Hofstede, Culture's Consequences: Comparing values, behaviors, institutions and organizations across nations. 2001:Thousand Oaks, Sage.

32. Fischer, R. and S. Schwartz, Whence differences in value priorities? Individual, cultural, or artifactual sources. Journal of Cross-Cultural Psychology, 2011. 42(7): p. 1127–1144.
33. López-Duarte, C., M.M. Vidal-Suárez, and B. González-Díaz, International business and national culture: A literature review and research agenda. International Journal of Management Reviews, 2015.
34. Kaasa, A., M. Vadi, and U. Varblane, European Social Survey as a source of new cultural dimensions estimates for regions. International Journal of Cross-Cultural Management, 2013, 13(2) 137–157.
35. Van de Vijver, F.J., D.A. Van Hemert, and Y.H. Poortinga, Multilevel Analysis of Individuals and Cultures. 2008: Lawrence Erlbaum Associates, New York.
36. Luo, Y. and J. Bu, How valuable is information and communication technology? A study of emerging economy enterprises. Journal of World Business, 2016. 51(2): 200–211.
37. Hofstede, G., Culture's Consequences: Comparing values, behaviors, institutions, and organizations across nations. 2001, Thousand Oaks, CA: Sage.
38. Aguinis, H. and K.J. Bradley, Best practice recommendations for designing and implementing experimental vignette methodology studies. Organizational Research Methods, 2014. 17(4): 351–371.
39. Sauer, S.J., Taking the reins: The effects of new leader status and leadership style on team performance. Journal of Applied Psychology, 2011. 96(3): p. 574–587.
40. De Meulenaer, S., N. Dens, and P. De Pelsmacker, Which cues cause consumers to perceive brands as more global? A conjoint analysis. International Marketing Review, 2015. 32(6): 606–626.
41. Aguinis, H. and K.J. Bradley, Best practice recommendations for designing and implementing experimental vignette methodology studies. Organizational Research Methods, 2014. 17(4): 351–371.
42. Pereira, V., S. Munjal, and M. Nandakumar, Reverse dependency: A longitudinal case study investigation into headquarter-subsidiary relationship in the context of an emerging economy. International Studies of Management & Organization, 2016. 46(1): 50–62.

4

EX-ANTE: METHODOLOGICAL ISSUES IN CROSS-CULTURAL BUSINESS RESEARCH

The search for equivalence and comparability across nations and cultures is a natural undertaking in cross-cultural research, whether in psychology, sociology or business studies. If researchers want to compare across cultural contexts, they need to use concepts and research instruments that are understood in similar ways in all of the cultures studied. Moreover, they need to check that the same data collection procedures do not result in biased findings in one or more of the contexts under investigation. This chapter describes what can be done *before* data collection (*ex-ante*) to ensure and enable comparison of data across cultures *after* data collection (*ex-post*).[1] *Ex-post* assessment of equivalence/invariance in data after it has been collected will be the focus of Chapter 5.

In the first section of this chapter, we introduce the concepts of comparability and equivalence, and give some examples of different types of etic research in international business (Section 4.1). Section 4.2 of this chapter presents the different facets of *ex-ante* meaning equivalence (conceptual, functional, categorical, and translation equivalence). Research instrument equivalence is dealt with in Section 4.3, while *ex-ante* precautions for sampling (anticipating differences) and data collection (anticipating respondent's participation and cooperation) are considered in Sections 4.4 and 4.5 of this chapter.

4.1 Introduction to *ex-ante* methodological issues

4.1.1 The search for comparability in international business research

The search for equivalence is the most important methodological aspect of cross-cultural business research; without it, data should not be compared across samples. It would be like comparing apples with cows. Researchers who strongly favour purely emic techniques (taking the perspective that phenomena are expressed in a unique way in each culture) may forget that there is always a need for a minimal level of comparability between cultural groups. However, due to the standardised instruments commonly employed in research of an etic nature (taking the perspective that phenomena are relatively universal), we necessarily go into the detail required for this type of research. As such, most of this chapter addresses issues around etic research, highlighting where the issues also apply to research of a more emic nature.

As discussed in Chapter 2, a vast majority of the knowledge base in business is mainly from western nations and the USA in particular, which while valuable, is not enough to understand developments in international business. Performing studies in non-western markets is essential for generating new insights into the applicability of theories and practices in emerging and developing markets.[2] To be able to capture what is going on in other cultures and countries we need to establish equivalence of the concepts and measures used, while also being open to phenomena that might be unique to specific markets.

The determinant of the decision to search for cross-cultural equivalence in a comparative design is whether the research is perceived to be 'culture free' versus 'culture bound'. It cannot be decided arbitrarily and has to be based on observation, honest self-questioning and discussion with insiders of the target cultures. Cross-cultural studies require the establishment of equivalent measures; this is a time-consuming and complex task which is done more often than it used to be, but is still not common practice.[3] Even studies in which respondents are from one nation may need to be assessed for equivalence, as multi-item scales used to measure constructs often originate in the USA. When questions designed and tested in one culture are transferred to another, it is necessary to check the equivalence of the items and constructs, before any comparisons can be made.

In this chapter, we do not take the view of *tabula rasa*, based on the assumption that everything is idiosyncratic, where no single piece of managerial or consumer behaviour could be compared. As a general statement, this is not true and would lead to inertia. Rather, we argue in favour of being aware of equivalence issues across national and cultural contexts and making conscious choices to deal with this in the research design and analysis (Chapter 5). While some areas of equivalence are relevant for comparisons made from an etic or emic perspective, this and the next chapter focus in more detail on the etic approach where addressing equivalence is vital. In survey research, for instance, questionnaires tend to impose strong (standardised) frames on respondents, in comparison to in-depth interviews or observation, where respondents are able to respond and act in a relatively free manner.

4.1.2 Examples of different types of etic studies in international business research

Studies on international business can have (1) a focus on domestic respondents only, (2) a focus on respondents from many countries surveyed in the same language, or (3) a focus on groups of respondents who come from different countries with the aim of comparing cultures. Only in the last type of study an explicit comparison between countries or cultures is made. An example of the first type of study (domestic respondents only) in international business is that of Sichtmann and von Selasinsky[4] who studied the drivers of service export performance in a sample of German business-to-business providers. The setting is international, but the methodology can be similar to that of a domestic study as all respondents (managers) were from the same country.

An example of the second type of study (respondents from many nations surveyed in the same language) in international business is that of Lawler and colleagues (2011).[5] This study focused on implementation of high-performance work systems (HPWS) in subsidiaries of American-based multinational enterprises in Asia, Africa and Europe. Human resource managers in the companies received a questionnaire in English on the subsidiary they worked for. The authors conducted conducted multilevel analyses, where the characteristics of the parent company and the domicile were included to explain cross-national differences in implementation of HPWS. In this study, the equivalence of the measures across countries was assumed. This might be justified, as the questions pertained to factual information, and neither attitudes nor opinions were asked. However, it cannot be assumed that respondents in the various nations understood the questions in the same way. Further, the use of English language questionnaires for non-natives can lead to significant bias.[6]

In these two examples, comparisons between groups of respondents from different nations are not explicitly made; the cultural background is either similar for all respondents or the cultural background is included as a background characteristic equivalent to occupation. In contrast, in the third type of study comparisons are made between two or more nations and any observable differences are interpreted as being a result of these cultural differences. As an example, Sharma (2011)[7] compared consumers in two developed (UK, USA) and two emerging (China, India) nations. The study investigated the influence of country of origin on consumers' purchase intention and actual choice of car brands. The author assessed equivalence of the translations and samples and also tested for construct and measurement equivalence across the four nations. He carefully checked for equivalence to ensure that differences found can be attributed to differences between the emerging and developed markets. It is this type of cross-national comparative study, in which groups of people from several nations are included, that will be the main focus of this chapter, as it is a very commonly employed method in international business research.

4.1.3 Existing information available

As researchers are developing their questions and designing their studies, they should be aware of what is already available in terms of published research and reports, as well as sources of secondary data that can be used to help with research design and potentially answer research questions without further need for data collection. There is a great deal of information available on the Internet and through library resources. In particular, before designing field-work, researchers can consult existing large databases (e.g., national statistical agencies, the Worldbank, or PewCenter), where a great deal of useful information on country characteristics, etc. can be obtained free of charge. Even more information is available at a fee. For instance, the Euromonitor GMID database provides aggregated, and in some areas disaggregated data, from consumer and industry markets in more than 100 nations worldwide. While the focus of this book is to provide information that will help researchers conduct a research project involving the collection and analysis of data, it is important to note that data collection is not always required.

4.1.4 Types of cross-cultural equivalence discussed in this chapter

As discussed in Chapter 3, researchers must decide on a *thesis* and choose relevant constructs and relations to examine. Next, they must decide how data will be collected to investigate the phenomenon. This is when equivalence must first be considered. Each of the *ex-ante* equivalences issues are discussed in detail in this chapter. There are, of course, many other resources that can be consulted for more detail on specific issues of cross-cultural equivalence and we would encourage researchers to read widely.[8]

It is important to note that equivalence in cross-cultural research is most often discussed ex-post; in the analysis phase, after data has been collected. However, for many aspects of equivalence this is far too late. If the meaning of a word or concept is fundamentally different across cultures, then treating people's answers as if they are talking about the same thing is ludicrous. Equivalence of meaning, of instruments and measures and of samples should all be dealt with *ex-ante*. However, since it is difficult if not impossible to establish equivalence at the start, it is necessary also to check *ex-post*. To be able to check *ex-post*, the research design needs to fulfil the requirements of any necessary analyses. For instance, for assessing invariance of constructs across cultures, constructs need to be measured by multi-item scales consisting of at least three items. The last part of this chapter discusses this issue in more detail. A summary of how equivalence can be established *ex-post* by statistical analysis procedures will be addressed in Chapter 5.

In the following sections, we begin with two key areas, conceptual and functional equivalence, which allows assessment of whether the theories used will be transferable across borders without major changes. This is followed by categorical equivalence, which refers to the categorisation of behaviours and products in society. The equivalence of measures used for secondary data or for surveys (units, scales, etc.) is examined. Then, we discuss the issue of finding comparable samples; both sampling cultures, as well as sampling individuals within these cultures, are addressed. We end with a discussion of issues in data collection: respondents' motivation, differences in scale use, familiarity with research techniques, and willingness to participate in surveys.

4.2 Meaning equivalence

A basic issue in cross-cultural research is the determination of whether the concepts used have similar meaning across the cultures studied. In the seminal book on international marketing research by Craig and Douglas,[9] three levels of meaning equivalence are defined: conceptual, functional and categorical equivalence. Each of these is discussed and examples given in this section, along with translational equivalence which is also essential in the understanding of meaning.

4.2.1 Conceptual equivalence

Conceptual equivalence refers to 'the interpretation that individuals place on objects, stimuli or behaviour, and whether these exist or are expressed in similar ways in different countries and cultures'.[10] For instance, a concept such as 'innovativeness' might be defined in the same way across cultures; however, in the USA when people are asked about consumer innovativeness they might think about those who purchase new state-of-the-art products, whereas in a developing nation when people are asked the same question, they might think about people who use an existing product in different ways (e.g., baking powder as an air freshener). Similarly, basic concepts such as autonomy, leadership, trust, satisfaction and well-being are often used in business research. They may be defined in similar ways in various language dictionaries. However, equivalence of meaning cannot be simply assumed. These constructs are related to self-image and interactions with other people in particular social and cultural setting, which may systematically differ across cultures. Thus, it is always advisable to check with local researchers *ex-ante* to examine the conceptual equivalence of important constructs, especially when designing a cross-cultural questionnaire.

Assessing conceptual equivalence helps to avoid problems with interpretation, but it might also mean that additional aspects of the concept emerge in other cultures. If these additional aspects are incorporated into the research, it will likely produce better cross-cultural data and add substantially to the impact of the research. As an example, Gardberg (2006)[11] studied the equivalence of corporate reputation as a construct and the 'Reputation Quotient' instrument as a multi-item measure in focus groups; extending initial research in the USA to six others. Generally, she found support for the concept and the scale; however groups in the Netherlands and UK suggested additional items to make the scale more representative of the complete domain (e.g., adding an item related to crisis management). Further, the antecedents of corporate reputation appeared to differ across countries; in both the Netherlands and Belgium, country-of-origin of the company was mentioned as an antecedent and in Australia the non-profit status of the company was also mentioned. Improvements were then made to a new version of the scale to enhance its equivalence in meaning.

Another example is the concept of trust which is being increasingly used in international business research, especially in the areas where intercultural interactions are frequent (e.g., joint ventures and international business negotiations). For instance, Gounaris (2005)[12] discussed the role of trust and commitment on customer retention in Greece and Jain and colleagues[13] investigated how power affects trust and how these relationships are affected by commitment in Taiwan. In fact the concept of trust has been used in thousands of studies in many countries; however, its operationalisation often differs. Despite this, trust is often considered as being conceptually equivalent across cultures and the linguistic equivalence of the concept of trust across cultures is rarely questioned.

By looking at how trust is expressed in five languages (English, French, German, Japanese, Chinese), we can derive some insight into which aspects of the concept are put to the forefront by the corresponding cultures. The English concept of *trust* is reliance on and confidence in truth, worth and reliability of a person or thing. Reliance is central to the Anglo-Saxon concept of trust, which is why the legal institution of trust has been highly developed in the common law tradition, whereas it was non-existent in the Roman-Germanic tradition until very recently. The German concept is based on two verbs, *trauen* and *vertrauen*, both of them meaning literally to trust. But in fact the Germans use the first form, *trauen*, mostly in the negative sense, *Ich traue Dir nicht* (I do not trust you), and the second in the positive sense, *Ich vertraue Dir* (I trust you). The prefix *ver* indicates a transformation and this informs us about the picture behind the German concept of trust: the initial position is distrust; only after a favourable change has occurred can trust be established. The French notion of *confiance,* as in other Romance languages, is based on the Latin *confidentia*, a compound of *cum* (with, shared) and *fides* (faith, belief): the notion of sharing common beliefs, religion or group membership is central to the Latin concept of trust. The Japanese word for trust is *shin-yô* meaning literally sincere business: it is based on a compound of *shin*, a character for 'sincerity' and *yô* which means literally 'something to do, a business'. Finally, Chinese language has one word for Trust (xìn rèn, 信任), combining trust and commitment, and another for Confidence (zì xìn, 自信), describing self (zì)-confidence (xìn).

Despite these differences, we can assume that the central concept of trust is likely the same cross-culturally, but that languages favour a facet of it. The concepts of trust largely overlap across cultures, but the dominant emphasis may be revealed by linguistic investigation, at least as a potential trail to be verified. A first possibility is to gather insights from the different language/cultures reviewed, to derive the facets of the concept of trust:

1. Trust is reliance on and confidence in the truth, worth and reliability of people, words and things.

2. Trust is inseparable from distrust: since obvious showing of distrust is detrimental to the establishment of trust, every culture has to deal with the paradox of their inseparability.

3. Trust is about sharing common faith, beliefs, possibly education or group membership.

4. Trust is directed to common and future achievements, even though this does not deny the value of the lessons of the past.

Another avenue is to build on the etymology of the word trust in various cultures and discuss its variations. With the English 'trust', remitting one's interests into another's hands, one may wonder to what extent trust is seen as reciprocal and under which conditions and circumstances. In cultures with a stronger doing orientation (i.e., the doing orientation defines the self by what the self does), this might lead to a tendency to write long and detailed contracts that remove at least some of the need for implicit trust. The French *confiance*, as shared beliefs, insists much more on being and membership, implying that if they are to trust each other, people must share a common religion, the same educational or social background, and possibly a common national or ethnic affiliation. This poses the question of the extent to which similarity between partners is a condition for a trusting relationship.

The German *Vertrauen* evokes the process of changing an initial trustless situation into one where the parties have built confidence into the relationship. It is very much akin to the human nature orientation of Kluckhohn and Strodtbeck (1961),[14] with an implicit view that the starting base of human nature is bad.

Generally speaking, in the west the default is 'trust'. I'll give you the benefit of the doubt, and consider you basically trustworthy until you do something that breaks our trust. In China, the default tilts more toward 'distrust' – I only award you my trust after you've proven yourself worthy of it. This attitude is illustrated in an eloquent way by the popular Chinese saying that 'early birds get shot' (*qiang da chu tou niao*) – which reflects the strong desire to avoid any social risks. Clearly such an attitude does not invite people easily to engage in a more western-like trust giving process.[15] Further, the Japanese *shin yô* insists on the orientation of trust towards the future, a common enterprise and the sincere expectations of the parties. Time orientations play a role in shaping cultural views of trust building. Both past performances and long-term orientation and continuity over time are essential in the Japanese conception of trust.

Researchers should be able to see that it is a useful game to question words and expressions and try to find the real concepts (shared meaning in the cultural and language group) which is conveyed by them. Shenkar and Von Glinow note, for instance, that when interviewing Chinese employees, a word such as 'autonomy' which is a key concept in organisational research 'cannot be adequately translated into Chinese, or that alternate Chinese terms, such as 'right of self-determination' (*zi zhu quan*) convey a quite different meaning.[16] Examples in previous chapters illustrate the practical difficulties in dealing with the conceptual equivalence of constructs, especially when they are used in survey research.

A particular concept may also partly lose its initial meaning, because it is transferred into another context. For example, the construct of 'consumer ethnocentrism'[17] and the corresponding psychometric scale (CETSCALE) refer to situations where consumers associate the purchase of foreign products with the potential loss of jobs in domestic industry and, consequently, refrain from buying foreign products and services. It applies fairly well in developed countries to regions in industrial decline where some people, especially the working classes, may resent foreign-made products because they feel that their jobs are threatened by competitive imports. The same logic may prevail in some large industrial nations, which is probably why a number of studies[18] have successfully replicated the one-dimensional CETSCALE in Australia, France, Germany, and Japan. However, replication of the CETSCALE has not been successful in many other nations. For example, in the Netherlands,[19] the CETSCALE produced a two-dimensional factor structure; one factor related to the core of consumer ethnocentrism, whereas the other factor focused on purchasing only those foreign products that are not available in the country. In some other developing and emerging economies the CETSCALE also produced two-dimensional solutions; however, they were not the same two dimensions as those found in the

Netherlands. Thus, it is likely that the basic rationale underlying the concept of consumer ethnocentrism may be somewhat different across nations.

As a last topic of conceptual equivalence we address perception differences across cultures. There is a wide range of practical research issues where perception has an influence. For instance, research that deals with a comparison of working conditions may need to consider the impact of perception; the ways in which people perceive space, shapes, materials and smells and interpret them within the native cultural community will have a deep influence on their evaluation and assessment of their own working conditions as respondents. Colours are also differently perceived across cultures. For example, Cyr and colleagues[20] found that a grey website is more appealing to Canadians than to Germans, who prefer a blue website, with yellow websites being the least liked by German, Canadian and Japanese respondents. The same is true for smells.

First, people do not necessarily perceive smells in the same way, physically and mentally, as they have been trained in the use of their olfactory apparatus in different conditions. Second, the kind of interpretation of smells can be very different. When researching packaging and perfumes for washing liquids or other products where perceptive clues are important for product evaluation, a key research issue is to formulate the questions so that interviewees can express their native views on the smell or colours. Rather than ask them whether they like the scent of lavender, it is better to ask them first to recognise the smell, then to comment on what it evokes for them.

4.2.2 Functional equivalence: similar concepts performing different functions

Concepts or constructs used in international business research range very widely. They can be activities, outcomes, products, practices, rites, rules, relationships, and so on. They may be conceptually similar but they might not perform the same function. For example, a product can be identical, such as a basic bicycle, but serve a different function in another cultural context. In the USA a bicycle is often used solely for recreational purposes, whereas it is usually used for transport in the Netherlands and China. The primary purpose of meetings can be to solve precise tasks in the agenda or to be social gatherings aimed at building and maintaining group consensus. Other basic concepts in management such as reports, deadlines, while conceptually similar, can serve different functions according to the cultural context. The difference in functional use of common concepts is not necessarily dichotomous, but rather the dominance of a particular functional aspect in a particular culture. The function of friendship is essential to the Chinese for doing business, while it is considered somewhat unfair to exploit friendships for business purposes by many westerners.[21]

If similar activities perform different functions in different societies, their measures cannot be used directly for the purpose of comparison. A concept such as authority (the right to give orders and the power to ensure obedience) can be conceptually equivalent, but the functional use of authority can be different according to the context; whether authority is used directly by giving detailed instructions, or indirectly by setting target achievements and leaving room and autonomy to the employee for implementation. These are interesting cross-cultural differences. Activity concepts frequently used in marketing surveys, such as choosing products in a supermarket, are not necessarily functionally equivalent across countries. When asked what products a consumer chooses, women who do the shopping themselves and women who employ servants to do the shopping respond differently. For the first group, grocery shopping is a household chore, for the latter group it is a largely unknown activity.

Products are good examples of the problems of functional equivalence across cultures, because their use is context-embedded: a watch, for instance, may be used as wrist jewellery or an instrument for handling time and daily schedules. Another functional equivalence issue can be seen by taking the example of hot milk-based chocolate drinks. Whereas in the Netherlands they are considered best before going to sleep, in France hot chocolate is a breakfast drink for children. The use is not functionally equivalent in either neither in the consumption time period nor in the purpose for use (waking /energiser versus sleep/relaxer).

Many other examples could be given, such as wine (everyday beverage accompanying meals versus beverage for special occasions), beer (summer refresher versus all-year standard 'non-water' beverage), and perfumes (covering bodily odours versus adding a nice smell after a shower). The word 'coffee' covers a range of beverages that is enjoyed in very different social settings (at home, at the workplace, during leisure time, in the morning or at particular times during the day), in quite different forms (in terms of quantity, concentration, with or without milk, cold or hot), and prepared from different forms of coffee (beans, ground beans, instant). The function of the Brazilian *cafezinho*, very small cups of rather strong coffee drunk every hour in informal exchanges with colleagues, cannot be compared with the US coffee which is much lighter and drunk mostly at home and in restaurants or as a 'take-away' beverage. One of the best ways to investigate functional equivalence is to examine the social settings in which an activity takes place and what it means for the people involved.

4.2.3 Categorical equivalence

Categorical equivalence 'relates to the category in which objects or other stimuli are placed'.[22] Categorical equivalence refers to comparability in product category definitions, and in socio-demographic classes that exist between nations.[23] Unfortunately, demographic definitions do not correspond exactly from one country to another; age itself does (at first sight), but categories of occupation, education and socio-economic status usually do not. The meaning of age may differ across nations. For instance, 'retirement age' is highly different across nations and it might also differ over time. In several western nations retirement age has recently been moved from 65 years to 67. Furthermore, the age children go to secondary school differs across nations: In Germany that age is 10, in both the Netherlands and in Australia it is usually 12. Additionally, the category 'secondary school' is quite different across nations.

It is advisable to ask age in years in cross-national research; researchers then have the opportunity to recode the data into the categories they need. If data are presented in categories, say age bracket, these may differ across countries and will lead to inequivalence if you later want to compare sample to census data or other studies. To enhance understanding of differences between groups within a nation, religion and ethnic group may also need to be added to the demographic questions, as they are of the utmost importance in some countries (even if this appears politically incorrect to some researchers).

4.2.4 Translation equivalence

Issues around language were elaborated in Chapter 2. However, there are some simple guidelines, presented in Table 4.1, that will help researchers in their pre-translation wording. The remainder of this section specifically addresses issues of translation equivalence.

Table 4.1   Some translation guidelines

---

1. Use short and simple sentences and avoid unnecessary words (unless redundancy is deliberately sought).
2. Employ the active rather than the passive voice because the latter is easier to comprehend.
3. Repeat nouns instead of using pronouns because the latter may have vague referents; thus, the English 'you' can refer to a single or to a group of persons.
4. Avoid verbs and prepositions telling 'where' and 'when' that do not have a precise meaning, such as 'soon' and 'often'.
5. Avoid possessive forms where possible because it may be difficult to determine the ownership. The ownership such as 'his' in 'his dog' has to be derived from the context of the sentence and languages vary in their system of reference.

Adapted from Van de Vijver and Hambleton (1996); Brislin (1986, pp. 143–150) [24]

The back-translation technique[25] has been the most widely employed method for reaching translation equivalence (mainly lexical and idiomatic) in cross-cultural research[26]. See Table 4.2 for an overview of translation techniques. Back-translation helps to identify potential translation errors. One translator translates from the source language (S) into a target language (T). Then another translator, ignorant of the source-language text, translates the first translator's target language text back into the source language ('S'). Then the two source-language versions are compared. When back-translating, discrepancies may arise from translation mistakes in either direction, or from actual translation equivalence problems which are then uncovered. Then a final target-language questionnaire (T_f) is discussed and prepared by the researcher (who speaks the source language) and the two translators. It is advisable that one translator should be a native speaker of the target language and the other a native speaker of the source language; thus they translate *into* their native language rather than *from* it, which is more difficult and less reliable. When back-translation is strictly done across many nations a translation might become dull and insensitive.

However, back-translation does not guarantee that there is conceptual equivalence; simply knowing that words are equivalent is not sufficient. Literally equivalent words and phrases must also convey equivalent meanings in the two or more languages or cultures. Another technique, parallel translation, consists of having several translators translate independently from the source language into the target language(s). The different target versions are compared and a final version is written. Parallel or double translation (i.e., two translated versions) has been advocated as a preferred method of achieving equivalence in meaning.[27] Parallel and back-translation can also be merged, as shown in Table 4.2. When two languages and cultures present wide variations, such as Korean and English, combining parallel and back-translation provides a higher level of equivalence.

These methods can also be used in conjunction with a committee approach to review the meaning and equivalence of translations and to select the 'best' translation.[28] In the committee approach, translators discuss the meaning and equivalence of the translated items to select the preferred translation.[29] An adapted version of this procedure is used in the large scale European Social Survey. In this survey, the TRAPD procedure is used in the translation of the survey in more than 20 languages.[30] TRAPD stands for Translation, Review, Adjudication, Pre-testing and Documentation. TRAPD can be efficiently used when translating a questionnaire in 10 or more languages; one language is used as the source language from which all other translations are made. In TRAPD, key roles are available for the translators, the reviewer and the adjudicator. The translators need to be trained in the translation of questionnaires; the reviewer is a person who not only has good translation skills, but is also knowledgeable of survey design; the adjudicator is responsible for the final decisions about the translation (see Harkness, 2007 for further details).[31]

Translation techniques, even sophisticated ones, might still prove incapable of achieving full comparability of data. A different solution to the problem of translation has been suggested by Werner and Campbell (1970).[32] Research instruments should be developed by collaborators in the two cultures, and items, questions or other survey materials should be generated jointly. After back-translation, or after

Table 4.2 Advantages and drawbacks of translation techniques

Technique	Direct translation	Back-translation	Parallel translation
Process	S – – >T	S – – >T ; T – – >S' comparison S to S' – – > final version T_f	S – – >T ; S – – > T' comparison T to T' – – > final version T_f
Advantages	Easy to implement	Ensures the discovery of most inadequacies	Easier to implement in S country with T translators
Drawbacks/ Constraints	Leads to translation errors and discrepancies between S and T	Requires the availability of two translators, one native in S and one native in T languages	Leads to good wording in T, but does not ensure that specific meaning in S is fully rendered

Legend: S = source language, T = target language (translators or versions)

an initial translation process has been performed, there is an opportunity to change the source-language wording. This technique, called *decentring*, not only changes the target language, as in the previous techniques, but also allows the words and sentences in the source language to be changed if this provides enhanced accuracy. The ultimate words and phrases employed will depend on which common/similar meaning is sought in both languages simultaneously, without regard to whether words and phrases originate in the source or the target languages. The decentring approach is useful to increase cross-cultural understanding and an optimal final questionnaire. However, it is only workable when translation is done from one language to another. When five languages are involved, decentring would imply that 10 combinations of two languages need to be decentred.

Further, we do not advocate that translation should be a mechanical approach where the context is ignored. Language itself can be seen as a cultural informant to generate insights into shared or specific facets of meaning, for gaining a deeper insight into cross-cultural differences in which both the etic and the emic aspects of both languages are taken into account.[33] In current business research, the emphasis is on English culture and an etic approach is the norm; however, the emic perspective can increase knowledge and understanding in international business.

4.3 Instrument and measurement equivalence

4.3.1 Calibration equivalence

Calibration equivalence is one of the first issues to tackle when comparing scores across nations. To calibrate is to mark the scale of a measuring instrument, so that comparisons can be made in appropriate units. Many different types of questions need calibration (e.g., income, weights, distances, volume, and perceptual cues, such as colour, shape).

Survey questions need to be designed in a way that they fit the local situation; for instance, income needs to be asked in the local currency. When local currencies are used in a questionnaire or compared with secondary data, these need to be calculated to one currency before any comparison can be made. A common procedure is to take the US$ as the unit of comparison across nations; however, many other solutions also exist, such as converting nominal GDP per capita to GDP per capita adjusted for purchasing power parity (PPP). The method depends on the interpretation researchers wish to make.

Calibration problems are also significant when using secondary data. Differences in the categories used, for instance, age brackets, income brackets or professions, or differences in base years, can cause calibration equivalence issues, especially when some countries have no recent data. A typical calibration equivalence problem relates to monetary units, especially in high-inflation contexts where daily prices change constantly and cannot be directly compared over time – even a year – with those of a low-inflation country. Exchange rates and units of weight, distance and volume need attention to avoid equivalence problems.

A good example of calibration equivalence is given by Marchand (1993)[34] when he discusses the issue of defining and measuring working time cross-nationally, and particularly the problem of assessing the length of working time in a way which makes it comparable across nations. Reasons for inequivalence can be related to different bases for computation: legal or conventional working time, length of working time for which one is paid, hours during which a firm is open for business, full length of the working day including break times and travel time from home to work, time devoted to training, and time given for vacation. The same holds true for pay systems as to whether they are based on hour, day, week or month, and whether they include benefits or bonuses (for instance, the treatment of semester bonuses in Japan). The search for equivalence of hourly wages for workers is especially difficult since the calibration of qualification levels and categories across countries will add complexity to the already observed sources of inequivalence in both pay and working time. Lastly, even when comparing Gross Domestic Product per capita in PPP, high inflation might affect calibration equivalence; purchasing power might decline faster than can be included in the national statistics.

Calibration equivalence problems also arise when different basic units are being used, as well as from compound units based on different computation systems. Most Europeans, for instance, use the metric system, counting distances in kilometres and liquid volumes in litres (one cubic decimetre). Fuel consumption is measured in litres/100 km at an average speed. In the USA, 'gas mileage' is based on the inverse calculation: how many miles can one drive with a definite fuel volume, namely a gallon. Calibration also needs to assess which gallon it is: the British or imperial gallon (4.55 litres) or the US gallon (3.79 litres), and which mile, a statute mile (1.609 km) or a nautical mile (1.852 km), and then make an inverse calculation and try to finish with 100 km as the denominator. Lastly, the same term can refer to something else. A 'billion' in British English used to refer to 1,000,000,000,000, but is now the same as in American English 1,000,000,000. However, in other countries it the larger figure represents a billion and the commas are replaced with decimal places. For instance, in Dutch the word 'biljoen' (pronounced the same as the English word) refers to 1.000.000.000.000. An English 'billion' is a Dutch 'miljard'. The difference in the use of commas and decimals can play havoc with statistical packages!

4.3.2 Time lags

Temporal equivalence is similar to calibration equivalence, but deals with the calibration of dates and time periods. Information ages differently across countries. In a country where the annual inflation rate is 1%, income and price data are comparable across years, whereas in a country with 200% annual inflation rate, it is necessary to indicate on which exact day or week the data were collected and what the price indexes and exchange rates were at that exact date.

Temporal equivalence also deals with differences in development levels and technological advancement. Certain countries are 'equivalent' to what others were 20 years ago. Assessing time lags may be useful for making analogies: such a market may now develop in South Africa as it did in the USA 15 or 20 years ago and the product life cycle may be similar, even though the two countries are at different points on the curve.

4.3.3 Meaning of numbers

The way people understand and think about numbers depends on the culture where they grew up. When obtaining school grades in Germany 1 is highest and 6 is the lowest; in the Netherlands, grades are given from 1 to10, within 10 being the highest grade; in France a scale from 0 to 20 is used with 20 being the highest. In this way, culture has an influence on the perception of what is a low or a high number. Further, Roy and colleagues discussed the problems that may occur when individuals tend to choose lucky numbers more often (such as 2, 8, or 9 in China) or to choose unlucky numbers less often (such as 4 in China).[35]

Difficulties can occur in determining lexical equivalents in different languages when numbers in a scale are given verbal descriptions. The use of verbal descriptions can also increase problems in ensuring that the distances between scale points (adjectives, for instance) are equivalent in the two languages (metric equivalence). It is naive to use a differential semantic scale originally written in English, French or any other language and translate it lexically (simply with dictionary-equivalent words) into other languages. This will likely lead to errors in translations, in particular when rating scales are used with seven or more response categories. In the ESS, only end-points of the rating scales are used; this avoids confusion and translating scale categories in more than 20 languages.

Sood[36] provides a nice example on translation of scale labels. He studied the comparability of nine scale terms (from 'excellent' to 'very bad') across eight languages (English, Arabic, Chinese, Farsi, French, German, Korean, and Spanish). He evidences two facts:

1. Some languages have fewer terms to express gradation in evaluation (for example Korean), whereas others have a multitude (French).

2. There are large discrepancies in the 'value' of these adjectives, measured on a 0–100 scale. For instance, the Spanish *muy malo* was 58% higher than its supposed English equivalent of *very bad*. Therefore, the best solution is not to try and translate scale terms but rather to start from local wordings based on scales used by local researchers.

However, when studies are done in many nations simultaneously local wording might lead to problems in translation. Differences in scale should also be assessed and taken into account after data collection; see the section on response styles in Chapter 5.

4.3.4 Metric equivalence

Metric equivalence refers to the specific scale or scoring procedure used.[37] In cross-cultural studies, scores on multi-item scales are often used to assess whether the groups are similar or different on the construct. When comparing scores on these scales, researchers need to be able to establish configural, measurement unit and scalar invariance (see Chapter 5 for technical details). To establish measurement invariance of multi-item scales *ex-post*, these scales need at least three items, preferably more.

4.3.4.1 An illustration of instrument (in)equivalence: The CETSCALE

A scale often used in international business is the CETSCALE. This scale was developed in the USA and a 17-item version and a 10-item version are available;[38] the construct is considered one-dimensional. Many researchers all over the world have since then used versions of the scale in their models.

Although the scale was developed in the USA, few scientists questioned its applicability in other nations. This is surprising as some items (e.g., 'American products, first, last and foremost'), may be less relevant in a nation that only manufactures a limited number of products (of course, the country name first needs to be replaced!). The differences that may emerge when the scale is used in another culture are shown in Table 4.3; some items do not load on this factor

Table 4.3 The 10-item CETSCALE in three different countries: 'X' stands for a positive factor loading on a one-dimensional factor, 'O' stands for a non-significant factor loading on this one-dimensional factor

10-item CETSCALE (Shimp and Sharma, 1987)	USA (S&S, 1987)	Netherlands (D&N, 2003)	South Africa (P. et al., 2013)
1. Only those products that are unavailable in the US should be imported.	X	O	X
2. American products, first, last and foremost.	X	X	X
3. Purchasing foreign-made products is un-American.	X	X	O
4. It is not right to purchase foreign products.	X	X	O
5. A real American should always buy American-made products	X	X	O
6. We should purchase products manufactured in America instead of letting other countries get rich off us.	X	X	X
7. Americans should not buy foreign products, because this hurts American business and causes unemployment.	X	X	O
8. It may cost me in the long run but I prefer to support American products.	X	X	X
9. We should buy from foreign countries only those products that we cannot obtain within our country.	X	O	X
10. American consumers who purchase products made in other countries are responsible for putting their fellow Americans out of work.	X	X	O

(i.e., items that are not significantly correlated with the factor), as indicated by 'O' in the other nations. Douglas and Nijssen (D&N, 2003)[39] investigated the 10-item 'borrowed' CETSCALE in the Netherlands and found that there were two factors in the one-dimensional scale. More recently, Pentz and colleagues (2013)[40] in South Africa found two factors: one they call 'economic ethnocentrism' and the other 'patriotic ethnocentrism' and researchers[41] in Zimbabwe found two dimensions, namely negative influence of foreign products, and preference for domestic products. In contrast, another study[42] found the expected one-dimensionality of the CETSCALE in New Zealand and Singapore. The different results in dimensionality illustrate that 'borrowed scales' cannot be considered equivalent in other cultures. Depending on the context, items (and therefore scales) might have a different meaning.

To measure constructs, researchers often use scales from the well-known measurement scales handbooks.[43] These scales are almost all developed in western nations (mostly in the USA) and then, if necessary, translated into other languages. Translation can be fine, but the interpretation of items can turn out to be different across nations. In particular, balanced scales, with positively and negatively formulated items can be understood differently in Asian nations compared to western nations. In the materialism scale,[44] the negatively formulated items were not seen as opposites by people in East Asia,[45] in contrast to what was expected based on earlier studies in western nations using the scale. Wong and colleagues suggest another question format with items framed as questions instead of statements to avoid problems with the negatively formulated items.

Another option to control for response bias *ex-ante* is to use best–worst scaling (BWS) rather than rating scales. BWS[46] is an extension of the paired-comparison method to the multiple comparison case. It has been successfully used in the measurement of personal values, including Schwartz values and the List of Values,[47] and to investigate consumer ethical beliefs across countries.[48] BWS controls for response bias by asking respondents to identifying the two extreme items (best, worst; most, least, etc.) in each of a number of experimentally designed comparison sets. As such, respondents from different cultures cannot use different parts of the scale. Further, there are only two verbal scale terms (e.g., most/least important) and no numerical anchors, which reduces potential problems with lexical and numerical equivalence on the scale. For those interested, Louviere, Flynn and Marley (2015)[49] provide an extensive discussion of how to represent and analyse BWS choices.

Most Important		Least Important
○	Successful, capable, ambitious.	●
●	Protecting the environment, a world of beauty, unity with nature.	○
○	Helpful, honest, forgiving.	○
○	Devout, accepting portion in life, humble.	○
○	Clean, national security, social order.	○

Figure 4.1   An illustration of a best–worst scale comparison set from Lee, Soutar, Louviere (2008)[50]

4.4 Preparing for sampling

Sampling is a key issue in data collection, and many techniques and procedures have been described in the literature. Public opinion research is at the forefront in sampling, as it is considered of key importance in this field to make inferences on the whole population in a nation. Nationally representative samples are the norm in public opinion and social research. In psychology on the other hand, comparable samples are the norm; such samples often are convenience samples consisting of university students. Cross-cultural research in business is in between these two positions, although non-student samples are becoming more the norm.

The starting point in sampling in cross-cultural research is determined by the problem statement of the research. In research that seeks to make inferences about differences between nations on potential sales, trust in institutions, or willingness to adopt a new payment system, the emphasis might be on representative samples, similar to the approach in public opinion research. In contrast, when the research is focused on comparing personality dimensions across nations, comparable samples, such as students, may be appropriate, as they are assumed to mainly differ on culture. Further, when the objective of the study is to assess what cultural differences exist between nations, homogeneous comparable samples in all nations are needed. In these studies, convenience samples of managers or students are typically used; examples include the seminal work by Hofstede[51] who focused on IBM employees, and experimental studies in cross-cultural consumer psychology using students.[52]

There is a trade-off: comparable samples comprised of homogeneous groups of people from respective nations are not representative of the population. On the other hand, nationally representative samples are hardly ever comparable across countries, even on commonly used background characteristics such as age or attained level of education. Countries naturally differ on these variables. Furthermore, experimental designs involving cultural groups differ from experimental designs in domestic settings in that random assignment of subjects to the conditions (cultures) is not possible; the best achievable design is a pseudo-experimental setting.

If sampling of representative samples is desired, as it is in many studies, some considerations need to be made. A complete census, where the whole population of interest is researched, is far too costly, even for most governments! Therefore it is advisable to infer the characteristics of the whole population from a limited sample. During this process the following tasks must be carried out:

1. Determine a sampling frame, of which the basic characteristics are known (a telephone directory, an electoral list, a business directory).

2. Draw a sample from this frame, by a method which is either probabilistic or non-probabilistic.

3. Check that the selected sample is representative of the population under examination.

4. Determine the required sample size.

In cross-national research, sampling is a two-step procedure: first, nations are chosen and second, respondents are selected within the respective nations. The choice of nations can be either driven by theoretical or managerial considerations. In managerial research, companies choose nations they consider managerially important for their business; for instance in marketing research, the larger countries in Europe, such as Germany and the UK, are chosen in addition to the USA and important emerging economies, such as China. In academia, the choice of nations is best driven by theory; for instance, when differences are expected between nations that are collectivist and individualist, sampling ideally includes nations that differ only on individualism–collectivism, and not on the other Hofstede dimensions.[53] For instance, when a researcher hypothesises that a difference in likelihood of purchasing luxury products can be explained by country level masculinity (MAS), they need to sample nations that only differ on this Hofstede dimension, but not on the other dimensions. When we take the USA with a MAS score of 62 as the first country, both Russia and the Netherlands nations are potential nations for comparison on MAS (see Table 4.4) as both nations have relatively lower scores on MAS. The best option for testing the hypothesis is the Netherlands; only MAS differs, the other three dimensions are quite similar. When considering Russia as a possible comparison, differences found between the nations might be due not only to MAS but also to power distance, individualism and uncertainty avoidance.

Table 4.4 Hofstede (2001) scores on four culture dimensions

	Power distance	Individualism	Masculinity	Uncertainty avoidance
USA	40	91	62	46
Netherlands	38	80	14	53
Russia	93	39	36	95

Note: PDI = Power Distance, IDV = Individualism vs. Collectivism, MAS = Masculinity vs. Femininity, UAI = Uncertainty Avoidance

We will illustrate sampling by examining a large cross-national survey using random probability sampling: the European Social Survey (ESS). The ESS is a multi-country study designed to measure contemporary social attitudes and how they change over time. The aim of the study is to meet the highest methodological standards to arrive at truly comparable information across nations. In the bi-annual ESS survey, conducted in more than 25 nations, the sampling frame consists of all people (15 years or older) who are residents of the country and live in private households. In the ESS, as many nations (in the European Union including neighbouring nations) are included as possible, the limitation is the willingness to cooperate in the respective nations; when cooperation is agreed upon, the procedures as set by the coordinating team must be adhered to. Per nation the sampling frames are taken that best enable the researchers to draw the random samples. For instance, in the 7th ESS round in 2014, random samples from the United Kingdom (UK) were selected from the Post Office address database across England, Scotland, Wales and Northern Ireland, and in Germany from the population register (*Einwohnermelderegister*). In each nation, all selected addresses must be visited and contacted; however, the number of recontacts differ: in the UK interviewers must make at least six visits to the address to try to contact the household; in Germany at least four visits are required. In the UK, after contacting the household, an eligible individual is selected from within the household, whereas in Germany the selected individual is specified beforehand. To avoid respondents' refusal to cooperate, interviewers get special instructions to motivate the respondents; for instance, interviewers offer to come back at a more convenient time. In addition, visits to contact the selected people are planned in the evening and on weekends to increase the response rates. Different procedures are used with the aim of obtaining comparable samples across the respective nations.

Sample sizes in cross-cultural research are comparable to sample sizes in similar studies in domestic research. When inferences on public opinion are the objective of a study, samples consisting of 1000 people or more might be needed (e.g., in the European Social Survey); when matched student samples are compared in an experimental study, as few as 25 students per culture might suffice for a very simple study on one or two factors. More information on determining the appropriate sample sizes can be found in handbooks and articles on sampling.[54]

4.4.1 Selection of respondents

An important criterion is the choice of respondents (e.g., individuals, households, managers, or people with a specific profession). Selecting a unit of analysis is a key issue in the conceptualisation of comparative research designs. For instance, the role of respondents in the buying decision process (organisational buying, family buying, information and influence patterns) may vary across countries. In the US, it is not uncommon that children have a strong influence on product purchasing, whereas in countries that are less child oriented, children's influence on buying decisions will be much smaller. The same holds true for the extended family in South East Asia, which influences what might be thought of as autonomous decision making in other countries.[55] It is therefore of primary interest to first assess the basic equivalent sampling units: for instance, when researching industrial markets, it is necessary to compare the position, role and responsibility of industrial buyers throughout different countries. Similarly, in the area of management, the role of direct supervisors may vary considerably across cultures depending on their responsibility for evaluating their immediate subordinates.

After defining the population of interest, the researcher draws a sample which represents this population. However, a sample split into 50% men and 50% women conveys a different meaning in a country where women's rights are recognised as equal compared to a similar sampling frame in more traditional countries, where women do not actively participate in the job market. As such, the expression 'representative sample' makes little sense if one does not clarify which traits and characteristics this sample actually represents. For instance, shopping behaviour is very different worldwide. In some countries men do most of the shopping, in others women shop for the family, in others it is more often a maid; this also depends on other factors such as income level, type of product, employment patterns, norms and values, etc. The samples must represent actual shoppers rather than men and women as they are in the general population of potential shoppers. Information on consumers' customs and habits can be found, for instance, in the reports and databases of Euromonitor International (http://www.euromonitor.com/).

4.4.2 Internet samples

There is, of course, limited availability of an exhaustive sampling framework that corresponds exactly to the characteristics of the population. This holds in developed nations and even more in emerging and developing nations. As representative samples are hard to obtain, many researchers in academia and in practice rely on Internet panels for their international research. Large research companies, such as Survey Sampling International (SSI), control panels in many nations worldwide and other research companies have designated partners abroad. People who belong to these panels are paid to answer surveys. As they are usually done over the Internet, in the comfort of the participants' own home, panel surveys offer cost, time and convenience benefits over many other methods.

However, the availability of Internet panels in many nations does not imply equivalence of these panels. In many nations, panels rely on volunteer respondents, or exclude groups in the population from participation (which is done when people do not have Internet access), as such they are often far from representative of any population.[56] Internet panels in which large groups of people participate may approach representativity in developed nations, where the Internet penetration is close to 100%; however, in nations with a relatively low Internet penetration, and in emerging and developing nations in particular, participants in a panel are likely to be younger and have a higher level of education than the average person. However, many companies have relatively large panels, from which a sample can be drawn to be representative on a selection of characteristics, such as age, gender, education and income. Some research companies have focused on this issue and developed probability based online panels; an example is Knowledgenetworks (GfK) in the USA.

Finally, one may decide that representativeness and comparability of cross-cultural samples can be better achieved by using different samples and sampling techniques which produce equivalent levels of reliability, rather than by using the same procedure across all nations. This might involve approaching younger people via a web survey and the elderly by telephone. When focusing on the younger, higher educated population only, one might best reach consumers in

South Africa via their smartphone and in the Netherlands via their PC; however, it should be noted that such different modes of web data collection methods impact survey design and response rates.[57] Nevertheless, such mixed-method approaches may be the preferred approach when (an approximation of) a representative sample is required across different nations.[58]

4.5 Anticipating data collection equivalence issues

4.5.1 Non-participation of potential respondents

In the literature, the three most cited theories for participation or non-participation of respondents in surveys are exchange theory (individuals are motivated to respond by returns or rewards they expect from others), cognitive dissonance (failure to respond creates a state of anxiety which will be reduced by answering), and self-perception (people respond to be consistent with their view of themselves as helpful and responsible persons). To obtain nationally representative samples non-response has to be minimised, which may imply contacting individuals in the sample several times.[59] Even then, contacting people might be impossible; and if they are contacted they might refuse to participate in the survey. In the European Social Survey (ESS) the target response rate is 70%, a rate that is only met in a few nations, as can be seen in Table 4.5. These response percentages are high in comparison to response rates in business surveys; Harzing[60] reported response rates in mail surveys to managers of less than 20%.

Non-response in international surveys can become worrisome when response rates differ enormously between nations. In 2014, in the ESS response rates differed from 31% in Germany to 66% in Poland, which implies that the composition of the samples differs between the nations. Options to deal with non-response are imputation and employing weighting, but these are not a complete solution for missing responses of people with many activities outside of their home, or for people who spend large periods of time abroad. Discrepancies in response patterns across countries may cause data unreliability and limit direct comparability.

Table 4.5   Response rates in the European Social Survey over time (%)

	2004	2006	2008	2010	2012	2014
France	43.6	46.0	49.4	47.1	52.1	50.9
Germany	51.0	54.5	48.0	30.5	33.8	31.4
UK	50.6	54.6	55.8	56.3	53.1	43.6
Netherlands	64.3	59.8	49.8	60.0	55.1	58.6
Poland	73.7	70.2	71.2	70.3	74.9	65.8

Source: www.europeansocialsurvey.org

4.5.2 Respondents' cooperation in surveys

Participation in surveys can be enhanced by contacting the potential respondent several times and by doing the interviews face to face.[61] However, surveys can be long and not all respondents are equally capable and motivated to answer many questions on sometimes complicated and boring topics. The design of the questionnaire and the way the questions are formulated may enhance willingness to cooperate and provide high quality answers. Further, show cards can be used to clarify the meaning of specific questions in the questionnaire; for instance, a country-specific list of types of education can be provided (for examples see the ESS documentation on their website).[62]

Differences in response rates may be especially problematic when including emerging and developing nations, where people may neither be used to survey research nor to western interviewers. Respondents may feel that the interviewer is intruding upon their privacy. They may prefer not to answer or they consciously bias their answers, fearing that their opinion could later be used against them. Furthermore, many cultures have strong privacy/intimacy patterns, where the family group is protected from external interference. In some countries, interviewing females may only be possible in a specific setting with other family members being present and only with a female moderator. High response rates can then only be achieved with great effort.

However, response equivalence problems not only emerge in willingness to cooperate, but may also appear when respondents from different cultures differ in willingness to answer specific questions they consider sensitive. Sensitive topics may differ from one culture to the other; sensitive topics might be for instance, religion, sex, or criminal behaviour. In many European nations, questions on income are considered sensitive and people are reluctant to provide information on their income. In the ESS in 2012, the average percentage of people explicitly refusing to answer the question on income was 11%, with percentages as high as 24% in Hungary and 16% in Italy and as low as 2% in Sweden. These differences in refusal might be due to the willingness (or lack thereof) to reveal their income to tax authorities. Furthermore, styles of dishonesty might differ across nations; for instance, Andrighetto and colleagues[63] found that Italians engage more frequently in fudging, while Swedes were more likely to be both perfectly honest and perfectly dishonest.

4.5.3 Involving local researchers

In the researcher's quest to embed the data collection process in the local context, they may be tempted to employ local researchers rather than from the home country. The strength of local researchers is that they know the country and its people, and can usually establish rapport easily. Knowledge of the local language allows the researcher to interact much better and to understand what is said.

Language can be an enormous barrier, as anyone who has tried to interview through interpreters would recognise. If local researchers are familiar with the country and language where the survey originated, they can also interpret the significance of what is said and explain differences across cultures. However, local researchers also have weaknesses. They often have less research experience than their counterpart in more developed countries. They may find it difficult to adopt the kind of neutral, objective stance with reference to informants or clients because they do not see the value of objective truth resulting from a distanced position in the interaction. They may want to be didactic in groups and may well prefer to distort findings to reflect a more educated picture of fellow countrymen than exists in reality. Alternatively, they may seek to distance themselves from the 'average consumer' by exaggerating their foibles and lack of sophistication, especially if the researcher is from an educated family and out of touch with his or her countrymen. Finally, the local researcher may be unwilling or unable, even for business reasons, to cross traditional barriers of class, tribe, or religion.

4.6 Conclusion

This chapter has presented what can be done before data collection to obtain equivalence in a cross-national study. The researcher must keep a critical eye on the pursuit of absolute cross-cultural or cross-national equivalence which may simply end in obscuring relevant information. There is something vaguely ethnocentric in the absolute pursuit of 'zero-bias' in cross-cultural research, inasmuch as differences are not meant as useful information, but rather as a disturbing phenomenon for the research process that must in some way be eliminated, so that concepts, instruments, respondents and their responses are made comparable across nations and culture and systematically viewed as different in degree rather than different in nature. However, it is important, if samples are to be compared across countries or cultures. Not only quantitative but also qualitative researchers must be concerned with conceptual and measurement equivalence, because in such approaches the researcher is the instrument. In the next chapter the emphasis will be on what a quantitative researcher can do to assess equivalence after the data have arrived.

Notes

1. Singh, J., Measurement issues in cross-national research. Journal of International Business Studies, 1995. 26(3): p. 597.
2. Steenkamp, J.B., Moving out of the U.S. silo: A call to arms for conducting international marketing research. Journal of Marketing, 2005. 49(6): 6–8.

3. He, Y., M.A. Merz, and D.L. Alden, Diffusion of measurement invariance assessment in cross-national empirical marketing research: Perspectives from the literature and a survey of researchers. Journal of International Marketing, 2008. 16(2): 64–83.

4. Sichtmann, C. and M. von Selasinsky, Exporting services successfully: Antecedents and performance implications of customer relationships. Journal of International Marketing, 2010. 18(1): 86–108.

5. Lawler, J.J., S. Chen, P.-C. Wu, J. Bae, and B. Bai, High-performance work systems in foreign subsidiaries of American multinationals: An institutional model. Journal of International Business Studies, 2011. 42(2): 202–220.

6. Harzing, A.W., Response Styles in cross-national survey research: A 26-country Study. International Journal of Cross Cultural Management, 2006. 6(2): 243–266.

7. Sharma, P., Country of origin effects in developed and emerging markets: Exploring the contrasting roles of materialism and value consciousness. Journal of International Business Studies, 2011. 42(2): 285–306.

8. Davidov, E., B. Meuleman, J. Cieciuch, P. Schmidt, and J. Billiet, Measurement equivalence in cross-national research. Annual Review of Sociology, 2014. 40(1): 55–75. doi:doi:10.1146/annurev-soc-071913-043137

   van Herk, H., Y.H. Poortinga, and T.M.M. Verhallen, Equivalence of survey data: Relevance for international marketing. European Journal of Marketing, 2005. 39(3/4): 351–364.

   van de Vijver, F.J.R. and K. Leung, Methodological issues in psychological research on culture. Journal of Cross-Cultural Psychology, 2000. 31(1): 33–51.

   Craig, C.S. and S.P. Douglas, International Marketing Research. Vol. 3. 2005, Chichester: Wiley.

   He, J. and F.J.R. Van de Vijver, Bias and equivalence in cross-cultural research. Online Readings in Psychology and Culture, 2012. 2(2).

9. Craig, C.S. and S.P. Douglas, International Marketing Research. 2000, Chichester: Wiley. XXII, 425.

10. Craig, C.S. and S.P. Douglas, International Marketing Research. 2000, Chichester: Wiley., p. 158

11. Gardberg, N.A., Reputatie, reputation, réputation, reputazione, ruf: A cross-cultural qualitative analysis of construct and instrument equivalence. Corporate Reputation Review, 2006. 9(1): 39–61.

12. Gounaris, S.P., Trust and commitment influences on customer retention: Insights from business-to-business services. Journal of Business Research, 2005. 58(2): 126–140.

13. Jain, M., S. Khalil, W. J. Johnston, and J. M.-S. Cheng, The performance implications of power–trust relationship: The moderating role of commitment in the supplier–retailer relationship. Industrial Marketing Management, 2014. 43(2): 312–321.

14. Kluckhohn, F.R. and F.L. Strodtbeck, Variations in Value Orientations. 1961, Row and Peterson, Evanston.

15. De Cremer, D. Understanding trust, in China and the West. HBR Executive Education 2015 February, 11, 2015; Available from: https://hbr.org/2015/02/understanding-trust-in-china-and-the-west

16. Shenkar, O. and M.A. Von Glinow, Paradoxes of organizational theory and research: Using the case of China to illustrate national contingency. Management Science, 1994. 40(1): 56–71, p. 67.

17. Shimp, T.A. and S. Sharma, Consumer ethnocentrism: Construction and validation of the CETSCALE. Journal of Marketing Research, 1987. 24(3): 280–289.

Nijssen, E.J. and H. van Herk, Conjoining international marketing and relationship marketing: Exploring consumers' cross-border service relationships. Journal of International Marketing, 2009. 17(1): 91–115.

18. Nijssen, E.J. and H. van Herk, Conjoining international marketing and relationship marketing: Exploring consumers' cross-border service relationships. Journal of International Marketing, 2009. 17(1): 91–115.

Josiassen, A., A.G. Assaf, and I.O. Karpen, Consumer ethnocentrism and willingness to buy. International Marketing Review, 2011. 28(6): 627–646.

Netemeyer, R.G., S. Durvasula, and D.R. Lichtenstein, A cross-national assessment of the reliability and validity of the CETSCALE. Journal of Marketing Research, 1991. 28(3): 320–327.

19. Douglas, S.P. and E.J. Nijssen, On the use of 'borrowed' scales in cross-national research: A cautionary note. International Marketing Review, 2003. 20(6): 621–642.

20. Cyr, D., M. Head, and H. Larios, Colour appeal in website design within and across cultures: A multi-method evaluation. International Journal of Human-Computer Studies, 2010. 68(1–2): 1–21.

21. Meyer, E., Getting to Sí, Ja, Oui, Hai, and Da. (cover story). Harvard Business Review, 2015. 93(12): 74–80.

22. Craig, C.S. and S.P. Douglas, International Marketing Research. 2000, Chichester: Wiley. XXII, 159.

23. Craig, C.S. and S.P. Douglas, International Marketing Research. 2000, Chichester: Wiley. XXII, 425.

24. Van de Vijver, F.J.R. and R.K. Hambleton, Translating tests: Some practical guidelines. European Psychologist, 1996. 1(2): 89–99.

Brislin, R.W., The wording and translation of research instruments, in Field Methods in Cross-Cultural Research. 1986, Sage Publications Thousand Oaks, CA: Newbury Park, CA. pp. 137–164.

25. Brislin, R.W., Back-translation for cross-cultural research. Journal of Cross-Cultural Psychology, 1970. 1(3): 185–216.

Werner, O. and D.T. Campbell, Translating, working through interpreters, and the problem of decentering, in A Handbook of Method in Cultural Anthropology, R. Naroll and R. Cohen (Eds). 1970, American Museum of Natural History: New York. p. 398–420.

26. Douglas, S.P. and C.S. Craig, Collaborative and iterative translation: An alternative approach to back translation. Journal of International Marketing, 2007. 15(1): 30–43.

27. Van de Vijver, F.J.R. and R.K. Hambleton, Translating tests: Some practical guidelines. European Psychologist, 1996. 1(2): 89–99.

28. Harkness, J.A., Questionnaire Translation, in Cross-Cultural Survey Methods, J.A. Harkness, F.J.R. Van de Vijver, and P.P. Mohler (Eds). 2003, John Wiley & Sons Inc.: Hoboken. pp. 35–56.

Harkness, J.A. and A. Schoua-Glusberg, Questionnaires in translation. ZUMA-nachrichten spezial, 1998. 3(1): 87–127.

29. Harkness, J.A., Questionnaire translation, in Cross-Cultural Survey Methods, J.A. Harkness, F.J.R. Van de Vijver, and P.P. Mohler (Eds). 2003, John Wiley & Sons Inc.: Hoboken. pp. 35–56.

30. Harkness, J.A., Improving the comparability of translations in R. Jowell, C. Roberts, F. R., & G. Eva (Eds), Measuring Attitudes Cross-Nationally: Lessons from the European Social Survey, London: Sage Publications, 2007: 79–95.

31. Harkness, J.A., Improving the comparability of translations. in R. Jowell, C. Roberts, F. R., & G. Eva (Eds), Measuring Attitudes Cross-Nationally: Lessons from the European Social Survey, London: Sage Publications, 2007: 79–95.

32. Werner, O. and D.T. Campbell, Translating, working through interpreters, and the problem of decentering, in A Handbook of Method in Cultural Anthropology, R. Naroll and R. Cohen (Eds). 1970, American Museum of Natural History: New York. pp. 398–420.

33. Usunier, J.-C., Language as a resource to assess cross-cultural equivalence in quantitative management research. Journal of World Business, 2011. 46(3): 314–319.

34. Marchand, O., An international comparison of working times. Futures, 1993. 25(5): 502–510.

35. Roy, A., P.G. Walters, and S.T. Luk, Chinese puzzles and paradoxes: Conducting business research in China. Journal of Business Research, 2001. 52(2): 203–210.

36. Sood, J., Equivalent measurement in international market research: Is it really a problem? Journal of International Consumer Marketing, 1990. 2(2): 25–42.

37. van Herk, H., Y.H. Poortinga, and T.M.M. Verhallen, Equivalence of survey data: Relevance for international marketing. European Journal of Marketing, 2005. 39(3/4): 351–364.

38. Shimp, T.A. and S. Sharma, Consumer ethnocentrism: Construction and validation of the CETSCALE. Journal of Marketing Research, 1987. 24(3): 280–289.

39. Douglas, S.P. and E.J. Nijssen, On the use of 'borrowed' scales in cross-national research: A cautionary note. International Marketing Review, 2003. 20(6): 621–642.

40. Pentz, C., N.S. Terblanche, and C. Boshoff, Measuring consumer ethnocentrism in a developing context: An assessment of the reliability, validity and dimensionality of the CETSCALE. Journal of Transnational Management, 2013. 18(3): 204–218.

41. Makanyeza, C. and F. du Toit, Measuring consumer ethnocentrism: An assessment of reliability, validity and dimensionality of the CETSCALE in a developing market. Journal of African Business, 2016. 17(2): 188–208.

42. Durvasula, S. and S. Lysonski, Probing the etic vs. emic nature of consumer ethnocentrism. Innovative Marketing, Vol. 10, No. 1 (2014): p.7–16.

43. Bearden, W.O., R.G. Netemeyer, and K.L. Haws, Handbook of Marketing Scales: Multi-item measures for marketing and consumer behavior research. 2011. Thousand Oaks: SAGE Publications, Inc.

44. Richins, M.L. and S. Dawson, A consumer values orientation for materialism and its measurement: Scale development and validation. Journal of Consumer Research, 1992. 19(3): 303–316.

45. Wong, N., A. Rindfleisch, and J.E. Burroughs, Do reverse-worded items confound measures in cross-cultural consumer research? The case of the material values scale. Journal of Consumer Research, 2003. 30(1): 72–91.

46. Louviere, J.J., T.N. Flynn, and A. Marley, Best–Worst Scaling: Theory, methods and applications. 2015. Cambridge: Cambridge University Press.
47. Zhao, X., J.G. Lynch Jr, and Q. Chen, Reconsidering Baron and Kenny: Myths and truths about mediation analysis. Journal of Consumer Research, 2010. 37(2): 197–206.
    Lee, J.A., G.N. Soutar, and J. Louviere, Measuring values using best–worst scaling: The LOV example. Psychology and Marketing, 2007. 24(12): 1043–1058.
    Lee, J.A., G. Soutar, and J. Louviere, The best–worst scaling approach: an alternative to Schwartz's values survey. Journal of personality assessment, 2008. 90(4): 335–347.
    Lee, J., J. Sneddon, T. Daly, G. Soutar, J. Louviere, and S. Schwartz, (2016). Testing and ex-tending Schwartz refined value theory using a best–worst scaling approach. (forthcoming) Assessment. DOI: 10.1177/1073191116683799
48. Auger, P., T.M. Devinney, and J.J. Louviere, Using best–worst scaling methodology to investigate consumer ethical beliefs across countries. Journal of Business Ethics, 2007. 70(3): 299–326.
49. Louviere, J.J., T.N. Flynn, and A. Marley, Best–Worst Scaling: Theory, methods and applications. 2015. Cambridge: Cambridge University Press.
50. Lee, J.A., G. Soutar, and J. Louviere, The best–worst scaling approach: An alternative to Schwartz's values survey. Journal of Personality Assessment, 2008. 90(4): 335–347.
51. Hofstede, G., Culture's Consequences: Comparing values, behaviors, institutions, and organizations across nations. 2001. Thousand Oaks, CA: Sage. XX, 596.
52. Gurhan-Canli, Z. and D. Maheswaran, Cultural variations in country of origin effects. JMR. Journal of Marketing Research, 2000. 37(3): p. 309.
53. Sivakumar, K. and C. Nakata, The stampede toward Hofstede's framework: Avoiding the sample design pit in cross-cultural research. Journal of International Business Studies, 2001. 32(3): 555–574.
54. Barlett, J.E., J.W. Kotrlik, and C.C. Higgins, Organizational research: Determining appropriate sample size in survey research. Information Technology, Learning, And Performance Journal, 2001. 19(1): p. 43.
    Thompson, S.K., Sampling. Vol. 10. 2012. NJ: Wiley.
55. Chen, B., M. Vansteenkiste, W. Beyers, B. Soenens, and S.V. Petegem, Autonomy in family decision making for Chinese adolescents: Disentangling the dual meaning of autonomy. Journal of Cross-Cultural Psychology, 2013, 44, 1184–1209.
56. Baker, R., S.J. Blumberg, J.M. Brick, M.P. Couper, M. Courtright, J.M. Dennis, et al., Research synthesis: AAPOR report on online panels. Public Opinion Quarterly, 2010. 74(4): p. 711-781.
57. de Bruijne, M. and A. Wijnant, Comparing survey results obtained via mobile devices and computers: An experiment with a mobile web survey on a heterogeneous group of mobile devices versus a computer-assisted web survey. Social Science Computer Review, 2013, 31: 482–504. doi:10.1177/0894439313483976
58. De Leeuw, E.D., J.J. Hox, and D.A. Dillman, Mixed-mode surveys: When and why. International Handbook of Survey Methodology, Psychology Press, New York, 2008: p. 299–316.
    De Leeuw, E.D. and J.J. Hox, Survey mode and mode effects in U. Engel, B. Jann, P. Lynn, A. Scherpenzeel, and P. Sturgis (Eds) Improving Survey Methods, Routledge, New York, 2014: p. 22–34.

59. Billiet, J., M. Philippens, R. Fitzgerald, and I. Stoop, Estimation of nonresponse bias in the European Social Survey: Using information from reluctant respondents. Journal of Official Statistics, 2007. 23(2): p. 135.

60. Harzing, A.-W., Response rates in international mail surveys: Results of a 22-country study. International Business Review, 1997. 6(6): 641–665.

61. Stoop, I.A., The hunt for the last respondent: Nonresponse in sample surveys. 2005, The Hague: Sociaal en Cultureel Planbureau.

62. http://www.europeansocialsurvey.org/

63. Andrighetto, G., N. Zhang, S. Ottone, F. Ponzano, J. D'Attoma, and S. Steinmo, Are some countries more honest than others? Evidence from a tax compliance experiment in Sweden and Italy. Frontiers in Psychology, 2016. 7: p. 472.

5

EX-POST: METHODOLOGICAL ISSUES IN CROSS-CULTURAL BUSINESS RESEARCH

As described in Chapter 4, dealing with before (*ex-ante*) data collection measures can be taken to enhance equivalence across nations. However, whether data are in fact equivalent across nations can only be established after data collection (*ex-post*). This chapter describes what can be done *after* data collection to assess and ensure comparability of data across cultures. When the data first come in, an international researcher needs to check for data equivalence, in addition to following the common procedures for data checking when doing research in one nation.

Data analysis in international research differs from data analysis in a one-country setting in that equivalence of the measures needs to be established before valid comparisons can be made. It needs to be verified that respondents in the respective nations understood the questions in the same way and have interpreted and used the response scales in a similar way. Discrepancies in response patterns across countries may cause variation in the reliability of variables and limit direct comparison. In addition, contextual elements in the data collection process such as taboo topics, social desirability, uncritical endorsement of the proposed statements, uncertainty about or reluctance to reveal one's position, or, more generally, lack of familiarity with the research instrument may have an influence on responses. Differences in response style may create discrepancies between observed and true measurement, that is, stylistic variance may be confounded with substantive variance.

After preliminary steps taken when the data comes in from the various data locations (Section 5.1), non-response patterns should to be investigated

(Section 5.2). The ways and means to deal with measurement bias and response styles (Section 5.3), and assessment of measurement invariance (Section 5.4) are the next steps in *ex-post* methodological issues in cross-cultural business research. Finally, in the multilevel structure of cross-national studies involving several nations with individuals or businesses nested within these nations is discussed; such a data structure requires a specific analytical approach.[1] In multilevel studies both individual level and national level factors affect the dependent variable of interest. In Section 5.5 we describe multilevel studies in more detail and show their importance in cross-national research.

5.1 Preliminary steps

Datasets from international research projects typically come in from many different countries, where local academics or local research agencies collected the data. Despite elaborate briefings of the collaborators[2] in the other countries, it cannot be assumed that the datasets are the same and can be immediately merged. Issues might arise with additional variables being included in some countries and not in others, variables in the datasets may also have different names and labels, and they may use different categories (e.g., income, age groups etc.). A first step is to review the data from each country separately, following guidelines for examining domestic data. Guidelines can be found in many texts.[3]

Examining univariate and bivariate distributions provides additional insight into the data; calculating frequency distributions, descriptive statistics and correlations provides preliminary information about similarities and differences between countries. For instance, a correlation between happiness and satisfaction with life should be positive. If not, it might be that an answering scale was reversed, with '1' equals 'totally disagree' in one country, whereas in the other '1' stands for 'totally agree'. In addition to descriptive statistics, creating boxplots for distributions and scatterplots for relationships between two variables are very easy and insightful to check whether outliers are present and whether the distributions are roughly similar across nations or not.

Figure 5.1 shows that the average number of years of education differs across nations; however, it also shows that in all countries there are outliers. In both the Netherlands and Germany there are individuals who completed about 35 years of education; in Germany, France and the United Kingdom some individuals seem to have had no education. The researcher needs to verify whether these data may be correct or whether the scores can be considered erroneous and need to be set to missing values. A first check might be to create scatterplots of age against years of full-time education. Scatterplots for two countries are shown in Figure 5.2.

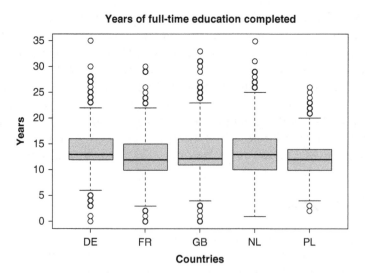

Figure 5.1 Boxplot showing self-reported years of full-time education completed in five nations. The data are from the representative samples in the European Social Survey (ESS) in 2012

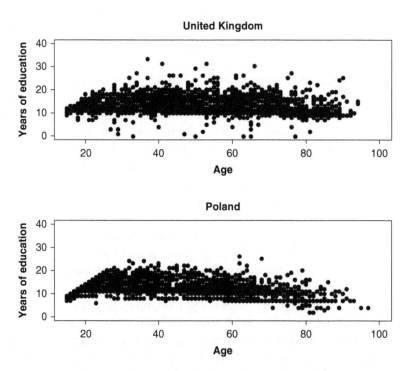

Figure 5.2 Scatterplots of age versus self-reported years of education completed. The data are from the representative samples in the European Social Survey (ESS) in 2012

Figure 5.2 extends the data in Figure 5.1 by combining years of education with age for the UK and Poland. This allows a further investigation of the outliers. For instance, in the United Kingdom a respondent of about 40 years old claims to have had 35 years of full-time education. Such observations need to be checked and decisions need to be made on whether the score found is plausible (e.g., a 40 year old who completed 25 years of schooling and indicated on another variable measuring education that he received a PhD) or whether the response needs to be coded as missing (e.g., a 40 year old who completed 25 years of schooling and indicated on another variable measuring education that he completed primary school only).

Checks on data quality are important. In face-to-face interviews or surveys done on a computer (CAPI or in web surveys) the time taken to answer the questionnaire can be registered. In Figure 5.3 the time taken by respondents in five nations is shown. Results show that not only the average time differs across nations, but also that some interviews took a long time to complete and others were done in a few minutes. Given that the ESS uses a long questionnaire with over 100 questions, the fast completion times need to be checked. The time

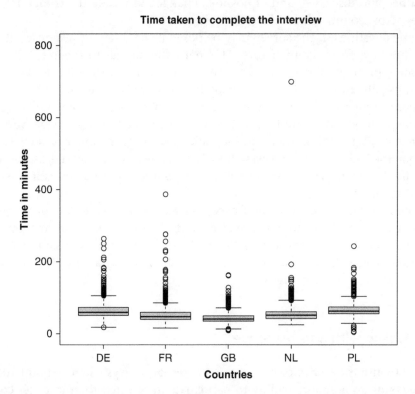

Figure 5.3 Boxplot of time taken to complete the survey in five nations. The data are from the representative samples in the European Social Survey (ESS) in 2012

taken to answer the questions in the ESS is expected to be at least 30 minutes. Thus, the measure of time taken might either contain a coding error, or it might be that the respondent did not take the time to carefully read the questions and answered them very quickly. Fast response times are likely to negatively affect the data quality.[4] Further, when the distributions of the same variables in data from different nations are dissimilar, there might be non-equivalence that needs to be checked before proceeding to more complex analyses.

It is important to check whether the codes and units used in the datasets are the same across nations. Researchers in the respective nations might not have used the same categories for the same variables. It might happen that the research agency in a country used the local norm for age groups or community size instead of the one used in your domestic survey. For instance, in coding community, the researcher may have used the code '1' for the smallest community being less than 1000 inhabitants in one country, but the code '1' for smallest community was for less than 5000 in another country; or they used the code '1' to represent 1000 inhabitants, whereas the code '1000' was used to represent the same number of inhabitants in another. Such differences need to be identified and discussed; and, if possible, changed to enable the comparison of scores across countries.

Some questions in the survey may be posed using different response categories, due to their inherent nature. This naturally applies to income, which is measured in the local currency. This variable needs recoding into the same currency, usually Euro or US$. The time period also needs to be checked as it may be more usual to measure annual income in one country, but weekly, fortnightly, or monthly in another. It is always advisable to create a new variable when recoding into another currency allowing comparisons at a later stage. Further, the coding for 'no answer', if included, needs to be checked, as the code (usually '9' or '99') will be simply used as a number in the analysis if it is not coded as missing.

When all data are checked and necessary recodes are made, the data can be merged into one large cross-national dataset. A last check before merging all national datasets into one international dataset is whether the same variable names were used in all country datasets and whether they are in the same positions in the respective datasets.

5.2 Dealing with non-response

Non-response is a source of bias in cross-national surveys when respondents in some countries are more willing to participate in research than in other countries, or when respondents may be unwilling to respond to some questions, such as those relating to age, education, income, age, or political questions. Some questions such as income or age, which appear as relatively easy to respond to in certain cultural contexts, are sensitive issues in others and cannot be asked directly. However, non-response is not only negative; it can also be a source of information for the researcher because it evidences possible inadequacies of the research instrument, which can be due to culture or language.

5.2.1 Survey non-response

After data collection it becomes clear to what extent people in the various nations have responded. Response rates may be highly different across nations (see Chapter 4). When the data are in, they can be checked to see whether non-response bias is present. This can be assessed by comparing early and late responders to the survey. The idea is that late responders have similar character-istics as non-responders; how this comparison can be made is described in Armstrong and Overton (1977).[5]

In many studies representativeness of the sample is a key issue; whether a national sample is representative can be checked by comparing background char-acteristics in the sample with background characteristics available from national statistical agencies (for links to national statistical agencies see e.g., http://ec. europa.eu/eurostat/web/links). However, it should be noted that genuine repre-sentative samples do not exist; that would require random sampling to ensure that every member of the population has equal probability of selection and inclu-sion in the sample group. When using Internet samples, genuine representative samples are impossible, as Internet penetration is less than 100% in all nations. Furthermore, Internet penetration is not random in the population; it is far from it. In 2013, in the European Union, 94% of 16–24 year olds were regular Internet users, whereas only 46% of the 55–74 year olds; also for high educated it was 93% and for low educated 48%. The 'digital divide' makes random sampling via the Internet impossible; however, it is also true of almost all other sampling tech-niques used in international business research. To gain insight into the Internet penetration of a particular nation, researchers may consult the website of *internet live stats* on http://www.internetlivestats.com/internet-users-by-country/

Apart from total non-response, there can be partial non-response in the data-sets. Some topics are more sensitive than others. For instance, income may result in a large proportion of respondents failing to respond to the question. For instance, in ESS round 6 (2012–2013) the missing percentage on households' total net income was as high as 53% in Portugal, 32% in Slovakia, but lower in the Netherlands (15%), France (9%) and lowest in Finland (6%). This might not be considered a problem if partial non-response would be random; however, often it is not. In the ESS non-response occurs significantly more often in younger than in older respondents. Non-response and partial non-response are common in large datasets. Before data analysis starts researchers need to check for differences in (partial) non-response between the nations. One option to correct for non-response is giving weights to respondents.

5.2.2 Response weighting

Non-response is rarely random. This results in a dataset where respondents who are easier to reach are overrepresented and respondents who are difficult to reach are under-represented in comparison to the general population in a nation. Thus, the data are not representative of the population in the respective countries. To make a sample representative, weighting is sometimes used. Weighting means that a people who are underrepresented in the sample will be considered as representing more than one person; people who are overrepresented in the sample will be considered as representing less than one person.

In face-to-face surveys where a random sample of the population is drawn, weighting can be used to approximate a representative sample. For example, in the ESS there are design weights to correct for the fact that in some countries respondents have different probabilities of being included in the sample (for details see: www.europeansocialsurvey.org). For instance, in Slovakia, a 15-year-old male living in a four-person household with parents around 50 years of age may receive a weight of 4.0 (meaning he counts as 4 people in the sample), whereas a 60+ woman living alone may receive a weight as low as 0.06 of a person. The weights are used to obtain valid (nationally representative) distributions of age, gender and education in each country.

5.3 Dealing with measurement bias

When examining distributions in different nations, it is not uncommon that respondents in one nation tend to give more positive responses on rating scales than respondents in another nation. For instance, in van Herk et al. 2004[6] Greek respondents had higher scores than the German respondents on all items independently of item content. Figure 5.4 shows differences in rating scale use between German and Italian respondents in the ESS on the set of 21 values items in the questionnaire. Italians not only tend to use the '1' more often, they also have more missing values, whereas Germans prefer choosing number towards the middle of the rating scale. There are obvious differences in rating scale use that are not warranted; absolute differences between values are theoretically not meaningful, only relative differences are important.

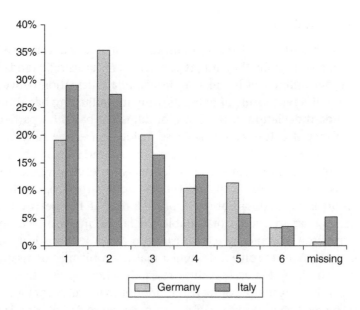

Figure 5.4 Propensity to choose rating scale categories in Germany and Italy (ESS, 2012). The items used are the 21 items measuring the Schwartz values; the rating scale ranges from 1 = 'totally like me', to 6 = 'not like me at all'

Before explaining response styles in detail, it is useful to outline different strategies based on the basic assumptions made by different researchers when dealing with response styles.

i. No check of response styles, they are just there. Differences in rating scale use are supposed to exist anyway and if deemed appropriate, standardisation techniques are applied.[7] For instance, standardisation is the treatment of response-style biases in Hofstede's work.

ii. No check of response styles as they are supposed to reflect substantive content. Trying to correct response set biases would then be at the risk of removing substantive variation related to culture. Response styles, rather than being bias obscuring true measurement, would be reflective of communication styles that are an integral part of culture. Therefore, Smith (2004)[8] emphasises that correction for response style needs not be done light-heartedly.

iii. Checking for response styles and considering them systematic (not random) variance that needs to be corrected for before valid comparisons can be made. This approach is based on the assumption that response styles can be computed and data corrected. This is the strategy predominantly explained in the subsections that follow.

iv. Approach (iii) is the predominant approach in cross-cultural comparative research in marketing research. A trend is to develop advanced statistical modelling techniques to separate substantive variance from response style variance.[9] These approaches require large datasets with many heterogeneous variables to enable estimation.

5.3.1 Standardisation

When researchers observe differences in means (or standard deviations) between data from different nations they might consider standardising. Standardisation is used to remove differences in mean and/or standard deviation between countries. There are different forms of data adjustment:[10] adjusting based on means, based on standard deviation, using both, or adjusting based on partial correlation or covariance structure analysis. These various corrective strategies can be performed either within subject (adjustment across variables for each individual), within group (adjustment across individuals for each variable), or within culture (adjustment across both individuals and variables). Within-subject standardization is called ipsatisation, a procedure that has been criticised for resulting in singular matrices not suitable for factor analytic techniques and because comparison of standardized measures in absolute terms is meaningless. Despite some proposals to solve the singular matrix problem,[11] ipsatisation is not widely used. An exception is in values research where ipsatisation is recommended;[12] in values, absolute comparisons are not made and from a theoretical perspective the relative importance of values make sense. When standardising it is crucial that researchers think about why they want to standardise and how it may affect further analysis. For further details on pros and cons of standardisation issue in cross-cultural research see Fisher 2004.[13]

5.3.2 Response styles

The different ways in which respondents use the points on a rating scale is called a response style. A response style can be defined as a person's tendency to respond to questionnaire items in a particular manner regardless of item content.[14] For instance, when answering questions, respondents may have the tendency to choose the highest categories of the response scale, have the tendency to choose the extremes of the scale or prefer the middle categories. These content-independent tendencies are referred to as response styles[15] and are

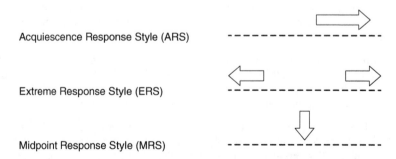

Figure 5.5 The main content independent response styles (ARS, ERS and MRS)

termed acquiescence (yea-saying), extreme response style, and midpoint responding respectively (see Figure 5.5). In addition to the response styles that are independent of item content, there is social desirability or the tendency to make oneself look good in the eyes of others.[16]

5.3.2.1 Response styles independent of item content: Prevalence of ARS, ERS and MRS

The most studied response styles are acquiescence and extreme response style. We will first focus on these and describe: (1) which people and cultures are the most prone to these response styles and (2) whether and how to make a correction for response styles. Acquiescent response style (ARS) is the tendency to use the positive side of the scale independent of item content. This response tendency has been found more often in older people,[17] and people with a lower education.[18] Regarding gender there is less consensus, some studies found more ARS in women,[19] others found no significant differences in gender.[20] Also cross-national studies have shown differences in ARS. People in collectivist nations have the tendency to acquiesce more than respondents in individualist nations.[21]

Extreme response style (ERS) is the tendency to use the extreme points of the rating scale, for instance, only the 1 and the 5 on a 5-point rating scale. This tendency is more prone in the lower educated,[22] and in older age groups;[23] in studies including a quadratic term for age, a positive effect is found, indicating that ERS is more prevalent in both the highest and the lowest age categories (younger than 25 years). Across nations, ERS differs between men and women, resulting in a difference between the genders in large cross-national studies.[24] At the culture level, ERS was found to be positively related to Hofstede's dimensions individualism[25] and masculinity;[26] however, for uncertainty avoidance, effects of ERS are less clear. De Jong et al. (2008)[27] found a positive effect, Harzing 2006[28] a negative effect and in Johnson et al. 2005[29] the effect was not significant. It should be noted that there are few studies relating culture to response styles; these studies require many nations and are therefore expensive and difficult to execute.

5.3.2.2 Response styles and questionnaire design

In the literature there is some indication of ways to reduce the effect of response styles. One effect might be the language used in the questionnaire. Harzing (2006)[30] found that extreme response styles were more likely to be present when the questionnaire was in the respondents' native language.

Furthermore, the type of scale and the mode of data collection impact the prevalence of response styles. The length of the rating scale used (e.g., 5-point or 7-point scale) might affect response style;[31] Weijters et al. (2010) the authors provide guidelines for choosing a scale format that will be least affected by response styles and, for instance, conclude that a 5-point fully labelled scale is best when measuring opinions in a sample from the general population. Regarding the mode of data collection, Weijters et al. 2008[32] found that responses in telephone surveys are more likely to be affected by response styles than responses in both paper and pencil, and online surveys. Unfortunately the latter study focuses on one nation only and whether the results are generalisable to other nations is not known. However, it is expected that modes of data collection also affect responses in other nations. Assessing whether response styles differ across the modes of data collection is advisable when researchers have used mixed methods, such as Internet surveys, pen and paper and face-to-face interviews.

5.3.2.3 Social desirability response style

Another kind of response style is content related. This response style is called social desirability or socially desirable responding (SDR). Social desirability is measured with a multi-item scale. According to Johnson and Van de Vijver[33] the Marlowe-Crowne scale[34] is one of the most employed scales to measure social desirability among American researchers. Although developed more than 50 years ago these scales (or slightly adapted forms of the scale) are still used in international business research. In the Balanced Inventory of Desirable Responding[35] distinguished two sub-dimensions of socially desirable responding: impression management and self-deceptive enhancement. Impression management is similar to what is measured in the Marlowe-Crowne scale; impression management refers to the tendency to present one's own actions in the most positive manner to express a favourable image. People high on impression management agree with items such as 'I never cover up my mistakes'. Self-deceptive enhancement (SDE) refers to the tendency to describe oneself in inflated and overconfident terms. An example of an item measuring SDE is 'I don't care to know what other people really think of me'.[36] In the study by Lawani et al.[37] it was shown that IM is more prevalent in Asian cultures (collectivist) compared to western cultures (individualist), whereas SDE is more prevalent in western cultures and less so in Asian cultures.

5.3.3 Calculating response style biases

Indices are calculated to assess the presence of the response styles such as ARS, ERS and MRS that are independent of item content. A prerequisite for calculating such indices is a set of heterogeneous items (a set of items that have low inter-item correlations). All indices are computed at the respondent level; calculations are based on *respondent's answers across all items* included in the set of heterogeneous items.

Researchers have used slightly different ways of computing the score for ARS (acquiescence); here we explain the procedure followed by van Herk et al. (2004)[38] for calculating an acquiescence index. To calculate an index for acquiescence, both the number of clearly positive scores and the number of clearly negative scores is counted. Then, the number of negative scores is subtracted from the number of positive scores. Thus, on 5-point rating scales, the values 1, 2, 4, and 5 are taken. Then the total number of 1 and 2 chosen was subtracted from the total number of 5 and 4. The resulting number is divided by the total number of items, resulting in an acquiescence index ranging from –1.00 to 1.00.

For extreme response style (ERS), the number of responses in the extreme categories is counted, for instance the number of 1 and 5 on all 5-point rating scales in the set of heterogeneous items. This number is then divided by the number of items resulting in an extreme response index ranging from 0.00 to 1.00. Midpoint response style (MRS) is calculated by counting the number of times the middle scale category is chosen by the respondent. This number is then divided by the number of items resulting in a midpoint responding index ranging from 0.00 to 1.00. Finally, social desirability response style is calculated by specific multi-item scales such as the Marlowe-Crowne scale.[39]

5.3.4 Effects of response styles on the findings

Response styles may inflate or deflate observed means of variables. This is a problem in cross-national comparative research. For example, the Net Promoter Score[40] is often used to compare businesses. The NPS uses willingness to promote the organisation as an indicator of customer loyalty. The measure is a single question: 'How likely is it that you would recommend [company x] to a friend or colleague?' and a response scale ranging from zero to 10, where 0 = 'not at all likely', 5 = 'neutral' and 10 = 'extremely likely'. In calculating the NPS the number of customers who respond with a 9 or a 10 is subtracted from the number of customers who respond with 0 to 6. When comparing the NPS across nations, it is assumed that the scale is used in the same way in these nations. As it is known that people in Northern Europe avoid extreme answers and that people in Southern Europe prefer to choose them,[41] response styles are likely to affect the comparison of NPS scores in these nations. This results in lower NPS scores in countries with low prevalence of ERS scores, as compared to countries with a high prevalence of ERS. Such differences may not be caused by observed differences in willingness to promote, but likely to be due to differences in ERS.

Inflation of scores due to response styles can be serious. Baumgartner and Steenkamp 2001[42] report that on average 8% of variance in scores on constructs measured can be attributed to response styles. However, not all scales are equally affected. For instance, for the scale on price consciousness, 4% of variance is due to response styles and for the scale on quality consciousness it is 14%. These are not negligible sources of variance in business research. Correlations between scales can be inflated when both scales are affected by response styles, which may even result in spurious relationships between constructs that are not actually related. That is, observed variance in a variable is due to (1) true variance, (2) random variance and when there is response bias, also (3) systematic variance due to the response style. Systematic variance from response styles affects all variables in a questionnaire. When 10% of the variance in scales is due to systematic variance, an observed correlation of .10 will already be present even if the scales are actually not related.

Thus, response styles may affect correlations between items or constructs. Correlations may be affected by acquiescence, because items keyed in the same direction will be equally affected by acquiescence; this is also true for items that are unrelated in content. Alternatively, correlations between items that are responded to in opposite directions (for instance, items in balanced scales) will be deflated. Thus, individual differences in response styles may significantly decrease the validity of correlational structures in datasets.[43]

5.3.5 Removing response styles from the data

When differences in response style are detected, researchers can decide to remove the response style bias from the data. A procedure to do this is purging response style variance from the constructs of interest. To purge the response style variance from a specific construct, a first step is to calculate response style indices using a set of heterogeneous items that do not overlap with the items in the construct.

Several response style indices can be calculated (ARS, ERS, MRS). Regressing the construct on the response style indices of interest (that can be one response style, but also several together) is then done to purge response style variance. The construct free from response style is the resulting regression residual computed by subtracting the score on the construct after regression from the original score on the construct before regression (see e.g., Baumgartner and Steenkamp 2001[44] and Weijters et al. 2008[45]). One advantage of this method is that it is simple to implement since it only requires response style index scores. One disadvantage of this method is that it assumes a linear relationship between the construct and the response style indices, which may not be the case.

Purging response styles from the data can result in an over-correction, or it can have hardly an effect. To check the effect of removing response styles, it is advisable to compare scores before and after correction. If the correction hardly changes the constructs, using the original scores is advised.

5.3.6 Current developments in response style research

Research on response styles still evolves. In psychology, He and colleagues advocate the use of a general response style (GRS) to take out the plethora of types of response styles. The GRS combines, ARS, ERS, MPR and social desirability in one GRS index.[46] The usefulness of GRS has been shown in large cross-national datasets such as the ISSP (International Social Survey Program). Another line of research in response styles focuses on more advanced statistical techniques to assess the presence of many different kinds of response styles (e.g., Van Rosmalen, et al. 2010,[47] Weijters et al.[48] and De Jong et al. 2010[49]). For instance, Van Rosmalen et al. use a complex latent class based model (LC-BML) to gain insight into the prevalence of many response styles simultaneously; Weijers et al. (2016)[50] developed the calibrated sigma method to remedy for between-group differences in response category use on Likert scales; De Jong et al. (2010)[51] developed a new item response theory-based methodology for measuring one response style, ERS.

Another development focuses on avoiding response styles by using other methods than rating scales. Interesting new developments are the use of best–worst scaling[52] in cross-national values research. In this approach respondents choose the statements in a set that best and least fit their opinions and differences in rating scale use are avoided, as discussed in Chapter 4. The applicability of this method in cross-national research is promising.

5.4 Assessing measurement invariance: dealing with construct bias

In cross-national comparative research, comparability of constructs and measures is a key issue. In the phase before data collection, researchers can reduce construct bias with preliminary data collection, such as cognitive interviewing and pre-testing (see Chapter 4). However, establishing whether respondents interpreted the items in a similar way needs to be established by means of measurement invariance (MI) testing. A MI test establishes whether the multi-item scale has the same statistical properties as in the nation in which it was developed: Are the items understood in the same way? Do differences in scores on the scale mean the same? Is the origin of the scale the same in all nations?

Table 5.1 shows an example of a commonly-used multi-item scale; the CETSCALE measures consumer ethnocentrism and was developed in the United States, where the scale is considered to have excellent statistical properties. The coefficient alpha[53] (Cronbach, 1951[54]) is around .95 in many samples in the USA, and it has good predictive validity. However, when this scale is used in other nations, it needs to be translated (see Chapter 4) and 'America' needs to be replaced by the name of the nation under examination. Careful translation (following recommendations in Chapters 2 and 4) does not automatically imply that the items have the same meaning across nations. That can only be tested

Table 5.1 An example of a multi-item scale: 10-item CETSCALE (Shimp and Sharma, 1987), measured on 7-point rating scale (1 = 'strongly disagree', 7 = 'strongly agree')

1. Only those products that are unavailable in USA should be imported.
2. American products, first, last, and foremost.
3. Purchasing foreign-made products is un-American.
4. It is not right to purchase foreign products.
5. A real American should buy American-made products.
6. We should purchase products manufactured in America instead of letting other countries get rich off us.
7. Americans should not buy foreign products, because this hurts American business and causes unemployment.
8. It may cost me in the long-run but I prefer to support American products.
9. We should buy from foreign countries only those products that we cannot obtain within our own country.
10. American consumers who purchase products made in other countries are responsible for putting their fellow Americans out of work.

after data collection, by checking whether the items form a uni-dimensional factor as in the original scale. Further, it needs to be checked whether scores on the scale mean the same across nations; that is, does an increase of one point on the scale refer to the same increase in ethnocentrism in different countries, and lastly can scores on the scale be directly compared across countries?

5.4.1 What is measurement invariance?

Variation in the validity and reliability of research instruments across contexts is a threat to cross-national/cultural comparability. Measurement invariance across all nations should be addressed in the sequential steps of configural, metric and scalar invariance, using multi-group confirmatory factor analysis.[55] Variables are considered as latent, unobservable constructs, measured on the basis of measurement indicators (items), thus taking into account measurement error. Measurement invariance can be established for complete research instruments, including several constructs, across several national/cultural groups by using nested models and comparing their fit indices.

In international business research, it is common to measure abstract constructs, such as satisfaction, trust, market-orientation and ethnocentrism. For these constructs, multi-item scales have been developed where the items together make up the construct. In the nation the multi-item scale was developed, all items have a high factor loading on the same factor and the variance extracted is high. Furthermore, it is considered a reliable scale with coefficient alpha well above .80. Such multi-item scales are considered the standard for measuring these constructs and in high quality publications they are the building blocks of models. However, the large majority of available multi-item scales originate in the USA and their validity is not guaranteed in other cultural contexts. For instance, an item measuring ethnocentrism with the CETSCALE (see Table 5.1) 'Purchasing foreign-made products is un-Dutch' might be inappropriate in the Netherlands where buying foreign is almost standard when purchasing clothing, consumer electronics, or cars.

Measurement invariance means that the multi-item scale has the same measurement properties across countries. There are three levels of measurement invariance:

1   configural or structural invariance;

2   metric or measurement unit invariance; and

3   scalar invariance.

Configural invariance is present when all factor loadings on the multi-item scale are significantly different from zero in all countries, implying that all items meaningfully contribute to the construct. Metric invariance is present when the factor loadings on the scale are 'the same' in all countries (i.e., there is no statistically significant difference), implying that the contribution of each individual item to the scale is the same across nations. When there is metric invariance, measurement scales have the same intervals and the scale can be used as input for analyses requiring interval measurement level, such as correlation or regression analysis. Finally, scalar invariance is present when the factor loading and the intercept are the same across nations (i.e., there is no statistically significant difference). This implies that the item intercepts are the same across nations and that the scale not only shares the same intervals across nations, but also the same origin. Scalar invariance makes it possible to perform analyses in which levels of scores are compared across nations, such as in a t-test. The three levels of invariance are nested: metric invariance can only be established when configural invariance is established, and scalar invariance only after metric invariance is established.

In cross-national studies, the highest level of invariance attained is often measurement unit (metric) invariance; scalar invariance is almost never reached.[56] Several authors have therefore argued that parameters need not be equal across all nations for all items. Valid comparisons can also be made if a subset of items is invariant, which is called partial invariance.[57] Researchers then attain partial metric invariance, meaning that not all factor loadings in a multi-item scale are invariant (equal) across nations; some factor loadings are allowed to differ[58] Steenkamp and Baumgartner (1998) suggest that two invariant items per construct are enough to establish partial metric invariance. The latter might be an issue; as this is likely to be a problem when the multi-item scale in question consists of, for instance, 10 items. In that case, two invariant items cannot represent the substantive content of the complete 10-item scale. It is always advisable to assess why so many items are not invariant in the scale and to interpret the invariance in terms of what it suggests about cross-national/cross-cultural differences (see also Poortinga, 1989[59]).

When performing a study on the relationship between two constructs in one nation, the model can be tested after the scales have been tested for uni-dimensionality and sufficient reliability. In a cross-national context, in addition to these steps, the cross-national measurement invariance of the scales needs to be established. As an example we consider the study by Sharma (2011)[60] in *the Journal of International Business Studies* in which the constructs of ethnocentrism, materialism, and value consciousness were used to explain differences in purchase intentions of foreign cars. The study was performed in two developed nations (UK and USA) and two emerging nations (China and India). The researcher first established that the three constructs had discriminant validity using a confirmatory factor analysis with three factors. Next, correlation matrices were calculated for each nation to obtain insight into the relationships between the three constructs and the purchase of a car from a specific country of origin. The correlation matrices already showed some interesting relationships: materialism was positively related to purchase intention of a foreign car in China but not in the UK. Next, he tested metric invariance to assess whether the scales had the same interval level measure in all four nations. The scales were partially metric invariant across the nations, but only after releasing equality constraints for five variables. For instance, one ethnocentrism item 'We should purchase products manufactured in [home country] instead of letting other countries get rich off of us' had to be allowed to have a different factor loading in the respective nations, as was the case for the item on 'I like to own things that impress people' in the materialism scale. To enable comparison between means, scalar invariance is required. To reach scalar invariance constraints for some variables in the model had to be relaxed. The established level of invariance was partial scalar invariance, allowing comparisons between construct means.

5.4.2 Prevalence of invariance testing

Testing measurement invariance is a prerequisite in culture comparative research to ascertain that researchers are comparing the same constructs across nations. Since the first articles on testing MI appeared in international business,[61] an increasing number of researchers have included MI testing in their research (for a recent overview see Davidov and colleagues (2014).[62] In the top journals in international business and international marketing (e.g., JIBS, AMJ, JM), invariance testing has become common practice; however, in other journals in international business, researchers often 'report insufficient information in relation to data equivalence issues thus limiting confidence in the findings of many cross-cultural studies'.[63]

5.4.3 Methods and techniques to assess measurement invariance

Multi-group confirmatory factor analysis (MG-CFA) is one of the most widely used methods for assessing measurement invariance. There are many software packages available for assessing measurement invariance such as LISREL, AMOS, and MPlus. Furthermore, in R the package Lavaan[64] can be used for multi-group measurement invariance testing. The latter is an asset, as R is open source, publicly available and free of charge, making it accessible for researchers in emerging and developing countries. Another option for assessing measurement equivalence might be exploratory factor analysis (EFA) followed by procrustean rotation (see Van de Vijver and Leung 1997[65] for details); this procedure is useful for getting insight into which items cause invariance. When comparing many nations EFA followed by procrustean rotation may be a good choice; however in top journals in business and marketing, the preferred approach and norm is MG-CFA.

To be able to assess measurement invariance, multi-item scales of at least three items should be available in order to undertake factor analysis. The usual analysis procedure is as follows:

1 To begin with, conduct EFA in each nation separately to gain insight into differences and similarities between nations; this might be followed by procrustean rotation.[66]

2 Next, conduct a multi-group CFA (MG-CFA) to assess whether the factor loadings are similar across nations (i.e., test for measurement unit invariance); once established, common techniques such as regression analysis can be validly applied to the data.

3 Finally, conduct multi-group CFA (MG-CFA) to assess whether both the factor loadings and the intercepts of the items are the same across nations (i.e., test for scalar invariance); once established, scores can be validly compared across nations and techniques such as t-test and ANOVA can be validly applied to the data.

In Lavaan in R, the function 'invariancetesting' can be used to assess all three levels of invariance in one run. For detailed insight into coefficients other routines are needed, but a first insight can be obtained very quickly.

5.4.4 Assessing measurement invariance: examples

In this section two examples will be given of how measurement invariance can be assessed and what the results look like.

Example 1: Compulsive Buying Scale

A popular scale for measuring compulsive buying is the Compulsive Buying Scale (CBS)[67] consisting of seven items. The items of the scale are shown in Table 5.1. The seven-item scale is one-dimensional (factor loadings ranging from .69 to.79) with a coefficient alpha of .95, indicating good scale properties. The CBS scale has been successfully used in many studies in the western world and in the USA in particular. For a valid use of the CBS scale in other nations it should be measurement invariant across nations. Using the data of Horváth and colleagues,[68] we demonstrate invariance testing of this scale. Following the guidelines for good cross-national research, the questionnaires were translated from English (the original scale) into Dutch, Spanish, Russian and Turkish. All respondents were women; the number of respondents was 103, 167, 122, and 150 in the Netherlands, Spain, Turkey and Russia respectively. In these nations, coefficient alpha was .83 in both the Netherlands and Spain, .86 in Turkey and .74 in Russia; all coefficients are acceptable,[69] but lower than that of the original scale.

What is important in cross-national comparisons is whether the scale measures the same underlying construct in all nations. This question is not answered by calculating the alpha coefficient, but by measurement invariance testing. To gain insight into the functioning of the CBS scale in the four nations, the first step is to perform an exploratory factor analysis (EFA) to assess whether the scale is one-dimensional. This can be done easily in a package such as SPSS. The results of the SPSS analysis in the respective nations are shown in Table 5.2.

Table 5.2 shows that the factor loadings in the Exploratory Factor Analysis (EFA) differ across nations. For example, in Russia, the item 'Made only the minimum payments on my credit cards' does not fit in the scale; the factor loading of −.02 is not significantly different from zero ($p = .90$). Although the factor loadings of items 1, 2, 3, 4 and 6 seem quite similar across nations, item 7 is not; in the Dutch sample, the factor loading is lower than in the other nations indicating a different interpretation. The EFA suggests that the scale is not similarly interpreted across the four countries.

Table 5.2 Factor loadings in exploratory factor analysis (EFA) of the CBS scale in four countries

	Netherlands	Spain	Russia	Turkey
1. Bought things even though I couldn't afford them.	.72	.84	.87	.84
2. Felt others would be horrified if they knew of my spending habits.	.79	.85	.84	.86
3. Wrote a cheque when I knew I didn't have enough money in the bank to cover it.	.84	.82	.76	.80
4. If I have any money left at the end of the pay period, I just have to spend it.	.82	.87	.71	.76
5. Made only the minimum payments on my credit cards.	.74	.06	.02	.70
6. Felt anxious or nervous on days I didn't go shopping.	.75	.84	.73	.73
7. Bought myself something in order to make myself feel better.	.25	.58	.52	.54

However, to objectively assess measurement invariance, multi-group confirmatory factor analysis (MG-CFA) needs to be performed. A first step is testing whether the factor loadings are all different from zero in all nations. In the multi-group CFA, the structures turn out not to have configural invariance; not only is the chi-square significant ($\Delta Chi^2 = 91.96$, df = 56, p < .001), but also the other global fit statistics do not meet the usual thresholds (RMSEA = .135; CFI = .915; TLI = .872).[70] The RMSEA is far larger than the maximum of .08 and both CFI and TLI are smaller than the required .95 (cf. Van de Schoot et al. 2012[71]).

Consequently, a researcher might consider testing partial configural invariance[72] by leaving items such as item 5 (and 7) out of the scale, but such a decision needs to be justified, as it might leave out items considered important in the scale. In particular, the item on credit card use may reflect availability of payment methods rather than compulsive buying across nations.

Example 2. Social trust (European Social Survey)

In the second example we employ data on social trust from the ESS in 2004. For reasons of parsimony we limit ourselves to six nations: Germany, France, United Kingdom, Netherlands, Poland and Turkey, with more than 1000 respondents in each nation. There are three items in the ESS to measure social trust: (1) 'Would you say that most people can be trusted, or that you can't be too careful in dealing with people?', (2) 'Do you think that most people would try to take advantage of you if they got the chance, or would they try to be fair?', and (3) 'Would you say that most of the time people try to be helpful or that they are mostly looking out for themselves?'. All items are measured on an 11-point rating scale ranging from 0 to 10, with the end points labelled. The factor loadings are shown in Table 5.3. These loadings are all higher than .70, indicating that there is a one-dimensional scale in all nations.

The results of the measurement invariance testing are shown in Table 5.4; this table shows the usual indices of fit that are expected when presenting MI outcomes. Fit statistics for the configural invariance are not included in the table, as the model for a single latent construct with three items is just identified and fit indices are not warranted. In the row labelled metric invariance

Table 5.3 Factor loadings (EFA) three-item scale on social trust (European Social Survey, 2004)

	Germany	France	United Kingdom	Netherlands	Poland	Turkey
Most people can be trusted	.80	.78	.81	.81	.77	.78
Most people try to be fair	.81	.79	.80	.84	.76	.83
Most people try to be helpful	.80	.71	.77	.74	.76	.81

Table 5.4 Measurement invariance results construct 'social trust' (ESS wave, 2004 see www.europeansocialsurvey.org) across six nations

	ΔChi-square	Δdf	p	RMSEA	CFI	TLI
Metric invariance	66.18	10	< .001	.053	.991	.984
Scalar invariance	598.53	10	< .001	.128	.898	.908

the global fit criteria show that the construct social trust is metric invariant across the six nations: RMSEA is smaller than .08 and both CFI and TLI are higher than .95 (cf. Van de Schoot et al. 2012[73]).[74] For a good fit, the Chi-square should be non-significant; here it is significant, but given the large number of observations in the ESS samples that is expected. There is no scalar invariance though, as is shown by the fit statistics for scalar invariance: RMSEA is far larger than the threshold value of .080 and both CFI and TLI are smaller than .95.

In fact, scalar invariance is hard to establish in large datasets such as the ESS. In almost all large cross-national studies, metric invariance (or partial metric invariance) is the highest level that can be established. When scalar invariance is required, researchers might explore whether scalar invariance can be established in subgroups of similar nations within the dataset. For instance, in the ESS datasets social trust can be investigated in a subgroup consisting of Germany and France. Results show that in this subgroup of two nations scalar invariance can be established (ΔChi^2 = 3.667, df = =2, p = .16; RMSEA = .032; CFI = .99; TLI = .99). The latter implies that when comparing Germany and France, differences in mean scores on social trust can be validly compared.

5.4.5 New developments in invariance testing: Bayesian invariance testing

Invariance testing using the MG-CFA stepwise procedure is increasingly used in business research, but this does not mean that establishing invariance is easy. When many nations are included in a study, it is difficult to establish full metric invariance or even partial metric invariance. To reach partial metric invariance, equality constraints are relaxed and researchers accept that only a few items of the scale are similar across nations. The latter means that the assumptions of equivalence are violated, which may have serious consequences for comparability of the data. Interesting new developments that might overcome the issues with traditional MI invariance testing include Bayesian methods for invariance testing in which background information is used to explain cross-national variation in item functioning.[75] These methods are new and have not been tested in cross-cultural studies in business; however, they seem promising towards establishing invariance in studies where additional background information regarding the constructs is available. These methods might also be useful for assessing measurement invariance in constructs measured by single items; a way of scale development that is advocated in marketing by Rossiter (2002).[76]

5.5 Multilevel issues in cross-national research

In multinational samples, individuals are nested within countries, meaning that they are not independent of each other; people in one country share more characteristics with each other than they do with people from other nations. These dependencies in the data need to be accounted for in analyses. For instance, multilevel regression analysis is an ordinary least square (OLS) *regression analysis* that takes the *hierarchical* structure of the data into account.

In recent years the use of multilevel models has expanded[77] and its potential for international business research is large.[78] Moreover, in the last decades, several datasets have become available free of charge in which individual-level variables are included for a large number of countries. Again, we used the European Social Survey (ESS) as an example, but there are more datasets available such as the ones from the World Values Survey.

5.5.1 Multilevel structures in data

In cross-cultural studies, respondents belong to a specific nation, where they have many things in common (e.g., the economic, legal, political and cultural environment). In this case, there are two levels: the level of the nation and the level of individuals nested within the nation (see Figure 5.6). Such nested structures are not uncommon in international business as it applies not only to individuals in nations, but also to subsidiaries in economic regions, or to managers within organisations within nations. While there can potentially be many levels, an examination of two levels is more common.[79] In multilevel analyses, variance can be explained at the two levels and explanatory variables can be included at both the individual and at the national level. Moreover, interactions between individual and nation level variables can be tested.

If researchers just compare individuals irrespective of the nation they are from they are ignoring the fact that individuals within a nation may be more similar to each other than individuals in different nations. The extent to which respondents within a particular nation are more alike than respondents in different countries can be measured with the intra-class correlation;[80] an intra-class correlation of 0.0 indicates that there is no shared variance between individuals from the same nation, a correlation of 1.0 indicates that all individuals within a nation are the same. In the latter case there is no variation within the nation, and researchers

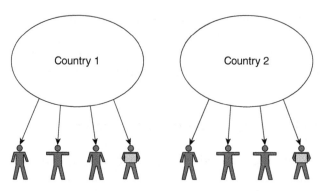

Figure 5.6 Graphical illustration of a two-level structure in multilevel analysis. Individuals are nested within countries

then (statistically) have one observation only; this situation is unlikely though, as nations are not homogeneous. When the ICC equals 0.0, there is no shared variance, and observations can be treated as independent in a regression; no multilevel analyses are needed and a common OLS regression suffices. However, total independence of observations is unlikely. In a meta-analysis of Hofstede's value dimensions, Steel and Taras (2010)[81] found that in the medium case, about 10% of the variance in the values was due to country and that the remaining 90% of variance was due to individual variation. About 10% is usual in business research. In organizational research, Hox (2010)[82] considers an intra-class correlation (ICC) of 0.05, 0.10 and 0.15 as small, medium and large respectively; an intra-class correlation of .05 requires a multilevel approach. How much variance is present at the different levels can be calculated by procedures in SPSS such as variance components. This is a first check to know whether multilevel analyses are required.

A multilevel study involving 2 levels (nation and consumer) by Steenkamp and colleagues[83] studied innovativeness in countries in the European Union. They found that innovativeness could not only be predicted by individual level constructs, such as ethnocentrism and openness to change, but also by the country-culture level variables such as individualism and uncertainty avoidance. Furthermore, a positive cross-level interaction effect between ethnocentrism and individualism was found. The latter illustrates a nice characteristic of multilevel models: variables at the nation level can attenuate or amplify relationships between variables at the individual level.

In multilevel analyses in international business involving individuals nested within nations, there is variance to be explained at two levels: (1) the level of the nation and (2) the level of the individual. For explaining variance at the individual level, variables such as a person's age, gender, attitudes, etc. are used. This is comparable to studies in which no levels are present. For explaining variance at the nation level, variables such as GDP per capita or Hofstede's culture dimensions can be used.

It is important to be aware of the difference in meaning that variables may have at the two levels. For instance, Hofstede defines an individualistic culture as a culture with 'a preference for a loosely-knit social framework in which individuals are expected to take care of only themselves and their immediate families'; however, this does not mean that *all* individuals within the nation are equally individualistic, there is a large variation within the country. The country level individualism score is an aggregate score across all individuals and should be treated at the nation level.

5.5.2 Examples of multilevel analysis[84]

Two reasons for doing a multilevel instead of OLS regression analysis in which all respondents are assumed to be independent observations are: (1) standard errors are suspect because the assumption of independent residuals is violated, (2) dependence is an interesting phenomenon and variability at the different levels is seen as an interesting phenomenon that needs further explanation.

In a multilevel analysis there is variance to be explained at both the individual and the nation level. To enable explaining variance at the nation level, there should be enough variance at the nation level. Therefore, at least 10 units at the highest level (e.g., countries) are needed, and for reliable results at least 20 units are needed.

In Figure 5.7 we illustrate possible relationships that can be assessed in multilevel analyses. In the figure there are three variables, two at the individual level (x and y) and one at the nation level C; both C and x are the independent variables, y is the dependent variable. There may be more independent variables at both levels, but for clarity we focus on one. In the Figure, the horizontal dashed line indicates the distinction between national and individual level. In situation 1, the relationship is only investigated at the individual level, the investigation is whether x has an effect on y; in situation 2, both the direct effect of x and the direct effect of C on y are studied; in situation 3, a main effect of x and the cross-level interaction effect (x times C) are included; in situation 4, both main effects at individual and nation level as well as the cross-level interaction effect are taken into account.

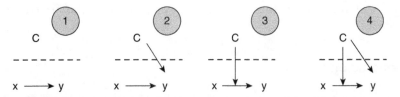

Figure 5.7 Multilevel analysis options: (1) individual level only; (2) direct effect of both individual level and nation level variables; (3) direct effect of individual level variable and a cross-level effect; (4) model including both direct effects and a cross-level effect

The first example focuses on main effects only (situation 2) and the second example includes both main effects and cross-level interactions (situation 4). The first example uses the study by Ralston and colleagues[85] on ethical behaviour including 16,229 respondents from 48 nations. The authors investigate the explained variance at both societal level and individual level, when predicting ethical behaviours of business professionals. For all four sub-dimensions of the subordinate influence ethics (SIE) instrument (see Ralston and Pearson, 2010)[86] the intra-class correlation coefficients (ICC) indicated sufficient between-group variance to warrant multilevel analyses (.32 for pro-organizational, .11 for image management, .14 for self-serving, and .13 for maliciously intended). Only one significant effect is found; collectivism is positively related to maliciously intended ethics behaviours. All other ethics behaviours are predicted by individual-level characteristics (e.g., individual-level individualism and age) only. In this study, no cross-level interactions were investigated.

Cross-level interactions in multilevel studies show whether relationships at the individual level are attenuated or enhanced by the context individuals live in. In van Herk and Poortinga (2012),[87] we investigated what explains differences in human values[88] in 165 within-country regions in Europe. Given the limited space in this chapter we focus on the higher order value of conservation. Main effects at the individual level show that age cohort and gender affect conservation; women and older persons score higher. At the region level both GDP per capita and former communism predict conservation; individuals in low GDP and in former communist regions are more conservative than individuals in high GDP per capita regions. The cross-level interactions between age cohort and the region level are also interesting; they show that the youngest age cohort in the low GDP former communist countries is less conservative than the same age cohort in other non-former communist low GDP regions. Taking into account the interactions between variables at different levels helps understand what is going on and provides insight into how the context people live in affects their attitudes.

To conclude, in multilevel regression analysis, as in ordinary OLS regression analysis, the terms main effects and interaction effects are used. The coefficients in a multilevel analysis can be interpreted in the same way as done in regression analysis. The difference is that estimates take into account the nested structure of the data.

5.6 Conclusion

Checking equivalence is a prerequisite. It is clear that respondents in many countries differ in their response styles; however, correction for response style needs to be done with great care as substantive content might be removed as well.[89] It is also emphasised that equivalence testing can be an opportunity to gain insight into cross-cultural differences. Often multi-item scales do not reach full metric invariance, implying that some items have a different meaning in another cultural context. A nice understanding of cultures may be obtained when looking at these differences. For instance, ethnocentrism or trust may be perceived differently due to the context people are in. Taking an emic perspective in interpreting the outcomes of *ex-post* cross-cultural invariance assessment can help increase our understanding of other cultures.

Notes

1. Van de Vijver, F.J.R., D.A. Van Hemert, and Y.H. Poortinga, Multilevel Analysis of Individuals and Cultures. 2008, New York: Lawrence Erlbaum Associates.
2. We assume here that there is a lead (dominant) country and research team. This is not always the case.
3. Hair, J. F., Black, W. C., Babin, B. J., Anderson, R. E., and R. Tatham, Multivariate Data Analysis (7th Edn). NY: Pearson, 2010.
4. Malhotra, N., Completion time and response order effects in web surveys. Public Opinion Quarterly, 2008. 72(5): 914–934.
5. Armstrong, J.S. and T.S. Overton, Estimating nonresponse bias in mail surveys. Journal of Marketing Research, 1977: 396–402.
6. van Herk, H., Y.H. Poortinga, and T.M.M. Verhallen, Response styles in rating scales: Evidence of method bias in data from six EU countries. Journal of Cross-Cultural Psychology, 2004. 35(3): 346–360.
7. Fischer, R., Standardization to account for cross-cultural response bias: A classification of score adjustment procedures and review of research in JCCP. Journal of Cross-Cultural Psychology, 2004. 35(3): 263–282.
8. Smith, P.B., Acquiescent response bias as an aspect of cultural communication style, Journal of Cross-Cultural Psychology. 2004, 35(1): 50–61.
9. See for example:
   Van Rosmalen, J., H. van Herk, and P.J.F. Groenen, Identifying response styles: A latent-class bilinear multinomial logit model. Journal of Marketing Research, 2010. 47(1): 157–172.
   De Jong, M.G., J.B.E.M, Steenkamp, J-P, Fox, and H. Baumgartner, Using item response theory to measure extreme response style in marketing research: A global investigation. Journal of Marketing Research, 2008. 45(1): 104–115.
   Weijters, B., H. Baumgartner, and M. Geuens, The calibrated sigma method: An efficient remedy for between-group differences in response category use on Likert scales. International Journal of Research in Marketing, 2016, 33(4): 944–960.
10. Fischer, R., Standardization to account for cross-cultural response bias: A classification of score adjustment procedures and review of research in JCCP. Journal of Cross-Cultural Psychology, 2004. 35(3): 263–282.
11. Cheung, M.W.-L. and W. Chan, Reducing uniform response bias with ipsative measurement in multiple-group confirmatory factor analysis. Structural Equation Modeling, 2002. 9(1): 55–77.

12. Schwartz, S.H., A proposal for measuring value orientations across nations, in European Social Survey, The questionnaire development package of the European Social Survey, 2003, Chapter 7, pp. 259–319.

13. Fischer, R., Standardization to account for cross-cultural response bias: A classification of score adjustment procedures and review of research in JCCP. Journal of Cross-Cultural Psychology, 2004. 35(3): 263–282.

14. Paulhus, D.L., Measurement and Control of Response Bias, in P.R. Shaver (Ed.). 1991, Academic Press, Inc: San Diego, CA, pp. 17–59.

15. Baumgartner, H. and J.B.E.M. Steenkamp, Response styles in marketing research: A cross-national investigation. Journal of Marketing Research, 2001. 38(2): 143–156.

16. Fisher, R.J. and J.E. Katz, Social-desirability bias and the validity of self-reported values. Psychology and Marketing, 2000. 17(2): 105–120.

17. Greenleaf, E.A., Improving rating scale measures by detecting and correcting bias components in some response styles. Journal of Marketing Research, 1992. 29(2): 176–188.

Ross, C.E. and J. Mirowsky, Socially-desirable response and acquiescence in a cross-cultural survey of mental health. Journal of Health and Social Behavior, 1984. 25(2): 189–197.

18. Narayan, S. and J.A. Krosnick, Education moderates some response effects in attitude measurement. Public Opinion Quarterly, 1996. 60(1): 58–88.

Rammstedt, B., L.R. Goldberg, and I. Borg, The measurement equivalence of Big-Five factor markers for persons with different levels of education. Journal of Research in Personality, 2010. 44(1): 53–61.

19. Ross, C.E. and J. Mirowsky, Socially-desirable response and acquiescence in a cross-cultural survey of mental health. Journal of Health and Social Behavior, 1984. 25(2): 189–197.

20. Johnson, T., Kulsea, P, Cho, Y.I., and S. Shavitt, The relation between culture and response styles: Evidence from 19 countries. Journal of Cross-Cultural Psychology, 2005. 36(2): 264–277.

21. Johnson, T., et al., The relation between culture and response styles: Evidence from 19 countries. Journal of Cross-Cultural Psychology, 2005. 36(2): 264–277.

Harzing, A.W., Response styles in cross-national survey research: A 26-country study. International Journal of Cross-Cultural Management, 2006. 6(2): 243–266.

Smith, P.B. and R. Fischer, Acquiescence, extreme response bias and culture: A multi-level analysis, in F.J.R. Van de Vijver, D.A. Van Hemert and Y.H. Poortinga (Eds), Multilevel Analysis of Individuals and Cultures, 2008: 285–314. New York: Lawrence Erlbaum Associates.

22. Greenleaf, E.A., Improving rating scale measures by detecting and correcting bias components in some response styles. Journal of Marketing Research, 1992. 29(2): 176–188.

Greenleaf, E.A., Measuring extreme response style. Public Opinion Quarterly, 1992. 56(3): 328–351.

23. Greenleaf, E.A., Improving rating scale measures by detecting and correcting bias components in some response styles. Journal of Marketing Research, 1992. 29(2): 176–188.

24. De Jong, M.G., et al., Using item response theory to measure extreme response style in marketing research: A global investigation. Journal of Marketing Research, 2008. 45(1): 104–115.
    Johnson, T., et al., The relation between culture and response styles: Evidence from 19 countries. Journal of Cross-Cultural Psychology, 2005. 36(2): 264–277.
25. De Jong, M.G., et al., Using item response theory to measure extreme response style in marketing research: A global investigation. Journal of Marketing Research, 2008. 45(1): 104–115.
    Chen, C., S.y. Lee, and H.W. Stevenson, Response style and cross-cultural comparisons of rating scales among East Asian and North American students. Psychological Science, 1995. 6(3): 170–175.
26. De Jong, M.G., et al., Using item response theory to measure extreme response style in marketing research: A global investigation. Journal of Marketing Research, 2008. 45(1): 104–115.
    Johnson, T., et al., The relation between culture and response styles: Evidence from 19 countries. Journal of Cross-Cultural Psychology, 2005. 36(2): 264–277.
27. De Jong, M.G., et al., Using item response theory to measure extreme response style in marketing research: A global investigation. Journal of Marketing Research, 2008. 45(1): 104–115.
28. Harzing, A.-W., Response styles in cross-national survey research: A 26-country study. International Journal of Cross-Cultural Management, 2006. 6(2): 243–266.
29. Johnson, T., et al., The relation between culture and response styles: Evidence from 19 countries. Journal of Cross-Cultural Psychology, 2005. 36(2): 264–277.
30. Harzing, A.-W., Response styles in cross-national survey research: A 26-country study. International Journal of Cross-Cultural Management, 2006. 6(2): 243–266.
31. Weijters, B., E. Cabooter, and N. Schillewaert, The effect of rating scale format on response styles: The number of response categories and response category labels. International Journal of Research in Marketing, 2010. 27(3): 236–247.
32. Weijters, B., N. Schillewaert, and M. Geuens, Assessing response styles across modes of data collection. Journal of the Academy of Marketing Science, 2008. 36(3): 409–422.
33. Johnson, T. and F.J.R. Van de Vijver, Social desirability in cross-cultural research, in Cross-Cultural Survey Methods, J. Harkness, F.J.R. Van de Vijver, and P. Mohler, (Eds). 2002, Wiley: New York. p. 193–202.
34. Crowne, D.P. and D. Marlowe, A new scale of social desirability independent of psychopathology. Journal of Consulting Psychology, 1960. 24(4): p. 349.
35. Paulhus, D.L., Two-component models of socially desirable responding. Journal of Personality and Social Psychology, 1984. 46(3): p. 11.
36. Mills, J.F., W. Loza, and D.G. Kroner, Predictive validity despite social desirability: Evidence for the robustness of self-report among offenders. Criminal Behaviour and Mental Health, 2003. 13(2): 140–150.
37. Lalwani, A.K., S. Shavitt, and T. Johnson, What is the relation between cultural orientation and socially desirable responding? Journal of Personality and Social Psychology, 2006. 90(1): 165–178.
38. van Herk, H., Y.H. Poortinga, and T.M.M. Verhallen, Response styles in rating scales: Evidence of method bias in data from six EU countries. Journal of Cross-Cultural Psychology, 2004. 35(3): 346–360.

39. Crowne, D.P. and D. Marlowe, A new scale of social desirability independent of psychopathology. Journal of Consulting Psychology, 1960. 24(4): p. 349.

40. Reichheld, F.F., The one number you need to grow. Harvard Business Review, 2003. 81(12): 46–55.

41. van Herk, H., Y.H. Poortinga, and T.M.M. Verhallen, Response styles in rating scales: Evidence of method bias in data from six EU countries. Journal of Cross-Cultural Psychology, 2004. 35(3): 346–360.

42. Baumgartner, H. and J.B.E.M. Steenkamp, Response styles in marketing research: A cross-national investigation. Journal of Marketing Research, 2001. 38(2): 143–156.

43. Rammstedt, B., L.R. Goldberg, and I. Borg, The measurement equivalence of Big-Five factor markers for persons with different levels of education. Journal of Research in Personality, 2010. 44(1): 53–61.

44. Baumgartner, H. and J.B.E.M. Steenkamp, Response styles in marketing research: A cross-national investigation. Journal of Marketing Research, 2001. 38(2): 143–156.

45. Weijters, B., N. Schillewaert, and M. Geuens, Assessing response styles across modes of data collection. Journal of the Academy of Marketing Science, 2008. 36(3): 409–422.

46. He, J. and F.J. Van De Vijver, Effects of a general response style on cross-cultural comparisons: Evidence from the teaching and learning international survey. Public Opinion Quarterly, 2015. 79(S1): 267–290.

47. Van Rosmalen, J., H. van Herk, and P.J.F. Groenen, Identifying response styles: A latent-class bilinear multinomial logit model. Journal of Marketing Research, 2010. 47(1): 157–172.

48. Weijters, B., H. Baumgartner, and M. Geuens, The calibrated sigma method: An efficient remedy for between-group differences in response category use on Likert scales. International Journal of Research in Marketing, 2016, 33(4): 944–960.

49. De Jong, M.G., R.G.M. Pieters, and J.-P. Fox, Reducing social desirability bias through item randomized response: An application to measure underreported desires. Journal of Marketing Research, 2010. 47(1): p. 14.

50. Weijters, B., H. Baumgartner, and M. Geuens, The calibrated sigma method: An efficient remedy for between-group differences in response category use on Likert scales. International Journal of Research in Marketing, 2016, 33(4): 944–960.

51. De Jong, M.G., R.G.M. Pieters, and J.-P. Fox, Reducing social desirability bias through item randomized response: an application to measure underreported desires. Journal of Marketing Research, 2010. 47(1): p. 14.

52. Louviere, J.J., T.N. Flynn, and A. Marley, Best–Worst Scaling: Theory, methods and applications. 2015. Cambridge: Cambridge University Press.

53. Cronbach alpha is commonly reported, but it has a number of serious shortcomings. For instance, the coefficient becomes higher with the number of items. When 10 or more items are included, it is likely that the coefficient will be above .70. We do not recommend using Cronbach alpha as a criterion in international research; however, as reporting the coefficient is the norm in scientific articles we mention it.

54. Cronbach, L.J., Coefficient alpha and the internal structure of tests. Psychometrika, 1951. 16(3): 297–334.

55. Rensvold, R.B. and G.W. Cheung, Testing measurement model for factorial invariance: A systematic approach. Educational and Psychological Measurement, 1998. 58(6): 1017–1034.
Steenkamp, J.B.E.M. and H. Baumgartner, Assessing measurement invariance in cross-national consumer research. Journal of Consumer Research, 1998. 25(1): p. 78.

56. Davidov, E., Dülmer, H., Schlüter, E., Schmidt, P. and Meuleman, B., Using a multilevel structural equation modeling approach to explain cross-cultural measurement noninvariance. Journal of Cross-Cultural Psychology, 2012. 43(4): 558–575.

57. Byrne, B.M., R.J. Shavelson, and B. Muthén, Testing for the equivalence of factor covariance and mean structures: The issue of partial measurement invariance. Psychological Bulletin, 1989. 105(3): 456–466.

58. Steenkamp, J.B.E.M. and H. Baumgartner, Assessing measurement invariance in cross-national consumer research. Journal of Consumer Research, 1998. 25(1): p. 78.

59. Poortinga, Y.H., Equivalence of cross-cultural data: An overview of basic issues. International Journal of Psychology, 1989. 24(6): 737–756.

60. Sharma, P., Country of origin effects in developed and emerging markets: Exploring the contrasting roles of materialism and value consciousness. Journal of International Business Studies, 2011. 42(2): 285–306.

61. Rensvold, R.B. and G.W. Cheung, Testing measurement model for factorial invariance: A systematic approach. Educational and Psychological Measurement, 1998. 58(6): 1017–1034.
Steenkamp, J.B.E.M. and H. Baumgartner, Assessing measurement invariance in cross-national consumer research. Journal of Consumer Research, 1998. 25(1): p. 78.
Vandenberg, R.J. and C.E. Lance, A review and synthesis of the measurement invariance literature: suggestions, practices, and recommendations for organizational research. Organizational Research Methods, 2000. 3(1): 4–70.

62. Davidov, E., Meuleman, B., Cieciuch, J., Schmidt, P. and Billiet, J., Measurement equivalence in cross-national research. Annual Review of Sociology, 2014. 40(1): 55–75.

63. Hult, G.T.M., Ketchen Jr, D.J., Griffith, D.A., Chabowski, B.R., Hamman, M.K., Dykes, B.J. and Cavusgil, S.T. An assessment of the measurement of performance in international business research. Journal of International Business Studies, 2008. 39(6): 1064–1080, p. 1027

64. Yves Rosseel. Lavaan: An R Package for Structural Equation Modeling. Journal of Statistical Software, 2012. 48(2): 1–36.

65. Van de Vijver, F.J.R. and K. Leung, Methods and Data Analysis for Cross-Cultural Research. 1997, Newbury Park, CA: Sage.

66. Van de Vijver, F.J.R. and K. Leung, Methods and Data Analysis for Cross-Cultural Research. 1997, Newbury Park, CA: Sage.

67. Faber, R.J. and T.C. O'Guinn, A clinical screener for compulsive buying. Journal of Consumer Research, 1992. 19(3): 459–469.

68. Horváth, C., F. Adigüzel, and H. van Herk, Cultural aspects of compulsive buying in emerging and developed economies: a cross cultural study in compulsive buying. Organizations & Markets in Emerging Economies, 2013. 4(2): 8–24.

69. Nunnally, J.C. and I.H. Bernstein, Psychometric Theory. 1994, McGraw-Hill: New York, NY.

70. For details on performing CFA and on the respective fit statistics we refer to Brown, T.A., Confirmatory Factor Analysis for Applied Research. 2015: New York, Guilford Publications.

71. Van de Schoot, R., P. Lugtig, and J. Hox, A checklist for testing measurement invariance. European Journal of Developmental Psychology, 2012. 9(4): 486–492.

72. Steenkamp, J.B.E.M. and H. Baumgartner, Assessing measurement invariance in cross-national consumer research. Journal of Consumer Research, 1998. 25(1): p. 78.

73. Van de Schoot, R., P. Lugtig, and J. Hox, A checklist for testing measurement invariance. European Journal of Developmental Psychology, 2012. 9(4): 486–492.

74. For details on performing CFA and on the respective fit statistics we refer to the book by Brown (2015) 49. ibid. on confirmatory factor analysis.

75. Verhagen, A.J. and J.P. Fox, Bayesian tests of measurement invariance. British Journal of Mathematical and Statistical Psychology, 2013. 66(3): 383–401.
Verhagen, J., et al., Evaluating evidence for invariant items: A Bayes factor applied to testing measurement invariance in IRT models. Journal of Mathematical Psychology, 2016. 72: 171–182.

76. Rossiter, J.R., The C-OAR-SE procedure for scale development in marketing. International Journal of Research in Marketing, 2002. 19(4): 305–335.

77. Peterson, F.M., J.-L. Arregle, and X. Martin, Multilevel models in international business research. Journal of International Business Studies, 2012. 43(5): 451–457.
Van de Vijver, F.J., D.A. Van Hemert, and Y.H. Poortinga, Multilevel Analysis of Individuals and Cultures. 2008, New York: Taylor & Francis Group.

78. Chabowski, B.R., S. Samiee, and G.T.M. Hult, Cross-national research and international business: An interdisciplinary path. International Business Review, 26(1): 89–101.

79. Peterson, M.F., J.-L. Arregle, and X. Martin, Multilevel models in international business research. J Int Bus Stud, 2012. 43(5): 451–457.

80. Kreft, I. and J.d. Leeuw, Introducing Multilevel Modelling. ISM. 1998, London: SAGE.

81. Steel, P. and V. Taras, Culture as a consequence: A multi-level multivariate meta-analysis of the effects of individual and country characteristics on work-related cultural values. Journal of International Management, 2010. 16(3): 211–233.

82. Hox, J., Multilevel Analysis: Techniques and applications. 2010: Milton Park, Abingdon: Routledge.

83. Steenkamp, J.B., F.t. Hofstede, and M. Wedel, A cross-national investigation into the individual and national cultural antecedents of consumer innovativeness. Journal of Marketing, 1999. 63(2): 55–69.

84. Explaining how to perform a multilevel analysis goes beyond the scope of this book. Multilevel analyses can be done with SPSS, but also with dedicated statistical packages such as HLM 62. Raudenbush, S.W., et al., HLM 6: Hierarchical Linear and Nonlinear Modeling. 2004: SSI Scientific Software International. are available. In R the package multilevel 63. Bliese, P., Multilevel Modeling in R (2.6) – A Brief Introduction to R, the multilevel package and the nlme package. 2016, October. is available to perform multilevel analyses.

85. Ralston, D.A., C.P. Egri, O. Furrer, M.H. Kuo, Y. Li, F. Wangenheim, and P.P. Fu, Societal-level versus individual-level predictions of ethical behavior: A 48-society study of collectivism and individualism. Journal of Business Ethics, 2014. 122(2): 283–306.
86. Ralston, D.A. and A. Pearson, The cross-cultural evolution of the subordinate influence ethics measure. Journal of Business Ethics, 2010. 96(1): 149–168.
87. van Herk, H. and Y.H. Poortinga, Current and historical antecedents of individual value differences across 195 regions in Europe. Journal of Cross-Cultural Psychology, 2012. 43(8): 1229–1248.
88. Schwartz, S.H., Universals in the content and structure of values: Theoretical advances and empirical tests in 20 countries, in Advances in Experimental Social Psychology, Vol. 25, M.P. Zanna, (Ed.). 1992, Academic Press: San Diego,CA. pp. 1–65.
89. Smith, P.B., Acquiescent response bias as an aspect of cultural communication style, Journal of Cross-Cultural Psychology, 2004, 35(1): 50–61.

6

STRATEGIES FOR IMPROVING THE RELEVANCE OF CROSS-CULTURAL RESEARCH IN INTERNATIONAL BUSINESS

Eighteenth-century writers were active in exploring fantasy foreign territories, such as Swift with *Gulliver's Travels* or Voltaire with *Candide*. In so doing, they began the first explorations of cultural differences. In the *Persian Letters*, Montesquieu (1721) wondered, humorously, how it is possible to be a Persian, while letting Rica write the following lines: 'They [Europeans] are very keen on the pursuit of knowledge here, but I cannot say that they know a great deal ... The majority of Frenchmen have a mania for being clever, and the majority of those who want to be clever have a mania for writing books' (1973, p. 134).[1] A culminating point of such phantasied travels was reached by Xavier De Maistre with *Voyage autour de ma Chambre* (journey around my room), published in 1795. De Maistre died in St Petersburg in 1852, which tends to show that, in the meantime, he had travelled. In fact, our fascination for overseas locations, foreign peoples and their strange ways is also located within the observer, within ourselves. When travelling internationally and collecting data constantly, we compare, confront and finally enrich our inner gestalts. Culture is in fact suffusing the whole scene; it is located everywhere, that is, not only in the object under investigation, but also in the observer and the context of the observation.

True international research must therefore be based on some awareness of one's own biases and a readiness to accept new ways of seeing the world. That is why deconstruction, in the sense of a radical questioning about the ideological foundations of one's own thoughts, is an absolute necessity (Section 6.1). If a researcher does not question him- or herself about his or her preconceptions, he or she is quite likely to impose preframed views upon the foreign reality.

Language, as we have argued throughout the book, is a key asset for discovering hidden meaning and searching for equivalence across contexts. In this section, we give examples of how language can be used to deconstruct preframed meanings and generate insights on differences in concepts.

Combining quantitative and qualitative approaches seems a significant avenue in cross-cultural business research, because both the assessment of differences in nature and the assessment of differences in degree make sense. As discussed in Section 6.2, this type of multi-method approach is difficult because the two 'religions', the positivistic/quantitative/etic and the humanistic/phenomenological/Emic research paradigms, are in somewhat constant conflict. Although the two traditions tend to remain largely separate, it is possible to use the two approaches in parallel. In Section 6.3, we explain what should be avoided in cross-cultural business research if one is to generate valid cross-cultural findings. That is, between which rocks or icebergs (a large part being invisible) the ship of the cross-cultural researcher should be guided. Finally, we suggest some ways and means to enlarge perspectives in cross-cultural business research.

6.1 The necessary deconstruction of multiple cultural realities

Culture, being socially constructed, is a highly complex kind of reality[2] and needs to question the dominant set of 'commandments' which have emerged from 30 years of a cross-cultural research field being dominated in business studies by the Hofstedian framework.[3] Culture is often opposed to nature with the Rousseauist view that people living near to the primitive simplicity of nature would be fundamentally 'better' than those who live in sophisticated modern cultures. This naive opposition hides the complex nature of arrangements between nature and culture within real-world human systems. Subjects and objects of culture are in the same global ocean and culture is highly 'natural' while nature is now highly 'cultured'. An example of this can be found in our relationship to the environment and the ecosystem, as it is constructed by the environmentalists, especially the highly environmentally conscious Germans with their concept of *Umweltfreundlichkeit* (the fact of being environmentally friendly). An initial preoccupation with nature ends in a typically German list of prohibitions when people trek in even a tiny piece of forest; at the same time thousands of cars can be stopped in a major traffic jam one mile away, polluting the whole area. That is why the first step is to be sceptical about what is natural and about nature itself. What is our true nature anyway? A similar question might be asked about culture.[4]

6.1.1 Introspective self-enquiry and fears of deconstruction

Taking the perspective of 'doing what comes naturally'[5] seems to be a friendly piece of advice, but is in fact somewhat dangerous for cross-cultural business research. What is natural is to use our own culture as an interpretive framework, because it is a system of preconceptions and prejudices which allows a short cut to conclusive findings based on self-fulfilling prophecies. In this respect, qualitative research is as susceptible to bias as quantitative research, and in some respects even more so, because the researcher is directly in charge of interpretation and bears even greater responsibility for possible biases. Some personal backgrounds can be useful for cross-cultural research because they are multicultural and multilinguistic in nature, such as those of Fons Trompenaars, with a French mother and a Dutch father, or Mary Yoko Brannen, who was raised in Japan until she was seven years old.

Most of the cultural fabric is invisible, like the immersed part of an iceberg. This is problematic for cross-cultural researchers, as situations involve encounters between instruments from one culture and informants from another, employees and managers from different cultures, etc. For this reason it is necessary to start with a phase of pre-research enquiry, which has a lot to do with self-enquiry. In this enterprise, the key word is 'foreign': what or whom is foreign to what or whom? Cultural deconstruction is not a philosophical enterprise (although the word 'deconstruction' seems to be proprietary to some French philosophers like Derrida), but involves a systematic investigation of the basis on which the research design will rest, including a self-assessment of the researcher's own part in the process, including their selection of underlying concepts and theories, as well as their attitudes towards research practices.

People are bound to produce a certain kind of research, in line with the local scientific culture; the dominant, national and professional culture in the field. This dominant culture can also be foreign. For instance, in business research, the dominant culture is American, as discussed in Chapter 2, requiring researchers from other countries to adapt to, or at least build on, the mainstream American paradigms if they want to publish their work in the major journals. Cultural deconstructionist investigations are few and far between in international business research, where researchers are reticent to challenge the dominant assumptions. Researchers outside the USA, often believe that the whole research system, and their own survival as an academic, is tightly bound to a certain style of research (e.g., required use of multi-item scales developed in the US). They fear that deconstruction may be destructive. This results in enormous mental blocks, whereby differences are prudently searched for in degree rather than in nature. We believe that this view is largely mistaken. The quality and the durability of the academic system rests only on the relevance of the intellectual debates, on the soundness of the theses, and the quality of the arguments, data or theory brought in favour of them. Open debate will make the academic system stronger rather than weaker in the long run.

Another fear has to do with the lack of directly applicable results coming from the deconstruction process. If it results in highlighting key explanatory variables that cannot be easily acquired (e.g., language competence), it is unlikely to be utilised. The lack of content orientation is also an apparent drawback of deconstructionist approaches. However, deconstruction is constructive, when one considers knowledge as basically process-oriented, local in nature, within an idiosyncratic approach to the progressive construction of knowledge. It can be a very positive initial step for designing cross-cultural research, for instance, through open discussion with colleagues from other cultures.

Deconstruction is a critical investigation into one's own research approach. For instance, a lack of data orientation, which may have some drawbacks, may be typical of a Latin intellectual style (see Chapter 2) However, this bias can be overcome by continuous exposure to other intellectual and research traditions. In the deconstruction process, it is also important to think about alternative assumptions and explanations[6] including multiple cultures, professional and corporate, as well as basic socio-demographic variables that can often explain much more than national culture.[7] In a sense, fundamental socio-demographic variables such as age or sex represent cultures in themselves. The contrast between gender groups is surely a fundamental sub-cultural divide, largely crossing the border of national cultures.

In 1948, Margaret Mead published *Male and Female,*[8] which drew on her in-depth knowledge of several South Pacific and Balinese cultures. The book depicts the organisation of relationships between men and women, the division of labour and roles in the community, and explains how these patterns may be compared to those of American society. Her text, *Male and Female,* is a detailed introduction to gender cultures. The difference between masculine and feminine cultures is in fact a most basic cultural distinction, fundamentally under-researched despite its in-depth influences on organisational life, leadership patterns, or conflict handling modes; there are some exceptions though.[9]

Another key sub-cultural grouping is that of age and generation, which has been studied in a variety of contexts, including the examination of a single generation across cultures,[10] as well as multiple generations and gender across countries. In today's societies, age cultures appear to be more important than previously thought. People are often grouped into age classes or 'tribes', where interaction with individuals from other generations is often considered as irrelevant, useless or even ill-mannered.

6.1.2 An example of western bias: cross-cultural research in risk and decision making (CCRDM)

The concept of risk is pervasive in the whole field of business. How risk is perceived and how it influences decision making has been studied in a cross-cultural perspective, starting 25 years ago from an American model of perceived risk by Slovic et al.;[11] for a review of risk perception research see Rohrmann and Rend (2000).[12] The Slovic model consists originally of a psychometric technique based on 81 risks and hazards grouped in nine dimensions of risk evaluation. These risks and factorial dimensions, with some variation in the number of hazards and dimensions across studies, have been further used for cross-cultural comparisons between the USA and Japan,[13] Hungary,[14] Poland,[15] and France.[16] Hovden and Larrson (1987)[17] started investigating, at a conceptual level, the cultural aspects of risk issues and their influence on decision making with a basic divide between risk exposure and risk handling, quite typical of the western linear model of 'think first, then act ', often a nice reconstruction of the real world. Later, the acronym for cross-cultural research in risk and decision making (CCRDM) was progressively introduced to propose a framework for research in the area.[18] However, the psychometric approach of CCRDM has been challenged by other methods, for instance, respondents being asked to list in their own words as many risks of personal concern as they can[19] which may be a better technique for generating cross-cultural contrasts in this field. Similarly, Holtgrave and Weber (1993)[20] have compared a model of conjoint expected risk (CER) with the Slovic psychometric model in order to see which one highlights more efficiently the dimensions of risk perception for financial and health risks. They conclude in favour of the CER model.

However, the dominant paradigm in the area is the Slovic et al. psychometric model, based on American items and a factor-analysis approach, centred therefore on the search for differences in degree rather than nature. When one looks at such research undertakings from a critical deconstructionist perspective, the cultural relativity of the starting assumptions is obvious. First, individualism is assumed in its strongest form. Risks are best understood as individual risks, experienced at an individual rather than family or group level; risks are at best shared with other individuals in a mutual form, that is, based on impersonal rather than personal solidarity. The individual is supposed to be future oriented and time projections are more or less assumed to be similar around the world. The 'doing' orientation[21] permeates the whole Slovic model. The seven variables are related to activities,[22] risk-takers being described as individualistic doers, rational masters of their own destiny, and utilitarian decision makers, far in fact from a collectivistic and fatalistic approach to life events:

- voluntariness (degree to which the *activity* is voluntary);
- dread (degree to which negative consequences of the *activity* are dreaded);
- control (degree to which the person engaging in the *activity* has control over the consequences);

- knowledge (degree of knowledge which the person engaging in the *activity* has about the associated risks);
- catastrophic potential (worst case disaster severity of the *activity*);
- novelty (degree to which the *activity* is new and novel or old and familiar);
- equity (degree to which the consequences of the *activity* are fairly distributed).

These items have little if nothing to do with being, identity, belonging, membership or status. Moreover, perception of risks has been shown by this literature to be situation specific, with an underlying model of individuals identifying and assessing particular risks related to their activities (especially through subjective probability assessment) and then handling these risks by some kind of hedging strategy. This whole model is typical of a purely rational human being engaged in mastering his own destiny.

CCRDM is mostly cross-national rather than cross-cultural research. This western framework which suffuses this research stream is not wrong as such. It is probably the best applicant for generality. However, there is no real discussion on the underlying assumptions and the western framework is imposed on other people; differences in nature are largely hidden, as well as the differences in degree. In a deconstructionist approach, the search for conceptual equivalence would have to be undertaken for the concepts of risk, hazard, peril, risk assessment and risk handling, and their articulation in either linear, circular or holistic models. In cross-cultural assessment of risk perception, the issue of the controllability of real-world situations cannot be addressed without referring to fatalism and to locus of control issues which may be key variables in such research. The over-rational approach is apparent in many ways:

1 *Risks can be dimensionalised*: the basic assumption is that of divisibility and relative independence of the parts into the whole, evidenced in psychometry by the search for relatively uncorrelated factorial dimensions (which is actually not the case).

2 *Measurement orientation*: to a large extent risk is viewed as measurable, with a strong emphasis on probability assessment and predictability of events.

3 *Risk handling*: the ways to cope with risk are limited to linear and sequential solutions and do not envisage flexible adaptation to reality based on context-embedded solutions, such as those which can be observed for motor insurance in developing countries.

4 *Cost-benefit analysis and economic rationality*: the expected value of risks can be balanced against the discounted value of insurance premiums over a period of time.

Fortunately new approaches to risk perception start to take into account a local perspective.[23]

6.2 Combining qualitative and quantitative cross-cultural business research

6.2.1 Going beyond the stereotypical opposition between words and numbers

Our next broad suggestion for becoming explorers of real meaning in the field of cross-cultural business research is to refrain from constructing false opposition between words and numbers. It is strongly ingrained in the collective and unconscious mind of academics that some of them deal with words, sentences and interviews and participate in 'real life stories', whereas others – the tribe on the other bank of the river of knowledge – deal with data in the form of numbers and statistics, and spend the whole day at their computers doing number-crunching. No need to say that members of the two tribes conceive of themselves as quite different human beings. If, once again, we refrain from thinking in territorial terms (a frequent bias in academic communities), it is easy to recognise that both words and numbers are carriers of meaning, and to this extent complementary rather than competing against each other. Therefore, it is highly artificial to oppose them; it is not only unnatural but also reductionist. The opposition between words and numbers is a social construction in academic cultures that must be constantly deconstructed. This social construction is based, however, on solid grounds. To understand phenomena in their full complexity, some are obliged to build on words and renounce quantification which may become difficult and even meaningless in the face of human complexity. Conversely, to put reality into quantifiable categories, one needs to simplify and focus on the 'what' rather than the 'why' questions. Personal intellectual interests and abilities largely explain the choices of individual researchers. However, this divide, which may make sense in the research process, requires cooperation rather competition. The very primitive aspect of academic tribes can be observed in the journal institution which testifies to high in-group orientation in the composition of editorial boards and the choice of authors. Back in 1991, Peng et al. stated: 'With the use of a combined quantitative-qualitative approach, we shall improve our capacity in revealing the holistic, naturalistic, and inductive aspects of the phenomena under investigation.'[24] Yet, there is still much progress to be made.

The ways to combine quantitative and qualitative approaches of cross-cultural business research are multiple. We will focus on three avenues. A first avenue is to start from a qualitative approach which brings insights into the research issues, especially how the target informants see their world, and then submit these exploratory findings to other researchers who can prepare a more quantified approach, but on a grounded basis. However, the reverse is more common: researchers often start from a quantitative questionnaire from their home or the dominant culture, replicate it in a different context and, at best, discover inadequacies at the translation stage, choose relatively naive solutions, and finally fail to establish measurement invariance. This means that findings are incomparable across nations and many be very difficult to interpret in any sense. If published, the discussion generally indicates that they have an insight that something in the method went wrong and an undeclared suspicion that most of the relevant meaning was lost in an inadequate process. Don't fall into this trap. Allow the necessary time to conceive and implement high quality cross-cultural business research. It will have more impact.

A second avenue is to triangulate investigation, using different types of data collection procedures and combining qualitative and quantitative methods.[25] For instance, when researching strategies of international banks from a cross-cultural perspective, interview bankers, investigate bank practices (e.g., credit decisions) and look at international banking data (e.g., corporate accounts of banks). Observation data related to meetings, reports, memos, and the like can be extremely useful to contrast with interview statements and actual behaviour, to confront conflicting interpretations or to validate self-reports made by certain actors in the case of intercultural conflicts. The research results will often be puzzling, since the datasets obtained from different collection procedures are quite likely to generate different insights and possibly contradictory ones. Returning to informants to check their views or for a new round of data collection will increase the depth of interpretation.

A third avenue is first to explore a problem quantitatively, that is, generate data based on concrete indicators and tangible evidence which allow assessment of whether the issue under investigation differs in some way across contexts (the 'what' question). Such an approach was used by Levine[26] in his interesting study of the pace of life across cultures. He conducted field study of bank clocks in the USA and Brazil, and tried to generate data on actual time use, while also looking at how much time beyond the schedule was considered locally as being late. The measurement of actual differences based on concrete indices is followed by four steps of investigations: (1) An account of how people interpret the actual situation within their own culture; (2) An account of how people interpret differences and similarities across cultures. Respondents in the various cultures were then asked to interpret the findings, that is elaborate on the 'why and how'. The initial quantitative step can be based on a multitude of actual indicators: evaluation sheets; payroll; mission statements; planners; work classifications; distribution of personnel by level of qualification; diaries of managers and time spent on particular tasks (time spent in meetings, on the phone, writing, and so on); number of days on strike, etc.; (3) Asking informants to elaborate on their own reality, providing them with both the image of their own reality and the contrast images found in other cultures. This can be done in many ways, by questionnaires, in-depth interviews, or critical suggestions about the researcher's approach. Allowing local informants to express views on their own reality does not imply that the researcher takes them for granted; (4) Interpreting and dealing with the reciprocal projections generated by such comparative investigations. They can be particularly helpful if the cultures under study are those of individuals in intercultural interaction (e.g., who are supposed to work together in joint ventures, to negotiate business, to work as expatriate managers, or as superiors of culturally alien subordinates).[27]

6.2.2 Ethnographic and anthropological research in international business

Herskovits (1952)[28] was an early figure in economic anthropology, a branch of comparative economics mostly based on the study of economic behaviour among non-literate, non-industrial and non-pecuniary societies. Very little international business research has built on this literature and research tradition. The role of machines, technology and money remains largely unquestioned in the world of contemporary business which proceeds to a large extent by comparing modern societies or at least the modern aspects of contemporary societies. The underlying patterns of exchange and economic interaction are held constant: for profit transactions are made by independent individuals or organisations within a combination of markets and provisional hierarchies. However, the use of anthropological approaches is extremely useful to broaden views. For instance, in the area of consumer behaviour and market exchange, Kopytoff (1986)[29] enlarges our perspectives about the commoditisation of goods by envisaging slavery, the trade of humans and slaves as merchandise. He shows in this way how, in modern societies, human beings have been strongly drawn out of the market sphere. This critical view allows a better understanding of modern phenomena which contain in reality much primitive behaviour which is normatively hidden.[30] Our mass market assumptions, for instance, hide the singularisation of goods by their owners, the private meanings invested in them, irrespective of their market value. The 'for money' orientation hides the fact that economic rationality is very far from being the sole source of rational behaviour in business exchanges. Despite the compulsory display of prices by vendors, bargaining still exists to a large extent in modern societies and fulfils social functions that go far beyond the mere discussion of price. Thus, anthropological approaches have the immense merit of bringing about broader and more context-free interpretations which are normally the ideal of quantitative research and, often, its unverified assumption.

A typical ethnographic approach is offered in *Logique de l'Honneur* by D'Iribarne,[31] who studied work relationships, management styles and organisation in three different factories of the Pechiney Group; one in France, another in the Netherlands and the third in Canada. Through an ethnographic approach, D'Iribarne was able to highlight the originality of the French system of organisation and motivation, built on a deep-rooted sense of rank within the organisation and an awareness of the duties attached to this rank, imposed by tradition rather than group pressure. The French, according to D'Iribarne are deeply attached to well-executed work and their intrinsic motivation factor 'is not so much what one owes to others as what one owes to oneself'.[32] Another typical example of an ethnographic approach in the area of management is that of Brannen,[33] who studied as a participant observer the takeover of an ailing US paper mill by a Japanese company over a four-and-a-half year period.

One may wonder why the anthropological approach and, more generally, qualitative studies are relatively underdeveloped in cross-cultural business research. Mendenhall et al. (1993)[34] in a study of international management articles between 1984 and 1990, find that only 14% use qualitative methods and, even worse in the perspective of combining qualitative and quantitative methods, only 4% use both approaches in a joint research design. While noting the important role of qualitative research in international business, Cuervo-Cazurra and colleagues[35] in a *Journal of International Business Research* (JIBS) editorial, state that the proportion of qualitative research in JIBS is lower than it should be. They give several reasons, including (1) limited qualitative training in many PhD programmes, (2) unclear standards for analysing and presenting data, (3) the time-consuming nature of the research journey, (4) the language challenges, and (5) difficulties in establishing the trustworthiness of the research. In fact, qualitative research is often attacked for their supposed absence of criteria of scientific validity. However, a number of authors have now proved that the criteria of scientific validity found in positivistic research find their equivalents in qualitative research. For instance, in the area of marketing, the progressive recognition of qualitative research as general and applicable knowledge is evidenced by the fact that articles appear in all of the major marketing journals, including the *Journal of Marketing Research*, which represents the mainstream tradition of marketing research, with a strong psychometric and experimental orientation, and frequent use of sophisticated statistical modelling.

There are also other reasons. Qualitative research is often viewed as documenting context dependent, inconsequential cultural facts about little-known people, especially in anthropological research. And, many capable researchers in international business have been preoccupied with standardised explanatory grids, in place of more sophisticated discourse on globalisation. The word-lovers and the number crunchers, generally avoid the cross-cultural encounter between their rival professional cultures. They rarely try to develop, and thus almost never succeed in developing joint research approaches. The differences are multiple and make joint research ventures inherently difficult. The research paradigms typically lead to quite different field research activities and the difference in intellectual focus, deep-seated meaning based on specific and local knowledge on the one hand versus general and applicable findings backed by numbers on the other, make the merger difficult. Further, theoretical linkage is painful since researchers do not share the same substantive paradigms, the same data collection techniques and not even the same conception of what is scientific knowledge.

6.3 What to avoid in international management research

The 'dos and don'ts' style of this section are in fact more in the don'ts style, highlighting precautions and offering some recommendations. We start typically on the negative side and continue on the positive, expressing positive statements as the result of double negations ('avoid doing what you shouldn't do').

6.3.1 Cross-cultural research as fashion and fad

Some researchers carry out cross-cultural business research because it is fashionable and easy because they join an existing network and serve as local data collectors. They may underestimate the real requirements for being involved in cross-cultural research, which is demanding and as such more adapted to relatively experienced researchers. Real cross-cultural rather cross-national research involves many nations; however, few studies include four or more nations and even fewer include 10 or more, which is needed to attribute the findings to culture and rule out alternative explanations.

Cross-cultural research has some drawbacks for careers, namely that it may take a long time to reach findings, is lengthy to implement, and is partly in opposition to the local academic culture and its hiring, evaluation and promotion criteria. It is also demanding in scientific terms. As argued in Chapter 2, culture is located everywhere not only in the object under investigation, contexts, situations or informants, but also in researchers and their instruments. Distancing oneself from one's own background may simply result in losing contact with firm ground and not knowing whether one is really writing something significant at least to some people. When the emphasis is on publish or perish within a relatively short timeframe, cross-cultural business research may translate into direct and flat replications with a reductive two-country design, little depth and many mistaken views based on data that are purely self-reported (by the informants) and self-interpreted (by the researcher), resulting in *ethnocentrism squared*.

6.3.2 Culture over-operationalized

The most simple and frequent case of over-operationalisation of culture is to take nationality as a direct proxy for culture with no underlying rationale based on the cultures or languages of the studied national groups (see Nakata, 2009).[36] A more sophisticated case occurs when the researcher tries to build some synthetic cultural indicator. For example, the cultural distance index of Kogut and Singh (1988)[37] calculates the distance between countries, based on the four cultural dimensions of Hofstede. In Kogut and Singh's article, this index was meant only to describe cultural distance 'from the United States'. However, some researchers have further used the Kogut and Singh index of cultural distance, but in a rather naive and dangerous way. They have forgotten that Hofstede's study[38] had been undertaken within an American multinational corporation and reflected world cultures in contrast to the USA, not all possible contrasts. If, for instance, cultural distance is computed from Peru, distances range from to 0 (Peru to Peru) to a maximum of 4.65 (cultural distance from Peru to Denmark). There are a large number of 'cultural distances to Peru' which seem fairly consistent but some obviously make little sense: South Korea has 0.02 cultural distance to Peru; Arabic countries 0.56; Iran 0.59; Taiwan 0.16; Thailand 0.28; Turkey 0.18 indicating high cultural closeness. Similarly, France, as the country from where cultural distance is computed, is culturally nearer to Turkey (0.45) or to India (1.27) than to the UK (2.19), Sweden (3.17) or Denmark (3.53). Finally, Japan is nearer to France (2.37) than to South Korea (2.68). The advice here is to avoid equating nation with culture and confusing the cross-national with the cross-cultural perspective. Using distance from the USA is very limited view of the world. It does not capture any of the complexities between countries. Further, this type of distance score equates all cultural dimensions equally. Yet, it is likely that some cultural distances are more important than others for a given behaviour. For instance, Siegel and colleagues[39] hypothesised and found that egalitarianism was significantly related to foreign direct investment, holding Schwartz's other cultural dimensions constant.

6.3.3 Ignorance of research instruments' influence on the findings

As emphasised by a strong proponent of cultural similarities '... the key to success in understanding the role of culture on organizational behaviour is not focusing on differences but on similarities'.[40] However, most cross-cultural researchers look for both similarities and differences, which seems at first sight to be a legitimate expectation. In fact, 'cross-culturally friendly' instruments are those research instruments which are nearer to phenomena and respondents, which allow differences to emerge more easily, especially when perceived by informants as enabling them to freely express contrast. On the other hand, 'cross-culturally unfriendly' research instruments are those which favour the emergence of similarities rather than differences. As such, the use of instruments which favour the emergence of similarities is not good or bad, true or false. But it is puzzling to confront results from typically different research instruments and this may give more depth to the investigation. A typical case is described by Brannen (1996).[41] After doing participant observation and in-depth interviews which generated certain findings (emphasising adjustment problems in the US–Japanese encounter), she undertook the administration of a questionnaire with a psychometric instrument on 200 subjects of the same corporate population. The findings of the survey were in flagrant contradiction with the observation and interviews. Re-examination of both the ethnographic and survey datasets allowed more in-depth insights.

6.3.4 Underestimation of cultural borrowing processes among foreign informants

Cultural borrowing on the part of foreign researchers and informants can be intense and blur the research process (e.g., the use of borrowed scales[42]). Cross-cultural research can be full of magic and mystery from the point of view of informants who do not really understand what the researcher means: 'What the hell is this guy talking about?' Informants, rather than expressing straight-forward disbelief or puzzlement, are most often concerned with damage to their self-image and fear of ridicule in front of the well-mannered and highly educated foreign researcher. Informants will more often than not construct an image that is self-protective and avoids humiliation both for themselves and for this gentle foreign scholar whose obviously sincere behaviour deserves helpfulness. Thus, imitation behaviour is likely to blur the execution of research, especially for informants in 'remote locations'.

Management time, which is an important field of study in cross-cultural business research, illustrates cultural borrowing. Everyday management behaviour involves appointments, schedules and meetings. Actual time behaviour of economically successful countries like the USA or those in Northern Europe has been imported by many other nations as the ideal pattern. For example, the PERT task-scheduling technique is based on graph theory with an appealing management science look and implemented mostly for its intellectual appeal rather than for actual project planning.

Not only is economic time borrowed as an ideal pattern, but non-economic/polychronic patterns also seem to be borrowed by those who are economic time minded. Usunier conducted some 20 in-depth interviews about business time across cultures.[43] Northern European (Swedish) students presented an ideal time pattern which was non-economic. They tended to develop an ideal view of time as unrelated to money, not an economic good, and fully available to them. Other nationalities surveyed in those in-depth interviews included Chinese, Brazilian, and Moroccan. They tended to show an ideal economic time pattern, agreeing with the statement that 'time is money'. They also described their activities as rather organised, with a planner, precise appointments, and so on, showing a high level of agreement with the desired value.

Cultural borrowing is extremely important for questionnaire surveys (see Chapters 4 and 5). When people self-report their values or behaviour, they tend to respond with their ideal rather than actual behaviour. Some observational data can help correct, and possibly challenge or invalidate the questionnaire data. For instance, looking at managers' diaries, at clocks, at the respect of time and dates for meetings, at actual delivery delays of local companies, may show a very different pattern than their answers in interview or surveys. When addressing cross-cultural issues, the researcher has to check how people in the target culture react to messages, words and theories from the source culture and how their answers are consequently transformed.

6.3.5 Comparative results too quickly transposed to intercultural settings

Most of the settings in cross-cultural business research are comparative in nature, because it is easier to theorise and less costly to collect data. A cooperative venture between researchers, doing the field research in their own country/culture, minimises travels and maximises the relevance of the data collection process vis-à-vis local informants. However, it is advisable to be prudent before directly transposing data on the business behaviour or strategies of the peoples and countries studied in intracultural settings, to what may happen when these diverse cultures are interacting (intercultural setting). For instance, in the case of business negotiations Japanese business people may not adopt exactly the same behaviour and strategies when they negotiate within their cultures as they do when they have to adjust to American negotiation partners. Adler and Graham (1989)[44] have addressed the issue of whether international comparisons are fallacies, when and if researchers are trying, finally, to describe cross-cultural interactions accurately. They demonstrate that negotiators tend to adapt their behaviour in intercultural negotiations and do not behave completely as predicted by observations in intracultural settings. They show that French-speaking Canadians are more problem-solving orientated when negotiating with English-speaking Canadians than they normally are when working together. Therefore, behaviour as observed in intracultural negotiations can only serve as a partial basis for the prediction of their style and strategies when negotiating with people belonging to different cultures. It does not mean that every finding obtained from intracultural comparison has no implication for intercultural interactions, but one needs to put in some caveats when extending intracultural findings to intercultural settings.

6.3.6 Underestimating the complexity of the data collection process

Underestimating the complexity of the data collection process is probably the main risk in doing cross-cultural business research. As discussed in Chapter 3, over-ambitious researchers may add depth to width and to height (in terms of Figure 3.2) and pile up problems of cross-cultural equivalence, which cannot be solved appropriately. This type of undertaking typically finishes unpublished. Robust designs in terms of data collection can either be quantitative or qualitative. Hofstede's design[45] is an example of a quantitative design that resulted in a limited number of dimensions. But Hofstede's research was made possible only because a large multinational company granted the budget for such an enterprise and allowed access to its employees as interviewees (116,000 questionnaires collected in 20 language versions). Furthermore, one dimension was kept constant, that of corporate culture; a single organisation was surveyed, thereby reducing the width and depth of the design.

In Nakata (2009),[46] a number of chapters provide a critical approach of Hofstede's contribution. The most critical is Chapter 3, entitled 'Beyond Hofstede: challenging the ten commandments of cross-cultural research', by Taras and Steel. They list and discuss 10 assumptions underlying the Hofstedean framework, including the identity between cultures and values, the extreme stability of cultures, their association with geographical boundaries and the possibility of representing them through questionnaires, mean scores, and matched samples. Assumption 10, namely that the Hofstedean framework is the only viable framework to study culture, would certainly not be supported by Hofstede himself. Chapter 4, authored by Cheryl Nakata and Elif Izberk-Bilgin – 'Culture theories in global marketing: A literature-based assessment' – is a content-analysis based literature review of culture theories. This systematic undertaking reviews 587 research studies in total, 141 of which use culture theories. Based on this empirical approach, Hofstede is arch-dominant with 68% of the articles being based on his 'universal culture paradigm', Edward Hall being the main challenger (14%) and Harry Triandis to a lesser extent (3%). However, the method followed may overestimate the dominance of Hofstede's framework in the cross-cultural literature in marketing and management.

The costs incurred with complex designs should not be underestimated: a single full translation process (including back-translation and checks) can already very costly. The complexity of cross-national research collaboration required for collecting data at relatively low cost should also not be underestimated. It includes language issues, the influence of cultural differences on communication misunderstandings within the research team, as well as problems related to authorship and property over materials to be published. To add to this, there are usually some problems with establishing equivalence as discussed in Chapters 4 and 5, that may eliminate some country comparison, or such a significant number of items that it renders the research not publishable.

6.3.7 Naivety about cultural convergence

Cross-cultural management has allowed important breakthroughs in the understanding of cultural differences as they pertain to managerial decisions and practices. However, certain questions are far from being completely resolved, such as that of the overlap between national culture (which is somewhat over-privileged by cross-cultural research) and corporate culture (see for instance research on multicultural teams),[47] or the conditions for successfully transposing management systems, which succeeded in quite different cultural contexts. One may also wonder whether cultural convergence will not progressively reduce the managerial relevance of cross-cultural studies in management. However, the globalisation process is complex and cannot be reduced to the dichotomous issue of difference and similarity, or even to its more sophisticated version, that is, looking at the magnitude of differences and their degree of impact on managerial practices to determine whether it makes sense to take into account cross-cultural differences.

The first argument is that complete convergence is certainly far in the future. Furthermore, apparent linguistic convergence produces fake perceived similarity since the language of convergence, English, is used with different underlying world views. EIL speakers transport the world view of their native language. This gives rise to an apparently de-babelised Tower of Babel; full of apparent understanding and real misunderstandings. The second argument is that the globalisation process is achieved mostly through business and consumption activities in companies, international organisations, by some media with a worldwide reach and the Internet. In this sense globalisation can be viewed critically as the 'McDonaldisation of society'[48] or as different possible avenues for ordering meaning in an increasingly compressed world.[49] What will emerge out of this process is not simply a world culture, which would be a reflection of common social adaptation to new technologies. In the globalised world, there will be a multitude of local villages with much interconnectedness, rather than a mere global village: cultural borrowing, creolisation, bricolage and kaleidoscopic behaviour will be intense, in a postmodernist way.

Whether we progress quickly in the direction of more cross-cultural understanding is not obvious. However, we are facing a very slow and complex phenomenon of global cultural convergence. International interactions are driven mostly by the expanding international trade, worldwide business activities, tourism and travels, and globalised communications. These mechanisms also result in more active confrontation between people from different cultures and lead to an increased awareness of differences. While the primary outcome of such a process may be cultural misunderstandings, they are necessary steps towards progressive understanding of other cultures' values and behaviour. In this sense, culture shock is a pre-requisite for adaptation to world diversity. This process can be accelerated if we systematically search for more in-depth understanding by frankly acknowledging the clash in values, rather than by trying to dilute cultural conflicts in well-intentioned, superficial empathy.

6.3.8 Forms of cross-border research collaboration and problems involved

It is a frequent practice to promote cross-border research cooperation in order to increase research feasibility, especially at the data collection level. This results sometimes in large research teams[50] which are not easy to manage, especially when one or several key researchers bring with them the research questions, underlying theories and research instruments and the collaborators bring mostly their capacity as local insiders and data collectors.

There are three basic situations in which collaborations function: (1) to develop culture-free theories (by replications), (2) to develop culture-specific theories (single-culture studies with a certain degree of cross-national collaboration), or (3) to develop new theories which integrate input from a variety of different cultural settings. In the first case, the primary research task is simply to replicate an earlier study in a new cultural setting. This is in fact the most frequent case in cross-national collaborations. Mutual learning is limited in this case. The second case of cross-national collaborations may substantially improve the understanding of the phenomenon under study, since the researchers can discuss their interpretations and make collaborative decisions. The third case (developing integrated contextual theories) assumes that there is equality between the research partners, source(s) and targets. This is the case that has the most potential for new insight, but it is also the most difficult one to coordinate.

In an email interview with Peter Smith, who has been involved in several large scale research projects in cross-cultural management, he was asked his opinions on the matter:

> I have now found some time to reflect on the questions that you posed to me concerning the management of large-scale, cross-national projects in our field. First, I would put what I might call the nature of colleagueship. The projects in which I have been involved have relied upon the creation of a network of peer relationships between investigators in a wide variety of cultures. However, the colleagues within that network have differing conceptions of what is an appropriate way to participate in such a network. Colleagues from low Power Distance nations expect to be fully involved in key decisions as to hypotheses and design. Those from high Power Distance nations are more likely to be deferent toward Western researchers and not to question designs or hypotheses, even though there may well be objectively stronger reasons why it would be good for them to do so. Where a project has a large scope, collective planning of the project becomes both very expensive and very difficult, and the most typical consequence is that one or two researchers from Western nations take on a major role in decision-making. This may well undermine the validity of the results to a certain extent, but it could also be a necessary price if the project is to come to fruition. We shall welcome the time when researchers from other parts of the world find themselves in these leading roles.

Second, comes the problem of sampling equivalence. The more precisely one specifies the desired sampling frame within a given nation, the more certain one becomes that it will be impossible to satisfy that criterion within at least some of the nations which it is desirable to include. Furthermore, matching respondents on something readily measurable like age may ensure that they are less well matched on other less tangible attributes like seniority, since age and seniority structures vary by culture. We have pursued a policy of not trying to match samples precisely, and I note that the GLOBE project have also specified a range of populations to sample rather than just one. It is however crucial to have a demographic profile of respondents. Third, I know of no way of evaluating the relative adequacy of different translations and back-translations. In each case one tries to ensure that the process is carried through thoroughly and professionally. But at the end of the day, some translations are probably a lot more difficult to do than others, and they introduce an unknown and uncontrollable amount of error variance.

Fourth, timing. All large projects take a long time to complete. Data are thus collected at different sites at quite different times, and may thus lose another dimension of comparability. When an international project becomes known, by being presented at conferences and elsewhere, additional researchers offer to join the project. Waiting for them to complete their part then delays final publication of results, which frustrates those who have contributed much earlier. My overall feeling is that the conduct of these types of project is fraught with all types of difficulty, many of them without any possible resolution. The best that we can hope for is that a series of studies each of which has its own weaknesses will nonetheless converge upon some relatively consensual findings. I see some progress towards that goal in recent years.

Starting from the beginning, the first question is how to find collaborations. We propose here a modest view based on human motivations, some of which are beyond the ideal world of research. In the first place, we assume cooperation between people who have some sense of their 'inequality', of the asymmetrical relationship as concerns the research process and the responsibility for finding a publication outlet. Good potential 'targets' are often young researchers who have done their PhD in the USA, England, Sweden or the Netherlands because they have a good command of English as the language of research and publication; and they were educated in the dominant research cultures. Targets are often recruited as cultural insiders from their country of origin. Either they have been recruited as assistant professor in the country where they presented their dissertation (and want to return home sometime) or they have been hired in their home country or elsewhere and want to keep a link with the place where they did their doctoral work.

Across countries there are huge gaps in resources for universities and research which create differentials in academic levels that are in practice difficult to overcome. That is mostly visible in three areas:

1. The emphasis on research versus teaching, reflected in annual teaching load and administrative charges related to teaching.

2. Access to literature, library stacks, journals received, library opening hours, information search systems, etc.

3. Access to databases, software and computation (packages, which are often expensive, are unavailable to researchers in many countries in the world).

The sophistication of research facilities increases almost continuously from an absolute low in very poor countries such as Mauritania, to industrialising countries such as Brazil, Thailand or Tunisia, to some Latin European countries and Japan, and at the top North America (US and Canada). However, changes in the world university rankings are reflective of changes in funding for some key universities in developed and developing nations outside the USA. Some countries have concentrated resources on two or three key places, often supported by both public and private funds, while the average university has limited funding for research and cannot easily participate in cross-national collaborations. Such is the case of Spain with well-funded places like IESE and ESADE in Barcelona, or Turkey with private universities like Bilkent University in Ankara or Boyazigci University in Istanbul which benefit from a favourable research environment.

GNP per capita is surely not the only reason for resources dedicated to research. Another reason is the place of management in the local academic scene. Despite the growing legitimacy of management research due to the globalisation of the academic model in business studies, it is still not recognised as a fully legitimate field of knowledge in some countries:

1. There is little local tradition for management education and research.

2. Management is mixed with money, and is seen as too earthly.

3. Management is seen as practical in focus and an art rather than a science.

Moreover the degree of involvement of the business community in the process of promoting management research, through financing or by offering a research field, varies considerably across national contexts. The Dutch, for instance, are very good at cross-cultural research exercises and their companies are supportive of such research undertakings (e.g., Shell in the case of Trompenaars[51]). The Dutch have a long tradition of cross-cultural research, probably because they are also superbly located, right in the middle of different cultures. Their businesses are spontaneously sensitive to cross-cultural and intercultural issues because they make sense for them. This is very different from Australia; the largest island in the world.

Cross-national differences in intellectual style must also be acknowledged when cooperating with colleagues. The issue of who adapts to whom is not a major issue for the time being because cooperation patterns are mostly asymmetrical. It could become a more critical issue in the future. However, similarity between researchers as pure individuals is a key asset which can compensate for the cultural gap and allow better cross-cultural dialogue. The lack of familiarity of some target collaborators with management research methods (not from intellectual knowledge but as a practical experience) must be considered in advance. The richer must not confuse poverty with inability: intellectual talents as such need little support. But the source researchers must be aware that levels of professionalism do differ in the sense of ability to mobilise resources along definite standards of quality and performance set by the profession. If a gap in professionalism exists, it must be filled in some way.

We now take the point of view of the potential target who seeks to be targeted. The task may appear difficult if the target is in a place with less lustre: he or she is in an unknown university, in a small country which is not well located, especially for after-hours activities. These potential targets still have a major competitive advantage because they are in remote locations which may offer excellent settings for cross-cultural research in terms of implied variance. The target will use existing questionnaires and concentrate on the quality of the data collection. Modesty is a key asset for targets whose imitation behaviour is necessary at the beginning. For targets who want to make contacts with potential sources, the solutions are multiple. The participation in international academic conferences is a good starter for de-provincialising oneself. Access to journals, even to only one international academic journal, is a must, since it generally allows the possibility of becoming a member of an academic association and being listed in its directory simultaneously. However, target researchers will go through a series of practical obstacles: email, for instance, is heavily controlled by public authorities in a broad array of countries, such as China or Tunisia. Participation in specific networks (such as 'marketing and development' or 'organisational symbolism and corporate culture') is also an interesting avenue, but carries the risk of belonging to too-narrow groupings which do not reach the critical mass of larger academic associations. For potential targets, the solution to invite academic 'stars' is not worthwhile for a one-day conference, rather a better solution is if the star can come to the foreign location for a period of weeks, because he or she may be interested in extending existing theories to a new challenging cultural context.

In cross-national research cooperations, the problem of equality between researchers is in fact constantly posed, even if implicitly. Ranking and competition are standard practices in international business research. It is popular to rank business schools or faculties according to their research publications records or teaching excellence. We would suggest that the research contract, even if not written, must be fairly clear from the start in order to avoid misunderstandings later in the process (objective, methods, research philosophy, distribution of tasks, authorship).

Writing the research can be problematic when researchers have quite different levels of language proficiency. The language gap can be somewhat problematic for Asians, except when they come from English-speaking areas, such as India or Hong Kong. Writing and dissemination can also be a problem when there are different requirements from the local audiences. The source researcher may be targeting a high level journal, which takes years before publication, whereas the target researchers may want a few quicker lower level publications. Publication in the form of co-authorship or acknowledgement in a footnote must be decided at the beginning, under condition that the respective assigned tasks have been properly performed. Financial aspects of the cross-national collaboration can be tricky; especially when the source researcher is not allowed to spend public research funds by transferring part of these resources to research associates abroad, which is the case in many countries. Some researchers are able to collaborate on the basis of peer exchange and joint publication. Elsewhere, resource shortages are acute and data can only be collected if some payments are made, either to researchers or their subjects. Since the cost of living is usually much lower within those nations which are most lacking in resources, the transfer of quite small sums of money can have a disproportionally positive effect.

6.3.9 Enlarging perspectives: strategies for cross-cultural business research

Cross-cultural research in management serves the purpose of creating unique and new insights, and generating broader concepts, rather than simply comparing what is alike and what differs across contexts. For instance, the cross-national and cross-cultural literature in accounting provides unique insights on the broader meaning of concepts such as 'information disclosure' or 'goodwill', or on the link between general accounting, fiscal accounting, and cost accounting. 'Reading' the research results necessarily requires an interpretation process which also involves learning from the research process itself, as well as from the research findings. Key findings may be attained when trying to translate and transpose instruments, or by checking from voluntary comments of respondents[52] how they have understood questions, why concepts were different, etc.

Cross-cultural research must include a strong critical component, and try not to sacrifice desirability to feasibility when trade-offs are necessary; for example, if intercultural research is more desirable, because it has more important implications, but intracultural comparative research is more feasible. Some topics would also deserve better coverage, such as research about cross-cultural interactions, cultural intermediation and cultural mediators, intercultural competence in a broader perspective than communication and basic adjustment (see Thomas and Fitzsimmons, 2008).[53] In the same vein, cross-cultural research should also focus on the unlearning as well as the learning processes. Unlearning is important because new cultural skills are not simply superimposed on previous knowledge, they largely take the place of former representations which need to be unlearned.[54]

Cross-cultural research should also focus on extreme rather than average situations. There is a human side to culture which is typically non average: human behaviour is a mix of programmed and non-programmed conduct. Creativity is central to real human behaviour but is generally suppressed rather than full creativity. Human aspects, which suffuse culture, are paradoxical, at times ambiguous, and partly unpredictable. Occasionally, the focus should be on predicting unpredictability, rather than basing prediction on estimated average values. That is why a sole combination of linear models and traditional statistical approaches cannot easily describe human behaviour; especially the 'fingerprint' aspect which is not susceptible to reduction to mean values. There are other ways to use statistical methods, with less 'mean' orientation and looking more at probability density over the whole spectrum, that would allow better analysis on the fringes rather than have the sole focus on the central tendency. Non-linear models and continuity/discontinuity patterns are relevant to cross-cultural business research such as research on discontinuities, broken relationships and cross-cultural failures, even though academics as well as business people prefer success stories to blunders and fiascos. Analysis generally tends to be based on what has worked rather than on the reasons for failures. Research about non-average behaviour is interesting because it can tell a lot about potential behaviour, future behaviour and repressed behaviour: the central tendency may only be the result of people not daring to do what other people allow themselves to do.

6.3.9 Some advice for exploring management practices in foreign contexts

Looking at different locations from the standard places where research is generally conducted also appears to be a promising avenue, although often a difficult one. There have been many recent calls from journals for research on emerging markets, which include these rapid growth, but lower-income markets, of developing countries in Asia, Africa, Latin America and the Middle East, as well as transitional countries such as the former Soviet Union and China. Early research into these markets took a distinctly western view, applying a range of theories, such as institutional theory, transaction cost theory, and agency theory, in an attempt to understand similarities and differences to western markets. Today, journals are calling for papers from scholars in the emerging markets, and collaboration between scholars from emerging and developed nations, to develop new theoretical insights, new concepts and models and new methods of data collection and analysis.

Rather than systematically testing the universal hypothesis, researchers can generate more insights by comparing particular cases, by looking at what is different in specific organizational practices and management institutions between emerging markets, as well as looking for stories which are extremely different. It is of the utmost importance that researchers from developed countries move beyond the Western model (applicable now, doing-oriented, task-related, over-pragmatic orientation), with its focus on the immediately relevant, operational, and understandable concepts, in an attempt to better understand remote and seemingly mysterious concepts. It is Possible to do this, while retaining most of the considerable strengths of the western model in terms of professionalism, open-mindedness, data and facts orientation and least bad applicant for the unreachable universality.

6.3.10 Data collection procedures: precautions, pluralism and coherence

Data collection is a limitation for cross-cultural research which has to be considered frankly from the very start. There is no ideal method and it is probably impossible for the researcher simultaneously to reach high performance on all the criteria of Figure 3.3, that is, to describe phenomena in their full complexity, to develop pure ideas, to use sophisticated instruments and totally to respect what informants have to say. Case studies are obviously a privileged source of in-depth understanding, especially in a multiple culture perspective (see, for instance, the case of international joint venture[55]). How theory can be built from case study research has been described by Eisenhardt (1989).[56] She argues that multiples cases are a powerful means to create theory because they permit replication and extension among individual examples, while maintaining a highly rigorous approach for the identification of research questions and the design of instruments. Others argue that single case studies are preferred, because they allow to delve into the full complexity of the materials studied, are superior for producing theoretical insights (see also Thomas and Peterson, 2014).[57] The researcher must have this sort of choice in mind when she starts her investigation. The choice of single versus multiple case studies has an influence on the kind of value built into the findings by the research process: a unique understandings of complex patterns, involving a multiple culture perspective in an intercultural setting (in favour of the single case study), and a better replicability and external validity of findings for multiple cases.

In cross-cultural business research there is ample room for original data collection procedures, such as those which help to 're-contextualise' decisions, especially when respondents are asked to express their views on situations which they do not actually experience. 'Event management' is an example of such an approach, whereby full segments of managerial life are presented to managers from diverse cultures. Similar methods that give some flesh and blood to hypothetical situations to which respondents are exposed are the in-basket instruments and vignette surveys.[58] In-basket instruments and vignettes allow re-contextualisation which is extremely important for such sensitive issues as business ethics. However, wording must be very carefully prepared since the proposed situations must not bias responses. Some of these original research instruments provide surprising results, such as the 'role playing executive',[59] an exercise used for contrasting Chinese and American preferences for reward allocations, where the Americans finally appeared as more humanistically and the Chinese more economically oriented.

Finally, the researcher must beware of a too hasty transposition of domestic research procedures to cross-cultural contexts. As emphasised in Chapter 4, transposed research techniques are sometimes not properly understood, difficult to implement because certain resources are absent (in quality or quantity) or bring about a feeling of artificiality among subjects. For instance, the sampling may be a problem, as well as response rates to surveys, or the control of respondents' qualification or motivation. In fact, there are no 'easy' data collection procedures when applied cross-culturally: interviews, questionnaires, Internet surveys, or participant observation will all face the barrier of language, both as a threat and as an opportunity for improving the cross-national or cross-cultural comparability of data.

6.4 Conclusion

To a certain extent cross-cultural business research marks the historical end of the colonisation process. Over two or three centuries the west has had a very profound impact on the shaping of what in the distant future could be a world culture, through the imposition of western social, political and technological models on other peoples. The difficulties contained in such a process are evident in the destruction of traditional cultures and the progressive elimination of their economic patterns. The globalisation of business, as political and military colonisation previously, has a necessary element of violence built in. However, this violence is self-contained because of the pragmatic nature of business and the free nature of markets. It entails 'theoretical colonization' (in the words of Mark Peterson and T.K. Peng),[60] a post-colonial enterprise doomed to failure in a world where most people will retain their native world views, even when they speak and write international English.

International business research must be the domain of open-mindedness in business research. This implies methodological ecumenism, that is, the combination of qualitative and quantitative research methods, tending to promote unity among churches in a scientific world which are sometimes in quasi-religious conflict. This open-mindedness implies to look at possible research options rather than engaging in readymade designs. It also bears as a consequence the renouncement of culture as a system of prejudices about the nature of reality, which could be extremely challenging and even a threat to the researcher's ego. This can be done only by confronting all sorts of biases and prejudices rather than by making language-free, prejudice-free, context-free and supposedly bias-free research.

Notes

1. Montesquieu, Persian Letters, [1973] 2009. BiblioBazaar, LLC.
2. Moore, F., Shifting perspectives: multiples cultures and community embeddedness in an Anglo-German MNC, in Beyond Hofstede: Culture frameworks for global marketing and management, C. Nakata (Ed.). 2009, Palgrave-MacMillan: London. pp. 201–221.
   Moore, F., Towards a complex view of culture. Cross-cultural management, 'native categories', and their impact on concepts of management and organisation, in The Routledge Companion to Cross-Cultural Management, N. Holden, S. Michailova, and S. Tietze (Eds) 2015, Routledge: New York. pp. 19–27.
3. Taras, V., J. Rowney, and P. Steel, Half a century of measuring culture: Review of approaches, challenges, and limitations based on the analysis of 121 instruments for quantifying culture. Journal of International Management, 2009. 15(4): 357–373.
   Taras, V., B.L. Kirkman, and P. Steel, Examining the impact of culture's consequences: A three-decade, multilevel, meta-analytic review of Hofstede's cultural value dimensions. Journal of Applied Psychology, 2010. 95(3): 405–439.
4. Poortinga, Y., Is 'culture' a workable concept for (cross-) cultural psychology? Online Readings in Psychology and Culture, 2015. 2(1): p. 14.
5. Lincoln, Y.S. and E.G. Guba, Naturalistic Inquiry. 1985: London, Sage.
6. Brannen, M.Y., Culture in Context: New theorizing for today's complex cultural organizations, in Beyond Hofstede: Culture Frameworks for Global Marketing and Management, C. Nakata, (Ed.) 2009, Palgrave-MacMillan: London.
7. Fischer, R. and S.H. Schwartz, Whence differences in value priorities? Individual, cultural, or artifactual sources? Journal of Cross-Cultural Psychology, 2011. 42(7): 1127–1144.
8. Mead, M., Male and Female, 1948, William Morrow: New York.
9. Özkazanç-Pan, B., Post-colonial feminist contributions to cross-cultural management, in The Routledge Companion to Cross-Cultural Management, N. Holden, S. Michailova, and S. Tietze (Ed.) 2015, Routledge: New York. pp. 371–379.
   Paludi, M.I. and J.H. Mills, Making sense of gender equality: Applying a global programme in Argentina, in The Routledge Companion to Cross-Cultural Management, N. Holden, S. Michailova, and S. Tietze (Eds.) 2015, Routledge: New York.
10. Zhongqi, J., Lynch, R., Attia, S., Chansarkar, B., Gülsoy, T., Lapoule, P., Liu, X. et al. The relationship between consumer ethnocentrism, cosmopolitanism and product country image among younger generation consumers: The moderating role of country development status. International Business Review, 2015. 24(3): 380–393.

11. Slovic, P., B. Fischhoff, and S. Lichtenstein, Behavioral decision theory perspectives on risk and safety. Acta Psychologica, 1984. 56(1-3): 183–203.
    Slovic, P., B. Fischhoff, and S. Lichtenstein, Characterizing Perceived Risk. Perilous progress: Managing the hazards of technology, 1985: pp. 91–125.
    Slovic, P.E., The Perception of Risk. 2000: New York: Earthscan Publications.
12. Rohrman, B. and O. Renn, Cross-Cultural risk Perception: A survey of empirical studies. 2000, Boston: Kluwer Academic Publishers.
13. Kleinhesselink, R.R. and E.A. Rosa, Cognitive representation of risk perceptions: A comparison of Japan and the United States. Journal of Cross-Cultural Psychology, 1991. 22(1): 11–28.
14. Englander, T., K. Farago, P. Slovic and B.A. Fischhoff, A comparative analysis of risk perception in Hungary and the United States. Social Behaviour, 1986.
15. Goszczynska, M., T. Tyszka, and P. Slovlc, Risk perception in Poland: A comparison with three other countries. Journal of Behavioral Decision Making, 1991. 4(3): 179–193.
16. Karpowicz-Lazreg, C. and E. Mullet, Societal risk as seen by the French public. Risk Analysis, 1993. 13(3): 253–258.
17. Hovden, J. and T. Larsson, Risk: culture and concepts, in Risk and Decisions, W. Singleton and J. Hovden (Ed). 1987, John Wiley & Sons: New York, pp. 47–66.
18. McDaniels, T.L. and R.S. Gregory, A framework for structuring cross-cultural research in risk and decision making. Journal of Cross-Cultural Psychology, 1991. 22(1): 103–128.
19. Fischer G.W., M.G. Morgan, B. Fischhoff, I. Nair and L.B. Lave, What risks are people concerned about. Risk Analysis, 1991. 11(2): 303–314.
20. Holtgrave, D.R. and E.U. Weber, Dimensions of risk perception for financial and health risks. Risk Analysis, 1993. 13(5): 553–558.
21. Kluckhohn, F.R. and F.L. Strodtbeck, Variations in Value Orientations. 1961, Evanston, Illinois: Row, Peterson.
22. Slovic, P., D. MacGregor, and N.N. Kraus, Perception of risk from automobile safety defects. Accident Analysis & Prevention, 1987. 19(5): 359–373.
23. Park, J., D.-Y. Kim, and C. Zhang, Understanding cross-national differences in risk through a localized cultural perspective. Cross-Cultural Research, 2016. 50(1): 34–62.
24. Peng, T., M.F. Peterson, and Y.P. Shyi, Quantitative methods in cross-national management research: Trends and equivalence issues. Journal of Organizational Behavior, 1991. 12(2): pp. 87–107, p.105.
25. Hussein, A., The use of triangulation in social sciences research: Can qualitative and quantitative methods be combined? Journal of Comparative Social Work, 2009. 4(1): 1–12.
26. Levine, R.V., The pace of life across cultures, in Joseph E. McGrath (ed.), The Social Psychology of Time, 1988, Newbury Park, CA.: Sage Publications, pp. 39–60.
27. Söderberg, A.-M., Indian boundary spanners in cross-cultural and inter-organizational teamwork: An account from a global software development project, in The Routledge Companion to Cross-Cultural Management, N. Holden, S. Michailova, and S. Tietze, (Eds). 2015, Routledge: New York.
28. Herskovits, Melville J., Economic Anthropology, 1952, New York: Alfred A. Knopf Publisher.

29. Kopytoff, I., The cultural biography of things: commoditization as process. The Social Life of Things: Commodities in cultural perspective, 1986. 68: 70–73.

30. Smith, K.T. and T. Betts, Your company may unwittingly be conducting business with human traffickers: How can you prevent this? Business Horizons, 2015. 58(2): 225–234.

31. D'Iribarne, P., La Logique de l'Honneur. 1989, Paris: Seuil.
    D'Iribarne, P., Managing Corporate Values in Diverse National Cultures: The challenge of differences. 2012, Abingdon: Routledge.
    D'Iribarne, P., The effect of culture on business ethics, in cross-cultural management, in Culture and Management Across the World, J.-F. Chanlat, E. Davel, and J.-P. Dupuis (Eds.) 2013, Routledge: New York. pp. 165–199.

32. D'Iribarne, P., La Logique de l'Honneur. 1989, Paris: Seuil, p. 59.

33. Brannen, M.Y., Culture in context: new theorizing for today's complex cultural organizations, in Beyond Hofstede: Culture frameworks for global marketing and management, C. Nakata (Ed.). 2009, Palgrave-MacMillan: London, pp. 81–100.
    Brannen, M.Y., Your next boss is Japanese: negotiating cultural change at a Western Massachusetts paper plant. PhD dissertation. 1994, Amherst: University of Massachusetts.
    Brannen, M.Y., Ethnographic international management research, in Handbook for International Management Research. 1996, Blackwell. pp. 115–143.

34. Mendenhall, M., D. Beaty, and G.R. Oddou, Where have all the theorists gone? An archival review of the international management literature. International Journal of Management, 1993. 10: 146–146.

35. Cuervo-Cazurra, A., U. Andersson, M.Y. Brannen, B. Nielsen, and A.R. Reuber, From the Editors: Can I trust your findings? Ruling out alternative explanations in international business research. Journal of International Business Studies, 2016, 47(8): 1–17, 881–897.

36. Nakata, C., Reflexive considerations of culture theories in global marketing, in Beyond Hofstede: Culture Frameworks for Global Marketing and Management, C. Nakata (Ed). 2009, Palgrave-Macmillan: London. pp. 247–277.

37. Kogut, B. and H. Singh, The effect of national culture on the choice of entry mode. Journal of International Business Studies, 1988. 19(3): 411–432.

38. Hofstede, G., Culture's Consequences: Comparing values, behaviors, institutions, and organizations across nations. 2001, Thousand Oaks, CA: Sage. XX, 596.

39. Siegel, J.I., A.N. Licht, and S.H. Schwartz, Egalitarianism, cultural distance, and foreign direct investment: A new approach. Organization Science, 2013. 24(4): 1174–1194.

40. Earley, P.C., So what kind of atheist are you? Exploring cultural universals and differences, in Beyond Hofstede: Culture frameworks for global marketing and management, C. Nakata (Ed.) 2009, Palgrave-Macmillan: London. pp. 19–39, p.35.

41. Brannen, M.Y., Ethnographic international management research, in Handbook for International Management Research. 1996, Blackwell. p. 115–143.

42. Douglas, S.P. and E.J. Nijssen, On the use of 'borrowed' scales in cross-national research: A cautionary note. International Marketing Review, 2003. 20(6): 621–642.

43. Usunier, J.-C.G., Business time perceptions and national cultures: A comparative survey. MIR: Management International Review, 1991: 31(3): 197–217.

44. Adler, N.J. and J.L. Graham, Cross-cultural interaction: The international comparison fallacy? Journal of International Business Studies, 1989. 20(3): 515–537.

45. Hofstede, G., Culture's Consequences: Comparing values, behaviors, institutions, and organizations across nations. 2001, Thousand Oaks, CA: Sage. XX, 596.

46. Nakata, C., Beyond Hofstede: Culture frameworks for global marketing and management. 2009: London: Palgrave-Macmillan.

47. Halevy, N. and L. Sagiv, Teams within and across cultures, in Handbook of Cross-Cultural Management Research, P.B. Smith, M.F. Peterson, and D. Thomas, (Eds). 2008, Sage Publications: Thousand Oaks: CA. pp. 253–268.

48. Ritzer, G., The McDonaldization of Society. 2011: Pine Forge Press, Thousand Oaks: CA.

49. Steger, M.B., Globalization: The Greatest Hits, A Global Studies Reader. 2013, Oxford: Oxford University Press.

50. Gelfand, M.J., J.L. Raver, L. Nishii, L.M. Leslie, J. Lun, B.C. Lim, and Z. Aycan, Differences between tight and loose cultures: A 33-nation study. Science, 2011. 332(6033): 1100–1104.
   Schwartz, S.H., J. Cieciuch, M. Vecchione, E. Davidov, R. Fischer, C. Beierlein, and O. Dirilen-Gumus, Refining the theory of basic individual values. Journal of Personality and Social Psychology, 2012. 103(4): p. 663.

51. Trompenaars, F., The Organization of meaning and the meaning of organization, Unpublished doctoral thesis, 1981, The Wharton School, University of Pennsylvania.

52. Usunier, J.-C., Language as a Resource to assess cross-cultural equivalence in quantitative management research. Journal of World Business, 2011. 46(3): 314–319.

53. Thomas, D.C. and S.R. Fitzsimmons, Teams within and across cultures, in Handbook of Cross-Cultural Management Research, P.B. Smith, M.F. Peterson, and D. Thomas, C. (Eds). 2008, Sage Publications: Thousand Oaks, CA. pp. 201–215.

54. Hislop, D., S. Bosley, C.R. Coombs, and J. Holland, The process of individual unlearning: A neglected topic in an under-researched field. Management Learning, 2013: doi: 10.1177/1350507613486423.
   Lee, V.S., Unlearning: A critical element in the learning process, essays on teaching excellence toward the best in the academy, 2009, 14(2), 2002–2003.

55. Dash, R., Life and Death of International Joint Ventures (IJVs): A review of literature and theories. 2013.

56. Eisenhardt, K.M., Agency theory: An assessment and review. Academy of Management Review, 1989. 14(1): 57–74.

57. Thomas, D.C. and M.F. Peterson, Cross-cultural Management: Essential concepts. 2014: Thousand Oaks: CA, Sage Publications.

58. Marschan-Piekkari, R. and C. Welch, Handbook of Qualitative Research Methods for International Business. 2004: Cheltenham, Glos, Edward Elgar Publishing.

59. Chen, C.C., New trends in rewards allocation preferences: A Sino-US comparison. Academy of Management Journal, 1995. 38(2): 408–428.

60. Peng, T., M.F. Peterson, and Y.P. Shyi, Quantitative methods in cross-national management research: Trends and equivalence issues. Journal of Organizational Behavior, 1991. 12(2): 87–107, p.105.

INDEX

equivalence of meaning *cont.*
  categorical, 86, 91–2
  conceptual, 86–90
  functional, 86, 90–1
  metric, 97–9
  temporal, 96
  in translation, 92–4
  see also sampling equivalence
Estonia, 12
ethics, 66, 136
ethnic perspective, 33–5
ethnocentrism, 47, 38–9, 62, 106, 127–8,
  137, 154
  of consumers, 89–90
ethnographic approach to management, 63,
  152–3
etic perspective, 31–2, 35, 47, 56, 62–4, 72–3,
  83–5, 94, 145
Euromonitor GMID database, 85
European Social Survey (ESS), 74, 93, 97,
  101–4, 114–18, 131, 133
European Union, United Kingdom
  withdrawal from, 65–6
'event management', 166
ex-ante assessment of data, 82–7, 99, 112
exchange theory (applied to potential
  research respondents), 104
experiential meaning of words, 53
exploratory factor analysis (EFA), 129–31
ex-post assessment of data, 82, 85–6, 112
extension of research, 66–7
extreme response style (ERS), 121, 123, 125

'fact', meaning of the word, 45
'feminine' societies and cultures, 18, 147
field experiments, 66
finance and accounting, research in, 5
Fisher, Glen, 52
Flanders, 45–6
'flat' data, 61
Flynn, T.N., 99
force majeure in legal contracts, 47
'foreign/imported' perspective on research,
  33–4
foreign-made products, 89
'foreign' national character, 40, 146
France and French culture, 20–1, 44–6, 48–9,
  53, 88, 91, 96–7, 113, 132, 152, 157
friendship, concepts of, 90
fuel consumption, 95
fuzzy data, 61

'Gallic' cultural group, 41–2
Galtung, J., 41–2

Gardberg, N.A., 87
Gedankennotwendigkeit, 42
Geertz, Clifford, 32, 40
gender groups and gender cultures, 147
gender of words, 43
general response style (GRS), 124–5
generalisability of research findings, 8–9
Germany and German culture, 20–1, 45–6,
  48–9, 53, 87–9, 96, 101–2, 113, 118–19,
  132, 145
Ghoshal, S., 3
global businesses, 5
global perspective, 33–4
globalisation, 9, 159, 167
GLOBE project, 14–16, 161
Goldman, A., 55
Gounaris, S.P., 87
Graham, J.L., 157
Greece, 87, 118
grounded theory, 63

Hall, E.T., 13–14, 19, 158
Harzing, A.-W., 104, 121
He, J., 124–5
Hedlund, G., 3
Helms, L.V., 40
Herskovits, Melville J., 152
hierarchical cultures, 17
hierarchical models, 74
high-performance work systems (HPWS), 84
Hirschman, E.C., 34
historical explanations, 71
Hofstede, Geert, 13–22, 33, 53–4, 62–3, 67,
  74–5, 78, 100–1, 121, 134–5, 145, 155,
  158
Holden, N., 36, 56
Holtgrave, D.R., 148
Hong Kong, 20, 164
Horváth, C., 130
House, R.J., 13–14
Hovden, J., 148
Hox, J., 134
Hungary, 12

ideographic writing systems, 56
idioms in language use, 48
immigrants, 39
impression management (IM), 122
in-basket research instruments, 166–7
in vivo and *in vitro* instruments, 77
income data, 116–17
India, 164
individualistic societies, 10–11, 16–18, 34,
  101, 121, 135, 148

information and communications technology (ICT), 34
Inglehart, R., 13–14
in-groups and *out-groups*, 16–17, 38
Inkeles, A., 13
innovation and innovativeness, 19, 134
integration of knowledge, 3
intellectual style, 41–2, 162
interaction effects, 74–5
intercultural interactions, 51, 87, 152
intercultural and intracultural settings and comparisons, 157
interdisciplinary research, 7
international business research 56, 68, 75, 126, 146, 152, 163, 167
  comparability in, 83–4
  contemporary, 2
  difference from one-country settings, 112
  examples of *etic* studies, 84–5
  formulation of questions, 64
  overview of, 1–5
  progression of, 2–3
  sources of, 6–8
  substantive areas in, 5
  topics in, 3–5
  what to avoid in, 154–67
International Social Survey Program (ISSP), 74, 125
Internet samples, 103–4, 117
interpersonal interactions
  equality or *inequality* in, 17–18
  with others and *for others*, 18
interviews for research purposes, 77–8, 105
  in-depth, 84
intra-class correlation (ICC), 133–4, 136
invariance testing, 125–32, 137
  Bayesian, 132–3
  prevalence of, 128
ipsatisation, 120
Islam, 11
Israel, 12
issues, 'high key' and 'lower key', 70
Italy, 118–19
Izberk-Bilgin, Elif, 158

Jain, M., 87
Janssens, M., 47
Japan and Japanese culture, 11, 18, 20, 33, 40, 42, 49–50, 54–6, 62, 88–9, 153, 157
Johnson, T. 121–2
joint research ventures, 153
Journal of International Business Research (JIBS), 153
Journal of International Business Studies, 5, 7–8

Journal of Marketing Research, 153
journals
  access to, 163
  coverage of, 165

Kaasa, A., 74
Kamba language, 44
Kikuyu language, 44
Kluckhohn, F.R., 13–14, 88–9
Knowledgenetworks (GfK), 103
Kogut, B., 155
Kopytoff, I., 152
Korean language, 93, 97
Kotler's *Marketing Management*, 34

laboratory-style experiments, 66
Lagerlöf, Selma, 10
Lalwani, A.K., 122
Lamb, P., 63
Lambert, J., 47
language
  as a cultural informant, 94
  and deconstruction of meanings, 145
  different approaches to study of, 63
  instrumental view of, 56
  as an issue in international business research, 31, 42–9
  linked with cultural representations, 43–4
  linked with world views, 53
  in relation to actions, thoughts and emotions, 45–6
  in the research process, 11–12
  spirit of, 45
  as a tool for discovering potential meaning, 49–50
  as used in international companies, 47
  as a window on world views, 51–3
language awareness, 31, 50
language barriers, 7, 56, 106, 164, 167
Larsson, T., 148
Latin concepts and intellectual style, 88, 147
Lawler, J.J., 84
leadership, concept of, 35
Lee, Julie Anne (co-author), xvii–xviii, 39
legal issues in research, 8–9
Levine, R.V., 44, 151
Levinson, D.J., 13
lexical equivalence of words, 48–9, 53
lingua franca, 49
linguistic astuteness, 47
linguistic convergence, 159
linguistics, *phonetic* and *phonemic*, 32
Linton, Ralph, 13, 22